Mainstream(s) and Margins

Recent Titles in
Contributions in Political Science

MAINSTREAM(S) AND MARGINS

Cultural Politics in the 90s

Edited by
Michael Morgan and Susan Leggett

Contributions in Political Science, Number 367

Greenwood Press
Westport, Connecticut • London

Library of Congress Cataloging-in-Publication Data

Mainstream(s) and margins : cultural politics in the 90s / edited by
Michael Morgan and Susan Leggett.
     p.   cm.—(Contributions in political science, ISSN 0147–1066
: no. 367)
     Includes bibliographical references and index.
     ISBN 0–313–29796–7 (alk. paper)
     1. Politics and culture—United States.   2. Marginality, Social—
United States.   3. United States—Civilization—1970–   4. United
States—Cultural policy.   5. United States—Intellectual life—20th
century.   6. United States—Social conditions—1980–   I. Morgan,
Michael.   II. Leggett, Susan.   III. Series.
E169.12.M3234   1996
306'.0973—dc20   95–37339

British Library Cataloguing in Publication Data is available.

Library of Congress Catalog Card Number: 95–37339
ISBN: 0–313–29796–7
ISSN: 0147–1066

First published in 1996

Greenwood Press, 88 Post Road West, Westport, CT 06881
An imprint of Greenwood Publishing Group, Inc.

Printed in the United States of America

The paper used in this book complies with the
Permanent Paper Standard issued by the National
Information Standards Organization (Z39.48–1984).

10 9 8 7 6 5 4 3 2 1

Contents

Introduction

Michael Morgan and Susan Leggett

The important cultural debates in contemporary society are no longer over "high" versus "low" culture. Instead, cultural inquiry has been reconfigured into a *political* question about the dynamic relationships among cultural strands and currents. But what is the mainstream of a culture? What are the margins? Where does the center end and the periphery begin—and how rigid is the division between them? How do ideas, artifacts, practices—and people—get assigned to one "location" or another, and once so assigned, must they remain there?

We refer to "mainstream(s)" in the semi-plural to highlight the notion that what is dominant is neither necessarily monolithic nor static, and hence, the contours of the "margins" need not be fixed. But how do mainstream(s) and margins determine, direct, and define each other? In an increasingly interconnected world, what are the implications of maintaining, breaking, or merging boundaries?

This book explores these questions and takes as its collective starting point the assumption that expressive practices do, in fact, matter. That is, social and cultural power is imprinted on, reproduced, and lived through such practices. As a group, the chapters examine two central issues: (1) the processes by which cultural mainstreams and margins are formed and resisted and (2) specific community and institutional responses to the resulting patterns and their consequences. The chapters show that cultural mainstream(s) and margins not only define each other but also reflect shifting political and ideological bases.

The authors of these chapters are steeped in disciplines from anthropology to communication to sociology to art history; thus, these essays are constructed on interdisciplinary, and sometimes conflicting grounds. Within these chapters, terms such as culture, media, and representation—which carry commonsense meanings in everyday and *intra*disciplinary discourse—become varied, diverse, and complex. Yet each author writes about these issues with such rigor, insight, and passion that the intermix of ideas forces us to consider these concepts in new but complementary ways.

The book is divided into two parts: "Political Strategies, Identities, and Movements" and "Audiences, Ideology, and Cultural Representation." Part I opens with a provocative and stimulating chapter by Poonam Pillai that demonstrates that mainstream and margin are not dichotomous, internally homogenous locations. Drawing examples from the role of women in India's 19th century nationalist movement, postcolonial theory, feminism, and the environmental crisis, she argues that the center and the periphery are shifting, interconnected, and multilayered. Most of all, they are discursively and therefore socially constructed. Pillai's conclusion provides a potent warning of the consequences if we fail to recognize our global linkage not only theoretically but also politically.

Rebecca Schneider takes the tack that one of the most emotional and mythological cultural boundaries, that between pornography and art, is highly problematic. She lays bare how constellations of mainstreams and margins form and intersect in her exploration of where art ends and pornography begins—and vice versa. The confrontation of aesthetic mainstreams and margins produces significant and resonant shocks to our systems. The "leakages" she describes evoke border crossings that both intersplice and transform the positions and roles of artist/model/nude and force us to confront our bodies and our art and our porn.

If Schneider demonstrates how things can leak across the boundaries of mainstream and margin (therefore disrupting those boundaries), Michael Fraser and Stephen Adair illuminate the powerful forces—ideological, representational, and political—which normally cement those boundaries. Both authors use case studies of social movements to examine what happens when marginal groups meet those mainstream forces. Fraser's study of Queer Nation argues that this movement itself poses a conceptual challenge for social movement theory. Adair shows us that a marginal activist group—in this case, the anti-nuclear power Clamshell Alliance—can ironically lose its coherency and power as it grows.

Similarly, Sandra Jamieson illuminates the persistence of mainstream power and casts the battle over "the canon" in a whole new light. She provides a thoughtful analysis of both the conceptual and practical problems of challenging boundaries. Although multicultural readers are feared by conservative elements in U.S. society, she argues that such texts are cultural artifacts that undermine their own stated project of empowerment. The central contradiction she exposes is that the readers are teaching women students and students of color that they cannot write academic essays at the very moment when it would appear that they are being given the skills to do so.

Susan Ross shifts the focus on questions of writing and identity from the classroom to the prison. She examines the writings of women sentenced to life in prison—a group on the margins of the margins. Their writings are surely poignant and startling for those on the outside. In them she finds concepts of power, authority, and self-concept. Yet the prison system as archetype of oppression reveals how the mainstream uses the "other" to define itself and to maintain its power. This chapter demonstrates at what human cost.

It is impossible to examine the mainstream of contemporary culture without being drawn, forcefully and repeatedly, to the commercial mass media. Several chapters in Part II explore an interesting mix of media-related issues and problems. The part begins with a chapter by Thomas Streeter that turns our attention from the social to the political to the material and back again. His detailed analysis shows how the story of media regulation and policy is embedded in cultural history. It also shows how a particular system of commercialized mainstream culture has become naturalized to the point where alternatives are precluded in the United States.

Relatedly, Kevin Carragee approaches the question at the heart of cultural studies of mass media: what is the relationship between audience and mass mediated text? In his focused examination of current theories about the production of meaning and resistance, Carragee finds key concepts to be undertheorized and detached from political contexts. Oversimplification of the process of resistance to hegemonic messages, he argues, underestimates the power of mainstream media.

Next, Andy Ruddock shows how media construction of a politically significant event—in this case, the British press coverage of the killings of suspected IRA terrorists by the British Army in Gibraltar in 1988— exploits and sustains dominant ideological assumptions and frames. The press coverage itself—not the material evidence (the victims, it turned out, were unarmed)—constructed the "Other" as dangerous to the mainstream social order. Opportunities for alternative interpretations of media coverage may always exist but, as Ruddock demonstrates, hegemony operates not as much by imposing uniformity as by limiting and managing potential contradictions and fissures.

Those phenomena the media choose *not* to emphasize can also teach significant cultural lessons—the mainstream is defined as much by what is excluded as what is included, as the next two chapters show. Gina Daddario analyzes the rare portrayal of female athletes in prime-time dramatic entertainment and finds that even when programs appear to be breaking stereotypes, they heighten fundamental cultural suspicions about female physical strength. Bridging feminist media criticism with feminist sports criticism, her rhetorical analysis exposes how the fare offered to viewers, and perhaps most importantly to adolescent girls, insists that appearance counts far more than athletic prowess. She convincingly shows that the fictional portrayal of female athletes reproduces masculine hegemony in the sports arena and marginalizes female achievement.

Similarly, James Shanahan's novel analysis of prime-time entertainment programs reveals that not only is the environment marginalized when it is portrayed at all, but it is trivialized. The mainstream messages may occasionally pay lip service to the idea of environmental concern, yet for the sake of profits, the commercial media must ensure that its messages do not interfere with the goals of its corporate sponsors (i.e., devotion to individualism and the celebration of consumption). The result is that television as an institution cultivates and naturalizes a symbolic environment that keeps the natural environment on the margins, even as the medium seems to be paying unprecedented attention to environmental issues.

The final two chapters also highlight political implications of cultural representations, but in cross-cultural contexts. Linda Steet revisits some key themes from earlier chapters, including colonialism, primitivism, the environment, and the body, in her assessment of Arab images in *National Geographic* from 1888 to 1930. The magazine's representations served not only to enhance the sense of distance that "civilized" readers felt between themselves and members of these cultures, but they also extolled the obvious superiority of Western ways. Ironically, the photographs cloak what would be a forbidden indulgence of Victorian prurience in terms of scientific objectivity and education; yet the images evoke a voyeuristic eroticism that objectifies women.

Finally, Stuart Kirsch raises powerful issues that percolate beneath the surface of social inquiry and academic life in general. In a chapter sure to provoke self-reflection among all those who would claim their work to have political import, he draws attention to the ways in which the subjects of academic work may be marginalized. It is not simply the obvious problem that the researcher and the researched are in an unequal power relationship and that the latter can be exploited; it is instead that the representations emerging from academic work may run counter to intended emancipatory aims, or worse, be dangerous to the "subjects." The highly charged questions of who says what, under what conditions, and with what import, are brought into full relief in Kirsch's case study of refugees along the border of New Guinea. Using examples from field work, his essay explores how "political," "critical," and "pragmatic" ethnographic representations can impact an entire population.

The politics of culture involves power struggles over discourse, ideology, identity, and the epistemology of representation. The authors in this volume examine some processes by which cultural boundaries are constructed, maintained, subverted, merged, and crossed. They provide fresh views on social institutions, on hegemony, and on what constitutes appropriate modes of scholarly inquiry. These chapters, of course, do not definitively resolve the difficult and critical issues they raise. But they significantly advance the debate, as much by their own insights and arguments as by the unusually dynamic mix of interdisciplinary approaches brought together in these pages. It is a truism that scholars working in distinct but related fields should talk to each other more. To us, this volume vividly demonstrates the valuable and exciting intellectual sparks that such encounters can ignite. We hope it leads to more.

ACKNOWLEDGMENTS

This volume grew out of a conference originally conceived by Poonam Pillai and Shakuntala Rao. We appreciate their inspiration along with Rao's assistance on the early development of the project. The conference was held at the University of Massachusetts in 1992 under the auspices of the Center for the Study of Communication of the Department of Communication. Major support was provided by Mediated: The Foundation for Media Education (Sut Jhally, Executive Director). The Department of Communication, chaired by Jarice Hanson, played an invaluable role. We gratefully acknowledge the time, effort, and support of Karen Schoenberger, Pearl Simanski, Joan Thayer, April Tidlund, Debbie Madigan, Maddy Cahill, Chuck Garrettson, Fanny Rothschild, and Carolyn Anderson.

Mainstream(s) and Margins

Part I

Political Strategies, Identities, and Movements

Notes on Centers and Margins

Poonam Pillai

Articulating the "metaphysics of presence" in *Writing and Difference,*
Derrida argues that

> It would be possible to show that all the names related to fundamentals, to prin-
> ciples, or to the center have always designated the constant of a presence—*eidos,
> arche, telos, energia, ousia* (essence, existence, substance, subject) *aletheia,* tran-
> scendentality, consciousness, or conscience, God, man, and so forth. (1967, pp.
> 410–411)

Presence, according to Derrida, implies immediacy or self-presence of
being to itself and characterizes the central organizing principle of Western metaphysics.[1] The latter is constituted by philosophical oppositions
such as speech/writing, presence/absence, intelligible/sensible, unity/dif-
ference, subject/object, which sustain a "violent hierarchy." The first term
of these dualisms is the "central term of the metaphysical system" and
is "prior and superior" to the other (Ryan, 1982, p. 9). The second term
is contingent and defined by the former. Derrida relates "centrism" to
the desire for unity, order, and self-presence.[2] Phonocentrism, for example, refers to the priority of speech over writing. It assumes the immediacy of speech where unlike writing, the relation between the

signifier and the signified is given and natural. Derrida's project is to reverse and displace the binary relation between center and margin.

The term "center," in most discussions such as the one just suggested, is assumed to be both dominant and defining.[3] For instance, Derrida's critique of the term presence assumes that it signifies both that which is normative, legitimate, and desired, and that which defines the status of "absences." In using the center/margin distinction to characterize unequal power relations, we often situate the oppressor at the center and the oppressed at the margins of social hierarchies. We tend to assume that there is an inherent or objective connection between centrality and power. The fact that centrality and marginality might themselves be complex and contradictory sites of human subjectivity is often ignored.

It is possible to understand centrality as dominant and defining and as dominant but not defining. This distinction constitutes a hierarchy of social relations. Despite being normative, centrality may be a site of certain forms of oppression, in which case it is not necessarily emancipatory or desirable. The location of middle-class Indian women during the 19th-century nationalist movement in India illustrates this point well.

One of the sites within which the question of women's rights emerged in 19th-century India was within the context of the nationalist discourse. As Partha Chatterjee argues in his essay "Nationalist Resolution of the Women's Question" (Chatterjee, 1990), the eventual resolution of the women's question was based on the division of the cultural sphere into the material and the spiritual. Whereas the West was assumed to be more advanced materially, India's cultural heritage was considered to be far superior spiritually. The "ideological justification for the selective appropriation of western modernity" (Chatterjee, 1990, p. 238) was grounded in the belief that political independence and cultural autonomy would only be possible if the West was imitated in the material sphere. Chatterjee argues that the nationalist discourse provided the articulating principle through which the distinction between the material and the spiritual emerged as a more stringent dichotomy between the inner and outer, home and the world, public and private. A rearticulated patriarchy marked the external, material world as the domain of the male, confining women to the private sphere. By linking the goal of national liberation with women's progress, the nationalist discourse subjected them to new forms of domination (p. 248). To quote Chatterjee,

The burden of the retrogressive effects upon men of being in the outside world were to be borne by women through spiritual purification. The new patriarchy advocated by nationalism conferred upon women the honor of a new social responsibility, and by associating the task of "female emancipation" with the historical goal of sovereign nationhood, bound them to a new and entirely legitimate, subordination. (1990, p. 250)

Although a detailed exposition of the exclusions through which the notion of an ideal Indian womanhood was constructed is outside the scope of this chapter,[4] the preceding discussion has important implications for the center/margin distinction.

It shows that the ideological and material containment of women was made possible through the consideration of home as *dominant* and *superior* to the public sphere. Although middle-class Indian women occupied a space that was considered superior to that occupied by men, they did not have the agency to choose or define it in relation to the public sphere. Thus, in spite of being located at the "center" of the nation's subjectivity, these women faced new forms of subordination. This suggests that centrality as a privileged space may also be a site of containment. Hence, the terms center/margin cannot unproblematically be equated with oppressor/oppressed and need to be rethought in terms of a more complex notion of location.

The problem with understanding cultural processes through binary oppositions such as inside/outside or core/periphery is that they do not adequately account for the interconnectedness and complexity among different histories, identities, and social formations. Often, positionalities signified by the terms center and periphery are regarded as autonomous and homogenous, and the historical trajectories through which they are constructed are neglected. For instance, many theorists of postmodernity, while engaging in sophisticated critiques of essentialism, ignore the history of colonialism in their analysis of metropolitan identities and social relations. David Harvey's *The Condition of Postmodernity* (1989) is one example where little or no reference is made to European expansionism in the analysis of the displacement from modernity to postmodernity or in the historical development of capitalism. The effect is not only to dehistoricize the emergence of postmodernity, but also to reconstruct "West" and East" as binary opposites. By insisting that "the founding moment of modernity was the moment of colonialism" (Bhabha, 1990b, p. 219) postcolonial theorists have drawn attention to the problems in counterposing "East" and "West" as independent social and cultural formations. Binary oppositions not only undermine the differences between but also those within centers and margins. As Trinh Minh-ha (1990) points out, "Differences do not only exist between outsider and insider—two entities. They are also at work within the outsider herself, or the insider herself—a single entity" (p. 375). Some cultural critics reject the use not only of a single center/periphery model but also the assumption of multiple cores and peripheries in articulating the dynamics of global cultural processes. Appadurai (1990) argues that understanding relations of power in terms of multiple centers and peripheries fails to account for the "fundamental disjunctures between economy, culture and politics" that have become integral to the dynamics of global cultural forces (p. 296).

What is at issue in rethinking identity and cultural practices away from the binary opposition between center and margin are questions of difference, power, and location. Many feminists and postcolonial theorists have recently drawn attention to the importance of positionality, theorizing it not as a pregiven and natural, but a space of cultural resistance and struggle. Instead of being understood as a stable, uniform site of identity formation, it is understood in terms of complex and nonsynchronous processes that position subjects in uneven ways. Far from being neutral, it is assumed to be inscribed within historically constituted relations of power. For Chandra Mohanty a "politics of location" refers to the "historical, geographical, cultural, psychic and imaginative boundaries which provide the ground for political definition and self-definition" (1992, p. 74). Chicana writer and activist Gloria Anzaldua expresses this through the notion of "borderlands."

Cradled in one culture, sandwiched between two cultures, straddling all three cultures and their value systems, *la mestiza* undergoes a struggle of flesh, a struggle of borders, an inner war. Like all people, we perceive the version of reality that our culture communicates. Like others having or living in more than one culture, we get multiple often opposing messages. The coming together of two self-consistent but habitually inconsistent frames of reference causes *un choque*, a cultural collusion. (1987, p. 78)

The consciousness of the borderlands is grounded in a tolerance for ambiguity, difference, and contradiction. It departs from habitual ways of thinking and is based on a "massive uprooting of dualistic thinking in the individual and collective consciousness" (p. 80). According to Anzaldua, it involves taking an inventory of history, a public acknowledgment of the history of cultural genocide, and documenting the struggle of oppressed peoples against the racism of white society. It implies rearticulating old myths and creating new ones. Ultimately, it demands "an accounting of all three cultures, white, Mexican, Indian" (p. 22). What is important about Anzaldua's retheorization of positionality through notions of hybridity is that it does not lose sight of differences in histories and power between white, Mexican, and Indian, between male and female, and between heterosexual and homosexual. It locates oppositional consciousness within the experience of displacement and oppression, and calls for more than a *discursive* shift from homogenous forms of identity politics. In this sense I find her theorization of hybridity much more enabling than Homi Bhabha's (1990a) in his essay "DissemiNation: time, narrative and the margins of the modern nation."

Bhabha's critique is directed against the homogenous, autonomous and linear ways in which the modern nation space/time is constituted. He rejects the notion of nation as an independent form of political rationality (p. 293). Drawing attention to the ambivalence of both the temporal and spatial dimensions of the narrative strategies through which the notion of nation is invoked and its subjects interpellated, Bhabha insists upon a strategy of writing the nation which rejects "a 'centered' causal logic" (p. 293).

The problematic that Bhabha addresses is how to rearticulate the nation space so that it is marked by cultural difference *"internally."* He theorizes this by arguing that the terms "the nation" and "the people" derive their narrative and psychological force not from their sociological or historical unity, but from the "ambivalence of nation as a narrative strategy—and an apparatus of power" (Bhabha, 1990a, p. 292). The "structure of ambivalence" through which the nation is narrated is a result of a tension between the "continuist, accumulative temporality of the pedagogical, and the repetitious, recursive strategy of the performative. It is through this splitting that the conceptual ambivalence of modern society becomes the site of *writing the nation"* (Bhabha, 1990a, p. 297).

In Bhabha's formulation, the "structure of ambivalence constituting modern social authority" (p. 297) is derived mainly from a linguistic model. The lack of certainty and "fullness" marking positions of enunciation and reception make any claim to cultural supremacy untenable. This allows him to argue that representational strategies invoking "the nation" and "the people" are the articulation not of any self-contained narrative, but of the ambivalence of the national address. This opens up the possibility of the narratives of other people and their differences *within* the nation space (p. 300). Thus, Bhabha brings liminality right into the nation space. "Cultural difference" is inscribed in the very act of enunciation and is no longer a problem of the people as "other" but the "people-as-one" (Bhabha, 1990a, p. 301).

In proposing "cultural difference" as a theoretical analytic, Bhabha suggests a strategy not of inversion but of reinscription. It is not to install the margins at the center, but to transform the very *topos* of articulation between centers and margins. This changes the positions of enunciation and address within it. By arguing that self-alienation is the very condition of living, he redraws the liminalities of the nation space, locating different forms of living and speaking *within* it.

Bhabha's strategy of bringing liminality into the nation space is very inclusive but limited. First, it does not provide insight into the social, economic or political conditions which continue to maintain center/margin relations as such. This is not Bhabha's project, but one needs to account for how discursive practices articulate with non-discursive relations of power in order to transform existing structures of social authority.[5] Language by itself cannot provide the conditions for the reinscription of the cultural and national terrain that Bhabha wants. In the absence of a theory of articulation between cultural, economic, and political practices, the reinscribed space/time of "cultural difference" simply becomes an effect of the ambivalence of narrative strategies.

Further, by locating the conditions of possibility of minority discourse within the ambivalent structures constituting the *narrative* of nation, Bhabha undermines the realm of social experience as a site of production of oppositional discourses and practices. Many feminists have struggled hard to validate experience as a legitimate site for the production of counter-hegemonic discourses, knowledge and resistance (cf. Anzaldua, 1987; hooks, 1990; Fuss, 1989; Mohanty, 1992; Scott, 1992). Critiquing Bhabha's theorization of hybridity, Rey Chow argues that his argument

> ultimately makes it unnecessary to come to terms with the subaltern since she has already "spoken," as it were, in the system's gaps. All we would need to do would be to continue to study—to deconstruct—the rich and ambivalent language of the imperialist! What Bhabha's word "hybridity" revives, in the masquerade of deconstruction, anti-imperialism, and "difficult" theory, is an old functionalist notion of what dominant culture permits in the interests of maintaining its own equilibrium. Such functionalism informs the investigatory methods of classical anthropology and sociology as much as it does the colonial policies of the British Empire. (1993, p. 35)

Bhabha's (1990a) project, as I have suggested, is to theorize cultural difference so as to bring liminality *within* the nation-space. But, being internal to a given space is not always emancipatory or even desirable. As Chatterjee's (1990) analysis of the debate over women's rights in 19th-century India shows, women and minorities have often been marginalized in spite of being *within* the nation space. The question is on what/whose terms is one being included within any particular space. Who defines a community, controls membership, and wants to or does not want to be part of it? These questions are not interrogated in Bhabha's analysis. Finally, what is troubling about his "non-pluralistic politics of difference" (p. 305) is that we are into a realm of pure difference where there seems to be no legitimation for the conception of nation but only the living of the "*locality* of culture." In his formulation, I find no basis for solidarity or community except the temporality of Renan's daily plebiscite.[6] This ignores the coalition of women *as* women, of the indigenous *as* indigenous, or blacks *as* blacks, in a context in which women are oppressed *as* women and native Americans are oppressed because of the demands they make as indigenous people (cf. Churchill, 1993). To put it in terms of a politics of location, oppression has often been oriented around, but not necessarily limited to being situated *within* a gendered body, *within* a hierarchy of color, or *within* a certain culture, language, or territory. The politics and limits of being internal to any hegemonic space must be addressed in any discourse of hybridity and reinscription of center/margin relations.

One of the key issues underlying the ideological distinction between centers and margins is that of power, understood in terms of economic, political, and ideological practices. How can someone with power and privilege take responsibility for her own location? Adrienne Rich provides us with a blueprint in her classic essay "Notes Towards a Politics of Location" (1986). Situating herself as a white, lesbian, Jew, feminist, she criticizes white, middle-class, Western feminists for excluding the struggles of black feminists and women of color, and subsuming their differences under the homogenous category "Woman." "That only certain kinds of people can make theory; that the white educated mind is capable of formulating everything; that white middle-class feminism can know for 'all women'; that only when a white mind formulates is the formulation to be taken seriously" (Rich, 1986, p. 230). She locates the "whiteness" of Western feminist theory—its constitutive center—in such exclusions. Rich argues that in refusing to engage seriously with the work of feminists of color, "white feelings remain at the center. And yes, I need to move outward from the base and center of my feelings, but with a corrective sense that my feelings are not *the* center of feminism" (Rich, 1986, p. 231).

For Rich, location is not simply a matter of personal history, interest, and experience, but also a question of political solidarity. Hence, to take one's location seriously is not to construct a taxonomy of personal preferences, but to situate oneself historically within specific relations of power. Both literally and metaphorically her body becomes a starting point of struggle. It implies more than having "a vulva and clitoris and uterus and breasts. It means recognizing this white skin, the places it has taken me, the places it has not let me go" (p. 216). Characterizing the position of white Western women, she argues that although they have been marginalized *as women,* they have also been privileged by being situated within the Western tradition. It is for the meaning of "whiteness as a point of location" that they must take responsibility in order to construct a feminist consciousness that is not exclusivist. This is how Rich deconstructs her own position.

It was in the writings but also the actions and speeches and sermons of Black United States citizens that I began to experience the meaning of my whiteness as a point of location for which I needed to take responsibility. It was in reading poems by contemporary Cuban women that I began to experience the meaning of North America as a location which had also shaped my ways of seeing and my ideas of who and what was important, a location for which I was also responsible. (p. 220)

She argues that the possibility of social change lies "not in some debate over origins and precedents, but in the recognition of simultaneous oppressions" (p. 227). A failure to do so is perhaps hinged on the "confusion between our claims to the white and Western eye and the woman-seeing eye, fear of losing the centrality of one even as we claim the other" (p. 219).

What I find most persuasive about Rich's essay is her articulation of power. Even while recognizing the fear involved in losing one's privileges, she returns over and over again to the theme that "all privilege is ignorant at the core," of the "arrogance of believing ourselves at the center" (p. 223), and the need to move away from the center of one's location. In short, the necessity of those who are privileged, to account for their power and learn to question it. Rather than romanticizing one's ability to do so, Rich emphasizes the necessity of doing so in bringing about social change. This idea is also reiterated in Caren Kaplan's reworking of Deleuze and Guattari's notion of "deterritorialization" (1987, p. 191). Kaplan describes it as "the displacement of identities, persons, meanings that is endemic to the postmodern world system" (p. 188).

Arguing against simplistic evocations of embracing marginalities or "becoming minor" on the part of the first world critic, where "the margin becomes a linguistic or critical vacation, a new poetics of the exotic," Kaplan argues that there is a difference between "whether or not it is possible for me to *choose* deterritorialization or whether deterritorialization has chosen me" (p. 191). Within the present historical conjuncture, the challenge for the first world feminist is to construct a discourse that takes stock of the power relations she inhabits. "Any other strategy merely consolidates the illusion of marginality while glossing over or refusing to acknowledge centralities" (p. 189). Drawing on Minni Bruce Pratts' autobiographical essay, "Identity: Skin, Blood, Heart," Kaplan describes the process of "deterritorialization" or "becoming minor" as the process of leaving the security of home, of coming to terms with the absences within one's knowledge, and engaging with the different and unfamiliar. It involves a refusal of universalizing theories and a recognition that gender cannot be the common basis connecting all women. It is only through such a process of deterritorialization that one can reterritorialize.

Although critics like Rich and Kaplan attempt to deterritorialize in the sense of moving away from the centers they occupy, black feminist critic bell hooks does so by locating herself at the margins. For hooks, home/ marginality is constructed through the experience of pain, oppression and suffering, but it is also a "site of radical possibility, a space of resistance" (1990, p. 149). For her, the possibility of counterhegemonic discourse lies not in the character of the dominant discourse but in the lived experience of struggle and oppression. Hence, she does not speak of a "marginality one wishes to lose—to give up or surrender as part of moving into the center—but rather a site one stays in, clings to even, because it nourishes one's capacities to resist" (pp. 149–150) and create alternative ways of living. For hooks, a critic claiming a position of marginality, deterritorialization implies a movement away from home without forgetting the struggles that the margins have entailed. It involves politicizing one's memory in order to bring about political and economic change. As she argues repeatedly *"our struggle is also a struggle of memory against forgetting"* (1990, p. 147).

As we shift away from a dualistic center/margin framework and inaugurate ways of thinking about identity and positionality in more hybrid and discrepant ways, it is important not to lose sight of the broader relations of power and neocolonial hegemonies within which the production of identities and subjectivities takes place. Here are a few examples that might usefully problematize current invocations of hybridity.

More food is produced in the world today than is consumed. The rate of production of food is greater than the rate of population growth (cf. Bennett, 1987). Most people who die of hunger are children. A staggering 97 percent of them are in the so called "Third World." What does the theorization of hybridity have to do with the systematic ghettoization of hunger?

One of the major problems in the world today according to many mainstream environmentalists is population explosion, most of which is taking place in the "Third World." But, if population is assumed to mean not just numbers of people, but the amount of resources consumed by each person, the issue looks vastly different. Compared to the average person in Uganda or Laos, his/her counterpart in the United States consumes thirty times the amount of energy and resources. According to the World Bank's *World Development Report 1994,* the per capita energy consumption of a person living in America is equivalent to that of 12.77 Chinese, 32.6 Indians, or 50.7 people living in other low-income economies. From the perspective of a person living in China, the American population is about 3.2 billion, for an Indian it is 8.15 billion and for a person in one of the low-income economies it is 12.5 billion.[7] The number of people in the world in mid-1992 was 5.4 billion. Who lives off of whom?

Global warming, for example, is one of the biggest threats to human survival. Some of its well-known causes are rapid increase in greenhouse gases such as carbon dioxide, methane, chlorofluorocarbons, and nitrous oxide into the atmosphere (cf. Leggett, 1990). The increase in these gases is attributed primarily to industrialization, destruction of tropical rainforests, and the enormous dependence on carbon-containing fossil fuels, which provide almost four fifths of the earth's energy (cf. Flavin, 1989). Resulting climactic changes may lead to droughts and floods in many parts of the world, making others too hot to be habitable. In many rural areas in the Third World, where people are largely dependent on forests for their food and livelihood, deforestation has not only led to ecological destruction but has also displaced people and caused extensive malnutrition. In *It's a Matter of Survival,* Gordon and Suzuki note that

The Greenhouse effect is *us,* and it is specifically *us* in the Western world. More than 70 percent of the total global output of greenhouse gases comes from the industrialized world. Canada and the United States are two of the most energy-intensive countries in the world. Our per capita emissions of carbon are more than 16 times that of the developing world, twice that of Japan and Europe. (1991, p. 13)

Here it is important to ask, "Where am I in all of this?"

Although the short-term effects of environmental degradation are disproportionately being borne by the peripheries of both the rich and the poor nations, the *long-term* effects will be felt by everyone. The ability of the rich to insulate themselves is drastically being diminished. Perhaps the environmental crisis more than any other issue will make us realize that who we mean when we say "we" is not so ambiguous after all.

NOTES

1. An earlier version of this chapter, was presented at the Speech Communication Association (SCA) convention, November 1, 1991, Atlanta, Georgia.

2. See Gayatri Spivak, "Translator's Preface" in J. Derrida, *Of Grammatology,* Baltimore and London: Johns Hopkins University Press, 1976.

3. My point of course is not to critique Derrida but to point out a common use of the term "center."

4. See K. Sangari and S. Vaid, Eds., *Recasting Women: Essays in Indian Colonial History,* New Brunswick, N.J.: Rutgers University Press, 1990.

5. See Stuart Hall (1985) for an extensive discussion on the notion of articulation.

6. See Ernest Renan, "What is a Nation?" trans. Martin Thom, in Homi Bhabha, ed., *Nation and Narration,* London and New York: Routledge, 1990.

7. Of course, a similar calculation can be performed comparing a rich and a poor Indian, and so on.

BIBLIOGRAPHY

Anzaldua, Gloria. *Borderlands: The New Mestiza.* San Francisco: Spinsters/Aunt Lute, 1987.
Appadurai, A. "Disjuncture and Difference in the Global Cultural Economy," in

Featherstone, M., ed., *Global Culture: Nationalism, Globalization and Modernity*. London: Sage, 1990.

Bennett, Jon. *The Hunger Machine*. New York: Polity Press, 1987.

Bhabha, Homi, K. (Ed.). *Nation and Narration*. New York: Routledge, 1990a.

———. "The Third Space," in Rutherford, J., ed., *Identity: Community, Culture, Difference*. London: Lawrence & Wishart, 1990b.

Chatterjee, Partha. "The Nationalist Resolution of the Woman's Question," in Sangari, K. & Vaid, S., Eds., *Recasting Women: Essays in Indian Colonial History*, New Brunswick, N.J.: Rutgers University Press, 1990.

Chow, Rey. *Writing Diaspora: Tactics of Intervention in Contemporary Cultural Studies*. Bloomington: Indiana University Press, 1993.

Churchill, Ward. *Struggle for the Land*. Monroe, Maine: Common Courage Press, 1993.

Derrida, Jacques. *Writing and Difference*, Trans. Alan Bass. London: Routledge & Kegan, 1967.

Flavin, Christopher. *Slowing Global Warming: A Worldwide Strategy*. Washington, D.C.: Worldwatch Institute, 1989.

Fuss, Diana. *Essentially Speaking*. New York: Routledge, 1989.

Gordon, A. & Suzuki, D. *It's A Matter of Survival*. Cambridge: Harvard University Press, 1991.

Hall, Stuart. "Althusser and the Post-Structuralist Debates." *Critical Studies in Mass Communication*, Vol. 2, No. 2, June 1985.

Harvey, David. *The Condition of Postmodernity*. Cambridge: Blackwell Publishers, 1989.

hooks, bell. *Yearning; Race, Gender, and Cultural Politics*. Boston: South End Press, 1990.

Kaplan, Caren. "Deterritorializations: The Rewriting of Home and Exile in Western Feminist Discourse." *Cultural Critique*, Vol. 6, No. 6 (Spring 1987): 187–198.

Leggett, Jeremy. *Global Warming: The Greenpeace Report*. Oxford: Oxford University Press, 1990.

Minh-ha, Trinh T. "Not You/Like You: Post-Colonial Women and the Interlocking Questions of Identity and Difference," in Anzaldua, G., ed., *Making Face, Making Soul*. San Francisco: Aunt Lute Foundation Books, 1990.

Mohanty, Chandra Talpade. "Feminist Encounters: Locating the Politics of Experience," in Barrett, M. & Phillips, A., eds., *Destabilizing Theory*. Stanford, Calif.: Stanford University Press, 1992.

Rich, Adrienne. *Blood, Bread, Poetry*. New York: W.W. Norton, 1986.

Ryan, Michael. *Marxism and Deconstruction, A Critical Articulation*. Baltimore and London: Johns Hopkins University Press, 1982.

Scott, Joan W. "Experience," in Butler, J. and Scott, J.W., eds., *Feminists Theorize the Political*. New York: Routledge, 1992.

Spivak, Gayatri Chakravorty. "Translator's Preface," in J. Derrida, *Of Grammatology*, Trans. Gayatri Chakravorty Spivak, Baltimore: Johns Hopkins University Press, 1976.

World Development Report 1994. Oxford: Oxford University Press, 1994.

Mainstreams and Leakage: Interrogating the Margins of "Art" and "Porn"

Rebecca Schneider

There are any number of mainstreams—some, however, flow underground. Pornography might be considered an underground mainstream—a broadly based and integral part of the complex flow of social imagery, a kind of vast underbelly to the socially "appropriate" arenas of art and popular culture. More subterranean than marginal, there has been considerable traffic—often mimetic—between porn and the "higher," more socially acceptable flow of art. This chapter casts a broad net to explore some issues at the margins between porn and art, specifically the related images of the prostitute and the primitive as they have been imaged and employed in various venues from the high modernism of Manet to the confrontative historical avant-garde of Alfred Jarry to contemporary feminist and "post-porn-modernist" works.

The late 1980s and early 1990s have seen a burgeoning of confrontative, explicit body work in performance, photography, and studio arts. Much current work actively leaks across the margins separating porn and art. From Cindy Sherman to Karen Finley to Annie Sprinkle, artists have been employing their own physical bodies as visceral templates for cultural criticism in a new mise-en-scène of the socially engendered body. Photographer Sherman has taken self-portraits that range from the mimicry of starlets in movie stills to scenes of explicit display, disembodiment, and decay.[1] Performance artist Finley chants monologs describing horrific and abusive family scenes and sexual scenarios as she applies viscous substances to her body.[2] Pornographer Sprinkle has "come out" as a prostitute, publicly celebrating and explicating her profession while putting her body on display in art venues—from posing in standard porn style to inviting audience members up to the stage to view her cervix through a speculum.[3]

Much of this contemporary and confrontative "art" work is linked in important ways to the roots of the performative avant-garde dating to the last century in Europe.[4] Especially relevant to contemporary explicit body work is the historical thrall with the "savage" fetish as antithetical to art and the conjuncture of that fetish and the primitive generally with excretory and genital physicality. Exploring the art historical thrall of the primitive, and the related fascination with the prostitute, uncovers some important issues confronting current manipulation of the explicit female body in politicized—feminist—art contexts today and raises questions about contemporary fascination with the primitive and the prostitute as we imagine ourselves in postmodern and postcolonial contexts.

One of the hallmarks of modernism is the rise of realist depictions of "lowlife" subjects. The social and political upheavals of the mid-19th century gave birth to a movement that rejected all idealization in art and literature to depict concrete contemporary reality. Desire for democracy in the arts opened up a new range of subjects, previously considered unworthy of representation. Of course, although newly ennobled in representation and celebrated in the frame of art, in the frame of the everyday world actual lowlife remained socially and politically handicapped, subject to the social delimitations and environmental conditions of their class, gender, and race—conditions that had inspired artistic curiosity in the first place. With a particularly modernist twist, an artist's depiction of "lowlife" could reinscribe the "low" through mimetic representation while remaining at an aesthetic and quasi-scientific vantage point that actually buttressed the "high" of an artist's perspective and, by extension, the perspective of his art-appreciating audience. Especially with the rise of science-inspired naturalism, but also via science-inspired modernist formalisms,[5] lowlife could be brought into the frame and under the gaze of those who purveyed and those who owned art. As the subjects of modern "masters," lowlife (prostitutes, criminals, savages, etc.) could be framed—the socially inappropriate could be appropriated under the auspices and ultimate explications, however scandalous, of a master's eye.

The prostitute's body became an emblematic border crosser between high and low, art and porn genres. Widely imaged across modernist canvases and texts, the prostitute, like the racially marked "primitive," became a quintessential modernist subject manipulated in art and literature by Greats (especially French Greats) from Baudelaire to Degas, Zola, and

Picasso.[6] As a woman, the prostitute straddles the border of the appropriate (she is a human female) and the inappropriate (she is a whore).
So too the primitive or colonial subject is both appropriate (human) and
inappropriate (not-quite human).[7] Walter Benjamin cited modernist fascination with the prostitute as stemming from the general concern over
the place of art in commodity capitalism. Relative to that concern, the
prostitute appears to embody a paradox: she is both commodity and
seller in one—a bizarre collapse of active and passive, subject and object,
into a single entity.[8] Her inappropriate image was appropriated to signify
the "real" as opposed to the ideal or, as in Manet's 1863 paintings *Le
Dejeuner sur l'herbe* and *Olympia,* she became the strained site of tension, the paradoxical intersection between the historical beauty of the
ideal and the contemporary corruption of the real.[9]

It is often suggested that Manet's *Olympia* (1863) caused a scandal and
was proclaimed indecent in its day because it presented a prostitute who
"looks back" at her audience with disdain, seemingly denying her status
as low through her defiant sense of self, as if reveling with narcissistic
pleasure in her mimesis or pretense of the ideal. Georges Bataille argues
that modern art begins with Manet because Manet's subjects defy their
traditional contexts. For Bataille, Manet began the destruction of paintings' pretexts. In the case of *Olympia,* it is the social pretext of prostitution that is destroyed as the courtesan, through her gaze of seeming
self-possession, both indicates and denies the conventional reading of her
position. In Bataille's words: "The picture obliterates the text, and the
meaning of the picture is not in the text behind it but in the obliteration
of that text."[10] And yet it is worth noting that regardless of pretext and
anti-text, gaze and countergaze, the frame of "art" remains intact. Olympia's disdainful glance remains under Manet's authorizing signature, and
under the more invisible signature of those who determine membership
in the category of "great" or canonical art, making the painting a high
art depiction of lowlife pride. The prostitute herself, after all, has no
ultimate agency, regardless of the destruction of her "pretext." It is almost absurd to point out that neither said Olympia nor the model who
posed with said self-possession could co-sign the painting or wield even
an ounce of art historical agency, no matter how defiantly Manet may be
argued to have rendered her gaze. Following Sander Gilman's reading of
the painting, Manet's placement of the black serving woman in *Olympia*
can be read relative to pretexts of contemporary racisms as underscoring
the primitivized nature of female sexuality, rendering Olympia's suggested defiance as ultimately ineffectual in that the scene of her sexuality
is displaced beyond her person onto the symbolic body of her black ser-
vant.[11]

The point here is simply that regardless of the status afforded her defiance, modern *Olympia* is altogether different from postmodern avant-

garde works that do not attempt to represent the low within a high art frame, but actually attempt to wrestle with the frame itself, crossing the border between high and low. Something very different is afoot—more in line with Alfred Jarry's toilet brush/scepter, Dada's masks and drums, Marcel Duchamp's toilet seat—when a work does not depict a subject of social degradation, but actually *is* that degradation. Such an overlapping and contesting of the borders between low and high, between porn and art, is exhibited blatantly in the contemporary works of Annie Sprinkle, Robert Mapplethorpe, Linda Montano, Jeff Koons, Veronica Vera, and Sandra Bernhardt, to name a few. In the works of these artists, standard pornographic acts, images, or texts cross the border from low to high to be framed as "art" in galleries or museums or on art stages. In a similar move, "legit" artists cross from high to low, declaring themselves pornographers or porn queens as they cross the art tracks to pose for porno spreads.[12] In such work, distinctions between categories, and thus the categories themselves, come profoundly into question.

Concerned about the place of an artist in a burgeoning market economy, Baudelaire, in *Fusees,* answered his own question "What is art?" with the statement, "Prostitution." He also romanticized and identified with savage "apaches," low-class "ragpickers," and perverse "lesbians."[13] Yet Baudeliare's suggestion that the artist prostitutes himself when making art as a commodity remained metaphorical. Baudelaire did not become a literal whore any more than he became a lesbian. Neither did he really cross class, no matter what state of abjection he courted as an early "bohemian" artist.[14] Artistic slumming could suggest a border crossing, all the while building status. Metaphoric gesturing toward the whorehouse is one thing, but it is quite another thing when an actual prostitute attempts to claim the place of artist in the museum. That is, the artist can enter and manipulate the inverted make-believe and sadomasochistic play frames of the whorehouse, but the whore cannot as easily occupy the above-ground, hallowed halls of the museum. When the whore herself attempts to cross the border, the sacred divide between porn and art is thrown more immediately into relief. When Olympia defies the validating signature of the male artist and steps out of his frame to become a performance artist, perhaps stretching out live in the museum or gallery and claiming space as art *and* artist, she directly challenges the illicit relation between high and low, which doubles as a gendered relation and, in a complex concatenation, a race relation. The sexually active woman as both (lowlife) object *and* (high) artist straddles and challenges a deeply ingrained gender divide in which active or overt female sexuality is conceived as inherently debased.

Because female sexuality is socially, culturally, politically, and economically debased in patriarchal society—even while seemingly worshiped aesthetically—it is antithetical to the positively ascribed "virility" of an artist. In 1917 Duchamp could "create" a woman—Rrose Selavy—as the alter-ego of his artist self, sometimes signing his "Readymades" with her name.[15] Woman was, after all, a prime patriarchal readymade—or ready maid, if you will. As wielded by Duchamp, gender (especially the female gender) was denaturalized and rendered performative, readily made. Duchamp could cross between artist and woman with bravado and a bad-boy aplomb that bordered on grace, but it was something different for *women*, those bearing the literal markings of woman in their physical bodies, to cross as artists. We can look to 1963, exactly 100 years after *Olympia*, as a watershed point at which a number of women began to loudly defy the structural impossibility of being both passionate women *and* artists.[16] If Rrose Selavy was Duchamp's alter-ego, the 1960s saw the first rush of refusal to allow female embodiment to be "alter" to artistic identity as works began to appear that incorporated and emphasized the explicit body of the female artist in the art work. In her 1963 *Eye-Body*, Carolee Schneemann stretched out nude in her own installation, becoming both artist and object, both eye and body at once.[17] She was the artist *and* the nude. She was Olympia *and* Manet—a move that gave a certain agency and artistic authority to the defiant pride of those delimited as "low." In 1964, collaborating with sculptor David Morris, Schneemann actually performed a live version of *Olympia*, titled *Site*, in which the artist lay on Olympia's couch, dressed like Olympia in nothing but a black neck choker, while Morris built a wooden frame around her.[18] Schneemann's work was often dismissed as self-indulgent and narcissistic by the art establishment but other women, many influenced by Schneemann, began making similar work confronting the sacrosanct boundaries separating female sexuality and artistic authority. The roots of feminist performance art, which would flourish in the 1970s, took obstinate hold and many boundaries, closely linked to the socially demarcated margins separating artist/woman, high/low, subject/object dichotomies, began to leak and bleed together under the insistent banner of political purpose.[19]

A PROSTITUTE AND AN ARTIST

At least since Alfred Jarry's exclamation of "shittr" (*merdre*) in his riotous production of *Ubu Roi* in 1896, leakages and border crossings between high and low have been a staple of the historical avant-garde. That the current avant-garde continues to threaten the margins segregating above-ground and underground mainstreams is attested to by the National Endowment for the Arts (NEA) funding crisis over Robert Mapplethorpe, James Serrano, Karen Finley, Holly Hughes, Tim Miller, and John Fleck that brought the 1980s to a close.[20] It is the categories themselves that appear to be fundamentally threatened by the transgression of discretionary borders, as if art would cease to exist if porn or smut or obscenity lost definition, and vice versa. As long as porn keeps within its appropriate margins marked "low," art can somehow maintain its status as "high" even while reproducing that low within its own framings. Thus Olympia can be low within the controlling frame of high, but if she leaks outside the frame to manipulate the frame itself as artist then the high/low category is fundamentally threatened. When kept to its guttural place, the openly secret (and secreted) underground mainstream of pornographic images maintains its social sanction as the appropriate inappropriate, the sacred taboo. Maintained as inappropriate, pornography thus supports and maintains the categorical privilege of its social superior, which in turn continues to look into its gutters for "subject matter."

At issue in the demarcation of high and low is the social control of sexuality. But the display of sexuality itself is not the ultimate determinate of the border between high and low. Scratching even lightly at the surface of distinctions between art and porn reveals the fact that the explicit sexual body is nothing new to the hallowed halls of high art. There are countless examples of physical explicitude and seemingly pornographic content in the annals of art history. Bodily parts have been exposed for centuries in the art canon. The distinction between "art" and "outright pornography" at the Greco-Roman roots of Western civilization is particularly problematic, and even after the repressive triumph of Christianity in the Middle Ages, explicitly sexual physicality found expression as Art.[21] Historically the demarcation between art and porn has not been about the explicit sexual body itself, but rather about agency, which is to say about *who gets to be master and who must remain subject—who gets to make what explicit where.* More directed toward the control of the frame around the explicit gendered body than the category of the body itself, the issue really concerns who, or what interest group, gets to *explicate* the terrain of "the body" and appropriate bodily parts. Interestingly, the words explicit and explicate stem from the Latin *explicare,* which means, not without noted irony, to unfold. Who, the issue seems to be, gets to control the unfolding of sexual signifiers?

"My body is a temple" advertised pornographer/porn star/performance artist Veronica Vera. "My body is a temple" appeared in large bold type on a 1989 promo flyer that pictured a nude black man performing oral sex with Vera. In the picture, we see only the man's broad and muscular backside, his head bent to his task. With her black-lace-corsetted front to the camera, Vera's is the only face we see but her expression is so stock, so standard as to almost be unreadable. It is the stock porn-pleasure face, the semi-comatose, open-mouthed, tongue-draped expression signifying "X rated." Nothing out of the porn-ordinary at all. But despite the stock quality of the posing, Vera's promotion was not conventional porn promotion.

The photo is Robert Mapplethorpe's and Vera's flyer made the most of the Helms/Mapplethorpe funding controversy exploding at that time. A new label heralded the not-so-tongue-in-cheek politics of the porn she was wielding, and that label was the three-letter-word "art," giving validity to the four-letter "porn" by such up-scale avant-garde venues as The Kitchen, Franklin Furnace Gallery, and the New Museum in Manhattan. Work such as Vera's began to be shown in such venues in the mid-1980s,[22] where discretionary boundaries defining supposedly discrete centers—porn and art—were being laid over top of each other, resulting in an interrogation not only of the usual form and content, but also of function and frame. Important in this regard is that in much of this work it is the pornographized object, the woman in front of the camera, who is as reincarnated as artist, adding complex layers to the boundaries transgressed. Vera's piece, for instance, with its proclamation that the artist/porn queen's body is a sacred site, a "temple," plays provocatively with essentialist impulses in a medium (porn) embattled by the dual (and oddly coupled) fronts of liberal feminists and conservative fundamentalists.

Vera is one of several women in avant-garde performance who are further complicating our already embattled notions of what it means to "liberate" the body marked female from the confines of patriarchal delimitation. The clash of the rubrics "porn" and "art" do much of that complicating, raising Dadaesque questions about the *social functions* masked by the implicit "high" of fundable art and "low" of porn, questions that might double as interrogating the social functions of sexual economies such as gender, and in this particular flyer, race. But the questions are not clearly or even palatably posed. In the example of Vera's flyer, we read that Vera's body is a temple—a sacred place, yet clearly the iconography of that sacrality is the iconography of pornography, socially marked as base. Thus, to the degree that the artist's object, her body, fits the stock porn format, or works within the standard lexicon of porn significances, then sacrality doubles as its own social underbelly, the socially sanctioned realm of the base, the familiar and readable taboo of porn.

Flash the word "art" over the word "porn" and new ways of reading both begin to proliferate, if only in the teasing question: "How are you going to approach this one?" In the Vera/Mapplethorpe photo, for instance, is this an artwork to be taken solely for its formal elements so that we can ignore the blatancy of its contents, which make absolutely no deviation from porn standard? The argument that Mapplethorpe was a master of classical form won Dennis Barrie his acquittal when on trial for obscenity after mounting Mapplethorpe's *Perfect Moment* at his Cincinnati gallery in 1990.[23] In effect, Mapplethorpe's arguable mastery of formal properties excused, even eclipsed, the supposed obscene confrontation of his contents. And yet, despite the finding in Barrie's case, the supremacy of form over content seems so clearly to be one thing that the contents of much of Mapplethorpe's work mocks. The necessity of a social and political "decision" here, regarding art status and appropriateness of venue, leads to the proposition that framing or venue is ultimately that which determines artistic value. This would be to argue that any image framed in an "art museum" or an art historical textbook is art while the same image as a fold out in *Bazoombas* or *Hot Pussy* is, by virtue of the venue, porn. Thus it is not the contents within the frames but the frames themselves, and the social "appropriates" or "inappropriates" that those frames determine, that "artify" or "pornographize." The suggestion of a transgression of venue was precisely what caused the general Mapplethorpe uproar in the first place. Barrie's case had to be *decided* relative to appropriateness of venue, and it was the critical commentary (historical, social critical, formal, or otherwise) that could be extracted from Mapplethorpe's work in art historical banter that ultimately decided his case in the direction of "art." Thus, antecedent to framing or venue is art historical commentary and it might follow that art historical commentary is where art has always and only existed, and, further, that the social sanctioning of art has been an arena for social commentary on the socially, culturally, and politically appropriate (in both noun and verb senses of the word).

In terms of social and art historical commentary, the Vera/Mapplethorpe piece and the collapse of the space between porn and art which their collaboration invites can be provocative. Even the suggestion of collaboration is itself provocative. If Victorine Meurent, who posed as Olympia, had made a flyer of Manet's painting of her repose (which she may well have done for all history has allowed us to know), claiming artistic merit as *performer,* perhaps this issue would have been considered much earlier. In Mapplethorpe's picture and in Vera's modeling for and then reframing of that picture within a dual context of porn and performance art, the classical symmetry of Mapplethorpe's formal arrangement interacts with the unruly blatancy of Vera's content. Mapplethorpe's symmetry of form beckons the viewer to place his work alongside other formally correct canonical entries across the history of Western Art, such as ancient Greek sculpture (again, the Barrie trial serves as indicative).[24] And yet it is that very "placing beside" that becomes confrontative because the blatant content of Mapplethorpe's work, rife with contemporary taboos and subcultural references that disallow easy dismissal as simply or nostalgically Dionysian, can be seen to speak to or comment on the *social and political* history of formal artworks that ghost the piece.

But it is not only Mapplethorpe's form that is ghosted by canonical precedent. The content, too, can be said to be ghosted by art historical precedence, and such ghostings might suggest "ways of seeing" a piece such as *My Body is a Temple.* In Mapplethorpe's photo of Vera, it is not the black man's penis (invisible in the photo), that mytho-cultural locus of white male fear and envy,[25] that prompts the white woman's mimicry of pleasure, but his equally invisible tongue. Yet Vera's lax-mouthed expression seems to suggest that his unseen tongue *is* working—dare we read *speaking?* Looking to art canonical precedence, Vera's explicit literality as a templed goddess (her literal and particular body) finds unlikely company in the implicit symbology of the Virgin. Dissembling and disseminating through the aesthetic distance and supposed disinterestedness afforded the Symbol, the white dove stand-in for the holy Father repeatedly penetrates and impregnates the Virgin Mother through her unsuspecting (unconsenting) ear in paintings canonized in the halls of art museums around the Western world. In Vera's "art," however, a black man speaks into the cunt of the consenting prostitute/artist/model—not in the same frame, please! Keep the contexts discrete. Bleeding out of the socially sanctioned taboo of porn into the "light-of-day" of art, the content of those taboos (especially as they stick to the lexicon of porn) have the potential to become incendiary social commentary, especially to the degree that such works "talk back" to the sacred and the sanctioned, the canonical, unveiling a secret in the symbolism by *literalizing* that which it excludes, that is, *literalizing that which it secret(e)s.* Such literalization almost automatically triggers issues of the state, the family, gender, and race.

Collapsing the myth of disinterestedness, porn threatens to brings the domain of *literal* content (with its immediate and "interested" aim toward sexual, or visceral, tactile effect, and its tongue-in-cheek inversion of Freud's symbolic cigar: sometimes a penis is just a penis) raging into art contexts that have traditionally commanded the phallic domain of symbolic form (distanced by aesthetic "disinterestedness"). In the tangle of issues implied in such work, the overlap, indeed the collapse, of the symbolic into the literal and the literal into the symbolic (which doubles, interestingly as the collapse of obscenity into sacrality and sacrality into obscenity), is crucial and comments on the Helmsian anxiety over the transgression of the sacred social pact of keeping our porn porn, our art art.

Coming out of the porn industry, or "coming out" as porn queens in art spaces, Veronica Vera and Annie Sprinkle call themselves post-porn modernists. Others have crossed from the art and performance side of the tracks into the porn world wielding the same issues (aruably less successfully), such as performance artist/TV personality Sandra Bernhardt's recent self-exposure in *Playboy.* From the high-art avant-garde come explicit body artists such as Karen Finley and Linda Montano (who both trained at San Francisco Art Institute). All of these artists can be said to perform their "work" upon a bodily stage, wielding identity (and identity politics) as a manipulable mise-en-scène of physical properties in a kind of visceral cultural critique.[26]

PRIMITIVISM, THE AVANT-GARDE, AND THE EXPLICIT BODY

> Thus I learned to battle the canvas, to come to know it as a being resisting my wish (dream), and to bend it forcibly to this wish. At first it stands there like a pure chaste virgin . . . and then comes the willful brush which first here, then there, gradually conquers it with all the energy peculiar to it, like a European colonist . . .
>
> —Wassily Kandinsky[27]

For German expressionist Kandinsky, the strenuous achievement of "high art" created casualties of war: women and colonials, ultimately conquered into subservience through art. In fact, in literally making their bodies the stage or the canvas, the feminist performance artist can be said to be taking Kandinsky at his word—exploring the historical effects of such words through literalizing his credo. In becoming artist, the woman/colonial has to wrestle with the canvasing of her own body, and in such wrestling the historical terms on which art positioned female sexuality takes on an almost violent clarity.

In avant-garde movements inclined toward anti-aesthetics, from *Ubu* to Dada to Bataille to *Baal,* the body that repeatedly surfaces to confront the tenets of high art is a body made explicit—a body of physical functions, obscene specifics, and details of differences—gender, race, and class. Looking even cursorily at instances of primitivist shock in the modernist avant-garde and examining the collusions, in the effects of that shock, of the cultural narratives of sexology and ethnography, illustrates the deep imbrications of issues of race and sex (that is, the Question of colonials and the Woman Question) in the development of modern Western identity. Being almost exclusively composed of white male discontents, the modernist avant-garde largely utilized the hot spots of race, sex, and class for purposes of shock effect. Conversely, feminist postmodernists, although also discontent, utilize shock not for shock's sake, but to interrogate the properties of that shock: blind spots that surround the minefields of race, sex, and class.

In Carolee Schneemann's 1975 piece, *Interior Scroll,* Schneemann stood nude, in ritualesque body-paint before her mostly female audience and pulled a thin cord of text from her vagina. The text, which had been literally interiorized by that body, quoted the male-dominated establishment's unwillingness to respect women's art:

> we cannot look at
> the personal clutter
> the persistence of feelings
> the hand-touch sensibility

the diaristic indulgence
the painterly mess
the dense gestalt
the *primitive* techniques . . . [28]

Here I add emphasis to the word "primitive." I want to suggest that this confrontative, explicit body in performance relates in important ways to the shock of the "primitive" so intrinsic to our historical "avant-garde," so intrinsic to modernism. It bears clarifying that I use "primitivism" to mean a Western obsession with and nostalgia for the racial/cultural Other (and specifically the African Other) as "less developed," closer to the wild than the civilized—as an aspect of the history of Western patriarchal thought, art, and deed, not an aspect of an actual Other, the so-labeled primitive.

Turning to the historical avant-garde it is not insignificant to find that the confrontative body in art has been a body of details, of physical functions, and of differences—gender, race, and class. In fact, the scandal and appropriation of the primitive body and primitive "fetish" object in representation is a veritable history of modern art—especially of the avant-garde, and most especially in the performative avant-garde movements that confronted the institution of art itself.[29] In the history of performance, Alfred Jarry's staging of his *Ubu Roi* at Theatre de l'Oeuvre in 1896 is a famous case in point, and marks for theater historians the actual birth of the avant-garde. *Ubu* caused a riot on each of the three nights of its run because it was an affront to the prevailing artistic styles of the day—symbolism and naturalism. Through Ubu, Jarry spoofed the symbolist theater's attempts to accentuate a transcendental or dreamlike reality. In *Ubu Roi,* Jarry chose as his high holy symbol something so profane, literal, and explicit that it could not be transcendent, could not evoke any higher ideal. Jarry chose to loudly and repeatedly exclaim "shittr" (*merdre*) in the hallowed halls of the theater. That explicit excremental affront was coupled by an important parallel confrontation: the fat and whiney King Ubu (a name with an obvious Africanism) who uttered the recurrent expletive. The King Primitive's explicit body, in fact his own obsession with his bodily functions, disallowed distanced aestheticization, disallowed any redemptive dreamlike space. Ubu was the birth of the confrontative avant-garde, a confrontation that caused W. B. Yeats to write, disgruntled, after one performance: "After us [symbolists] the Savage God."[30]

The confrontative avant-garde as we historicize it was birthed as the Savage Art. But, as has recently been widely documented, the modernist's primitive Other and the symbol of the African fetish rapidly became the insignia of the modernist himself.[31] Even as *Ubu Roi* was causing its riots, Durkheim had turned his attention to primitive societies not to catalog exotic practices but to understand the modern's own ennui, to look for origins of the human sacred—to find the modern *in* the primitive. In *Ubu*'s year, as well, Freud wrote his "Aetiology of Hysteria" from which he would postulate the existence of a dynamic unconscious and eventually interiorize the primitive into the modern personality as the theoretical id from which we differentiate our egos. At the opening of the new century, the notion of the primitive was assimilated into our understanding of the modern self as its (repressed) driving force.[32]

Not surprisingly, then, ten years after *Ubu Roi,* what was anti-art was already being fully assimilated into art. The modern was being expressed *in* the primitive. Studio artists like Picasso were mimicking the artifacts that they observed in the Trocadero and collected in their studios. Now the savage body was no longer antithetical to the inner psyche, but was in fact *coming to represent it*—the inner psyche as the dark, unruly continent of the unconscious. With Surrealism the image of the tribal artifact met, most forcibly, the image of the female body—the fetish and the female had become the twin insignia of the unconscious.

Still, there was a big difference between the studio art, a medium that invites aesthetic distance, and performance, a medium whose live body arguably invites the illusion of intimacy, even of complicity in its "acts." In performance, the savage body was (and is) not so easily ingestible, not so easily assimilable. For example, twenty years after *Ubu,* Dadaism relied on the *performance* of "Africanisms" (as opposed to static representation of its forms) to drive home its anti-art credo. The rejection of aesthetic distance took the form of the big drum and "negro rhythms"; the dada dances with "dread masks of primitive peoples"; Tzara's gibberish plays full of "pseudo-Africanisms," Janco's African-style masks, and Hugo Ball's witch-doctor trance performance.[33] As Tzara illustrates in this manifesto, the static studio arts were linked with pretense and timidity, whereas performance was linked with assault on art:

MUSICIANS SMASH YOUR INSTRUMENTS
BLIND MEN take the stage [. . .]
Art is a PRETENSION warmed by the
TIMIDITY of the urinary basin, the *hysteria* born
in THE STUDIO
We are in search of
the force that is direct pure sober
UNIQUE we are in search of NOTHING
we affirm the VITALITY of every IN-
STANT[34]

Dadaist insistence on "the vitality of every instant" invoked a performative art and admonished a static studio art. It is important to note, however, that the search for an anti-art of vitality found its force (again) in allusions to bodily function, found its commentary on the corrupt institution of aesthetic "value" through a valorization of "waste," and found its critique of the Western status quo in a mimesis of tribal practice.

With the end of World War I, as the Zurich expatriates made their ways home, Dada transmogrified, becoming surrealism in France and Berlin Dada in Germany. In its surrealist manifestation, impulses from Zurich Dada were wed to psychoanalysis and, arguably, regained the aesthetic distance Zurich Dada had aimed to sabotage. Returning to France, Dadaist primitivism connected with Picasso's "Les Demoiselles d' Avignon" variety of appropriation of African form in which the mimetic impulse toward primitivism had immediately and consistently found a neat double in the discourse of sexology at the time—the "primitive" or primal landscape of the female body. With the surrealist lifting of the dadaist ban on studio art and with the reinstitution of aesthetic distance (and also with the migration of tribal artifact into the mainstream category of high art), allusions to primitive fetish no longer automatically flashed as anti-aesthetic. Instead, the fetish and the explicit body became mascots of a new symbolic landscape, linked to the fledgling science of the interior of the modern psyche—repressed desire, dream, wish. What once had confronted symbolism as Jarry's ribald literality, was now corralled to the service of a symbolism of the unconscious.

But even surrealism's symbology was vulnerable to excesses of savagery, and that excess found itself again coagulating around the issue of the explicit body. Reminiscent of Jarry's "savage god" affront to Symbolism, a number of dissident Surrealists, notably Georges Bataille, Michel Leiris, Andre Masson, Desnos, Queneau, and Artaud (whose theater was named Theatre Alfred Jarry), crossed the line of tolerability and found themselves excommunicated from the Surrealist ranks. The central issue of the rift concerned the significance to art of ethnological artifact and ethnological account in terms of transgressive social practice versus aesthetic or formal properties.[35] Fascinatingly, this dissident affront to the high art of Surrealism was staged, yet again, through conjoining the issue "primitive" (colonial) expression with "base" physicality and the transgressive properties of the sexual or excremental detail. Generally speaking, at issue across sides in the debate was the positioning of these details so as to either confirm or confront Western tenets of formal aesthetic distance. At issue was the sanctity of art.

Acceptable surrealist primitivism (that is, surrealism passed by Breton) was what Rosalind Kraus has called soft primitivism, "a primitivism gone formal and therefore gutless," part of the general "art for art's sake" aestheticizing discourse on the primitive. To this Kraus contrasts the dissident group's "hard primitivism," which sought in the primitive a kind of "primal vandalism."[36] For dissidents surrounding Bataille and the journal *Documents,* who came to make up the College de Sociologie, mimesis of primitive expression was a means of triggering a deep critique of positivist, "civil" identity. Hard primitivism was not a means of expanding the domain of Western aesthetic sensibilities but was a way of transgressing that domain and thus exposing its veiled but everpresent "sadistic" underbelly.

A lineage of manipulations of the explicit body intersect and wrestle across art and performance history. The battle around art and its appropriate/inappropriate appropriations continues today under the banners of feminism, postcolonialism, interculturalism, and now queer theory. We may struggle to understand ourselves as postmodern and postcolonial, nevertheless iconography of the colonial and "savage" body—the black body, the female body, and the queer body of explicit physical markings and implicit, hidden social questions and dangers—*still* circulates as that which potentially threatens civil identity. Although I have only been able to cursorily gesture toward an historical analysis in this chapter, the project of charting the confrontative moves of art against its own institutions underscores again and again the ways in which the twin primitivisms of gender and race prop the social distinctions between high and low, which in turn prop social hierarchies of civil identity.

What is it to recognize today the fascination with the primitive and the prostitute that was so much at the foundation of modernist expression? Where do we stand now in relation to that fascination, that modernism? In what ways, and for whom, are we beyond the fears and obsessions with primitivism and prostitution in our postcoloniality, our postmodernisms? The Ubu of the last turning century shocked at a time when colonialism—the question of who "discovers," who governs, who medicalizes, who anthropologizes, who controls the production of the racial other—was of great significance. Today's Ubus, perhaps an exposed black penis in a polyester suit photographed by Mapplethorpe, or Sprinkle's insistent cervix, have added the terms of the gendered body explicitly to the confrontation. We should remember that it is no coincidence that the body of genital detail should confront at a time when national concerns included control of the reproductive rights of women and people of color—a *Time Magazine* cover recently betrayed a current American fear with its headline: "What Color America in the Year 2000?"

And yet, today's Ubus are significantly different from yesterday's in at least one important respect, marking a significant shift in the use of the shock of the savage body in the avant-garde. Today, it is mostly women, artists of color, and gay and lesbian artists who, rather than solely utilizing shock, are interrogating the social properties of that shock. The terms of savagery and prostitution in the art gallery have become literal versus metaphoric—with voice and body often occupied by the primitivized and prostituted themselves who manipulate the frames around their primitivization. That is, the "primitives" themselves are reflexively representing the primitivizing process, pointing the finger at primitivism by exposing it as inscribed in a patriarchal vocabulary of difference, historically mapped upon their own specific physical markings—their explicit bodies.

NOTES

1. See Cindy Sherman's photography in *Cindy Sherman, 1975–1993*, text by Rosalind Kraus (New York: Rizzoli International Publications, 1993).

2. See Finley's *Shock Threatment*, (San Francisco: City Lights, 1990). See also C. Carr, "Unspeakable Practices, Unnatural Acts: The Taboo Art of Karen Finley" in *Acting Out: Feminist Performances* (Ann Arbor: University of Michigan Press, 1993); and Maria T. Pramaggiore, "Resisting/Performing/Femininity: Works, Flesh, and Feminism in Karen Finley's *The Constant State of Desire.*" *Theatre Journal* 44, no. 3 (October 1992): 269–290.

3. See Annie Sprinkle, *Annie Sprinkle, Post Porn Modernist* (Amsterdam: Torch Books, 1991). See also Linda Williams, "A Provoking Agent: The Pornography and Performance Art of Annie Sprinkle" in *Dirty Looks: Women, Pornography, Power*, edited by Pamela Church Gibson and Roma Gibson (London: BFI Publishing, 1993), pp. 176–191.

4. See Susan Rubin Sulieman, *Subversive Intent: Gender, Politics, and the Avant-Garde* (Cambridge: Harvard University Press, 1990).

5. For an analysis of the intersection between formalism and modern science see Paul Vitz and Arnold B. Blimcher, *Modern Art and Modern Science: The Parallel Analysis of Vision* (New York: Praeger, 1984). On the science inspired, Social Darwinist bases of naturalism, see Emil Zola's treatises "The Experimental Novel" and "Naturalism in the Theatre" in *Documents of Modern Literary Realism*, edited by George J. Becker (Princeton: Princeton University Press, 1963), pp. 197–229.

6. See Linda Nochlin, *Realism* (New York: Penquin, 1971). See also Marianna Torgovnick, *Gone Primitive: Savage Intellects, Modern Lives* (Chicago: University of Chicago Press, 1990); Hal Foster "The 'Primitive' Unconscious in Modern Art," *October* 34 (1985): 45–70; Susan Hiller, ed., *The Myth of Primitivism* (New York: Routledge, 1991); and William Rubin, ed., *"Primitivism" in 20th-Century Art* (New York: The Museum of Modern Art, 1984). See especially Rosalind Kraus, "No More Play" in *The Originality of the Avant-Garde and Other Modernist Myths* (Cambridge, MA: MIT Press, 1988), pp. 42–86.

7. See Homi Bhabha on the colonial subject as "almost but not quite" human and the mimetic construction of this "partial" status in literature in "Of Mimicry and Man: The Ambivalence of Colonial Discourse," *October* 28 (1984): 125–33.

8. Walter Benjamin, *Charles Baudeliare: A Lyric Poet in the Era of High Capitalism* (London: New Left Books, 1973), p. 171. See also Susan Buck-Morss, *Dialectics of Seeing* (Cambridge, MA: MIT Press, 1989), p. 443, n. 46.

9. See T. J. Clark, *The Painting of Modern Life: Paris in the Art of Manet and His Followers* (New York: Knopf, 1985). See also Henry M. Sayre's explication of Clark in *The Object of Performance: The American Avant-Garde Since 1970* (Chicago: University of Chicago Press, 1989), pp. 67–68.

10. Georges Bataille, *Manet* (Paris: Editions Skira, 1955), p. 62.

11. See Sander Gilman, "Black Bodies, White Bodies: Toward an Iconography of Female Sexuality in Late Nineteenth-Century Art, Medicine, and Literature" in *Race, Writing, and Difference,* edited by Henry Louis Gates, Jr. (Chicago: University of Chicago Press, 1986), pp. 223–261.

12. On Linda Montano's transformation from artist into "porn queen" see her "Summer Saint Camp 1987," *The Drama Review,* 33, no. 1 (1989): 94–119. Performance artist/pop culture icon Sandra Bernhardt posed for the September 1992 issue of *Playboy.*

13. See Walter Benjamin, *Charles Baudelaire: A Lyric Poet in the Era of High Capitalism* (London: New Left Books, 1973).

14. See Jerrold Siegel, *Bohemian Paris: Culture, Politics, and the Boundaries of Bourgeois Life, 1830–1930* (New York: Penguin, 1986), on the romantics of destitution in the historical avant-garde.

15. Rrose Selavy presents interesting questions at the intersections of feminist and queer theories as they unfold in the 1990s. See Amelia G. Jones who, in distinction to my reading, champions Duchamp's cross-dressing as inherently feminist in "The Ambivalence of Male Masquerade: Duchamp as Rrose Selavy" in *The Body Imaged: The Human Form and Visual Culture Since the Renaissance,* edited by Kathleen Adler and Marcia Pointon (London: Cambridge University Press, 1993), pp. 21–32.

16. There is no positive female-identified correlative for the word "virile," which aligns masculine sexuality with positive, powerful, "penetrating" creativity. According to Webster's Ninth, to be virile is to be energetic, vigorous, forceful, and to be "capable of functioning as a male in copulation." I have chosen the word passionate, though it is clearly inadequate to convey the notion of a positive and powerful woman-identified sexual force. See also Sally Banes's *Greenwich Village 1963: Avant-Garde Performance and the Effervescent Body* (Durham, NC: Duke University Press, 1993), on that watershed year in the arts.

17. See Carolee Schneemann, *More Than Meat Joy* (New Paltz, NY: Documentext, 1979), for original documentation of this piece. See Lucy Lippard, *From The Center: Feminist Essays on Women's Art* (New York: E.P. Dutton, 1976), p. 122, for the historical importance of this piece. See also Kristine Stiles, "Between Water and Stone" in *In The Spirit of Fluxus* (Minneapolis: Walker Art Center, 1993), p. 98, n. 80.

18. See Henry Sayre, *The Object of Performance* (Chicago: University of Chicago Press, 1989), pp. 67–73.

19. See Moira Roth, *The Amazing Decade: Women and Performance Art in America, 1970–1980* (Los Angeles: Astro Artz, 1983).

20. Although the usefulness of the modernist term "avant-garde" for aesthetic practices in the age of postmodernism has come under considerable debate, I agree with Susan Rubin Sulieman's maintenance of the term "however messy and full of dividing lines it may be." See Sulieman's explication of the tensions in the term in *Subversive Intent: Gender, Politics, and the Avant-Garde* (Cambridge, MA: Harvard University Press, 1990), pp. 11–12. On the NEA funding crisis see Peggy Phelan, "Money Talks," *The Drama Review* (Spring 1990): 4–15, and "Money Talks Again," *The Drama Review* (Fall 1991): 131–142.

21. Edward Lucie-Smith, *Sexuality in Western Art* (London: Thames and Hudson, 1991).

22. See Elinor Fuchs, "Staging the Obscene Body," *The Drama Review* 33, no. 1 (1989): 33–58.

23. See Phelan, "Money Talks Again."

24. On the issue of Mapplethorpe and classical symmetry see Peggy Phelan, *Unmarked* (New York: Routledge, 1993), pp. 45–47.

25. See Kobena Mercer, "Looking for Trouble," *Transition* 51 (1991): 184–197.

26. The issues raised by the transgression of art and porn are not completely separate from general "body issues" for women artists not involved in the porn industry. Whether or not "porn" is explicitly involved, the explicit manipulation of the gendered/colored/classed body raises the porn-related issue of the social relation between the appropriate and the inappropriate. Arguably, any body bearing female markings is automatically cathected to the dominant historical trajectory of the delimitation of that body for the signification of male sexual possession—either explicitly (literally) in porn or implicitly (symbolically) in art.

27. See Carol Duncan, "The Aesthetics of Power in Modern Erotic Art," in *Feminist Art Criticism,* edited by Arlene Raven, Cassandra L. Langer, and Joanna Frueh (New York: IconEditions, 1991), p. 63.

28. Quoted in Roth, *The Amazing Decade,* p. 14.

29. The scandalizing potential of primitivity is difficult to imagine from a late-20th-century perspective. Through modernist mimesis, "primitive" fetishes, initially confrontative to the tenets of high art, became hallowed objects in the halls of museums. It was Picasso's mimetic initiative in style that, in part, effected the long migration of African fetish objects out of ethnographic museums, such as the Trocadero, and into art museums. But in performance, mimesis of "primitive," or tribal "ritual" practice, remained antithetical to art practice.

30. Quoted in Roger Shattuck, *The Banquet Years: The Origin of the Avant-Garde in France, 1815 to World War I* (New York: Vintage Books, 1955), p. 209.

31. See Christopher Innes, *Avant-Garde Theatre* (New York: Routledge, 1993), for an analysis of primitivism as the driving force behind the avant-garde. Innes looks more to the nostalgic search for the primal in primitivism than the anti-art confrontation I would argue informed Jarry's allusions to primitivity.

32. Importantly, the primitive has also been employed in aesthetic sign-systems as a noble savage, as in the paintings of Gauguin. The noble savage differs in important ways from his ever-present double, the savage savage. The savagery of the explicit body still marks a site of cultural fascination, a hot spot, a scandal waiting to happen threatening all things "civil."

33. See Hans Richter, *Dada: Art and Anti-Art,* translated by David Britt (London: Thames and Hudson, 1965).

34. Robert Motherwell, ed., *The Dada Painters and Poets: An Anthology* (Boston: G.K. Hall, 1951), p. 82.

35. The intellectual center for this group was the journal *Documents* and ethnography was a core issue. See James Clifford, "On Ethnographic Surrealism," *Comparative Studies in Society and History* 28 (October 1981): 543–564, for a discussion of the way Bataille's thought was shaped by ethnography, particularly

Marcel Mauss. By 1931 Leiris had become an ethnologist. Carl Einstein, one of
the original Zurich dadaists, had published a study of primitive sculpture and was
also influential in the group.

   36. See Kraus "No More Play," pp. 51, 52, 54.

Identity and Representation as Challenges to Social Movement Theory: A Case Study of Queer Nation

Michael R. Fraser

We're here. We're Queer. Get Used to it![1]

CHALLENGE AND CHANGE: AN IN(TRO)DUCTION TO A MOVEMENT

In early April 1990, several members of the AIDS activist group ACT UP New York (the AIDS Coalition to Unleash Power) announced the meeting of a discussion group to address issues of gay and lesbian invisibility and homophobia. When sixty people attended the meeting, the facilitators were "shocked" at the size of the turnout (Trebay, 1990). Unaware of the impact this first meeting would have on gay and lesbian activism in the United States, the group decided to meet again. A second meeting, several weeks later, drew more than 100 people, many of whom brought with them ideas for actions and protests the group could carry out to promote gay and lesbian visibility and confront violence directed against them.

The summer of 1990 witnessed the transformation of this self-called "New Group" into "Queer Nation," a gay and lesbian urban activist organization that quickly spread nationally. The initial April discussions were a response to tensions and splits within ACT UP, as well as an attempt to create a radical gay and lesbian organization. These discussions led to the formation of a group of activists who wanted to concentrate specifically on issues of sexual politics and identity, not solely AIDS politics.

Queer Nation New York formed specifically to "fight against homophobia and invisibility" (Schwartz, 1990). The ideology and organization of Queer Nation spread to other cities where groups have stated similar goals. For example, Queer Nation Boston describes itself as "A confrontational direct-action group organized to combat homophobia and hate crimes that, locally and nationally, have spiraled" (Longcope, 1990). Queer Nation is comprised of gay, lesbian, and bisexual members who are familiar with the direct-action tactics of ACT UP and want to use similar protest actions to advance gay and lesbian visibility across the nation. Exactly how the group's objectives should be carried out is left to the individuals who make up each Queer Nation group.

A controversial document that appeared only two weeks after Queer Nation New York decided on its name, however, details the group's objections to mainstream society and states goals for queer activism. "Queers Read This," an anonymously published gay manifesto, was distributed at the New York City Gay and Lesbian Pride Parade in June, 1990 (Anonymous Queers, 1990; Kaplan, 1990). The document is a substantive and expressive statement of Queer Nation's ideologies, political stances, strategies, outrages, outcries, and more.[2]

"Queers Read This" purports to describe the current state of gay and lesbian existence in mainstream America. Assailing gays and lesbians who take an assimilationist approach to sexual liberation, the broadsheet explains the need for gays and lesbians to express themselves as "queers," and to not fit into a model of behavior that heterosexuals tolerate. The document defines what being "queer" means and posits that a "queer" lifestyle is a life at war with straight America:

Being queer means leading a different sort of life. It's not about the mainstream, profit-margins, patriotism, patriarchy or being assimilated. It's not about executive directors, privilege and elitism. It's about being on the margins, defining ourselves; it's about gender-fuck and secrets, what's beneath the belt and deep in the heart.

Queer Nation members view their group as one way to create a radical alternative to the way established gay and lesbian organizations operate. By consciously not using the older, more traditional gay and lesbian organizations that rely on "executive directors," legislation, or the political process to create change, Queer Nation works outside the conventional system to disrupt it. For example, the late activist Vito Russo noted that, "Queer Nation seems to be a response to the current gay mainstream:

NGLTF [National Gay and Lesbian Task Force] and GLAAD [Gay and Lesbian Alliance Against Defamation]. Those organizations can't do direct actions and street theater or zaps. That's not their agenda" (Russo in Trebay, 1990, p. 37).

Individuals in Queer Nation believe that the term *queer* best describes and unifies people with non-mainstream sexual identities because, unlike labels such as "bisexual," "gay," or "lesbian," queer cuts across these boundaries (as did the term "black" in the 1960s for all skin color shades of African-Americans). Queer Nation members believe they have taken a once derogatory, hurtful word and turned it into an enabling label for all gay, lesbian, and bisexual individuals. The label unifies a community of individuals who share a common identity: queer. A pamphlet distributed at a Queer Action Philadelphia march (M. Stein, 1990) defines the use of the term "queer" in its most inclusive sense:

[Queers are] . . . lesbians, gay men, bisexuals and homosexuals, transsexuals, transvestites, ambi-sexuals, effeminate men and masculine women, gender-benders, drag queens, bull dykes and cross-dressers, lezzies, diesels and bruisers, marys and faeries, faggots, buggers, hairy pit-bulls, butches and fems.

"Queers Read This" positions queers as a potential army, an army that must fight for freedom, civil rights, and the right to love, since "no one else is going to do it for us." The presumed need to use fear and violence to achieve Queer Nation's goals adds a militant tone to the document's overall statement, as illustrated in the following paragraph:

Fear is the most powerful motivator. No one will give us what we deserve. Rights are not given, they are taken, by force if necessary . . . we are being systematically picked off and we will continue to be wiped out unless we realize that if they take one of us they must take all of us. AN ARMY OF LOVERS CANNOT LOSE.

Queer Nation documents stress the need for gays and lesbians to take it on themselves to create change, and not expect liberation to come without militant action. "Queers Read This" calls for each queer to cast away the invisibility that keeps gays and lesbians "in the closet," and come out, fighting:

make every space a gay space. Every street a part of our sexual geography. A city of yearning and then total satisfaction. A city and country where we can be safe and free and more . . .

Queer Nation's ideology encourages activists to fight and free gays and lesbians from the state of invisibility many find themselves placed in by mainstream society. Queer Nation members state they reserve the right to use violence to stop violence, as one member frankly states in a newspaper interview (M. Stein, 1990): "coming out as a queer means making our presence known . . . [we are] pissed off . . . we want to let bashers know that when you fuck with one of us, you fuck with all of us."

"IN YOUR FACE": IDENTITY, REPRESENTATION, AND QUEER NATION

This chapter presents a case study of Queer Nation. Between June 1990 and April 1991 I reviewed public statements by its members in the popular press and in Queer Nation pamphlets, including articles about the organization in national and gay and lesbian newspapers. I also became personally involved with the organization through informal interviews with movement participants and through my own participation in movement events.[3]

Throughout this chapter I emphasize the subjective and reflexive activities of the Queer Nation movement. Past social movement theory has stressed objective and rational aspects of social movements to explain their origins, orientations, goals, and images. These conventional theorists have stressed the importance of material resources to a group, such as money, power, and the grassroots organization necessary to conduct a movement. Past theory has also stressed traditional sources of societal control, including the state, the economy, and the church, as the targets of a movement's protest actions and calls for change. The emphasis on the objective criteria necessary for movement efficacy has left identity issues out of past analyses of social movements, leaving actor subjectivities unexamined in the literature.

By focusing on identity and representation, this chapter attempts to move away from social movement theory, which has been dominated by this objectivist bias. Instead of looking for the material conditions requisite for movement organization, I focus on *identity* and *representation* as important aspects of movement organization and success. Although there has not been a total neglect of cultural, social, or subjective factors in movement theory, these aspects of movement development have only recently been considered in studies of social movements.

Josh Gamson's study of ACT UP moves social movement theory in this direction (Gamson, 1989, p. 53). Using ACT UP as a case study, Gamson illustrates how modern movements are complex organizations involving personal identities and interests, movement activities in relation to an audience (self and/or other), internal politics among members, tensions within movements, and exigent solidarity. Gamson's framework offers a window on personal and internal politics and the evolution of the movement and its organization. He suggests that the internal politics and the organization of a movement are the result of the interplay of individual and collective identities within it.

Gamson also introduces the notion that audience plays a vital role in the development of movement actions. He finds that actions that were planned by ACT UP often took place without consideration of who would be watching (Gamson, 1989). Instead, participants considered each other the "audience" for a given action. As participants' actions were mirrored by others during protest actions, individuals gained a sense of the movement's goals and a sense of their place within the struggle. Thus, protest actions act as reflexive devices for the actors themselves, empowering movement actors while simultaneously protesting against the target of the demonstration.

The recent reintroduction of social psychology to social movement theory (made explicit by Morris and McClurg-Mueller, 1992) has moved theorists toward examinations of how social movement actors make sense of their participation in a movement. Hence, many social movement theorists no longer take identity for granted, and instead have become interested in how heterogeneous groups of movement actors define what it means to identify as a member of a movement.

Past social movement theory has treated identity as the objective characteristics or attributes shared by movement actors. These characteristics generate solidarity within the movement because actors have a common bond; for example, we talk about the *black* civil rights movement, the *women's* movement, and the *student* movement. In this chapter, I attempt to move social movement theory to a place were theorists can begin to address the way in which identity is *shaped*, as well as *shared*, during participation in a movement.

Identity unifies a social movement but is also uniquely expressed and interpreted by individual movement actors. Although activists take on the social position, or "role," of movement participants, identity is what makes this social position unique; identity fills the "empty container of the role" with individual experiences and elaborations (Hewitt, 1989). In Queer Nation the identity of each actor is based on each individual's self-definition as "queer" as well as the collective definition of belonging to the group "Queer Nation." Thus, queer identity has two implications, the first is for one's own, personal identity and the other is the social or collective identification with the movement itself.

The title of Trebay's article on Queer Nation in *The Village Voice* provides an example of the importance of identity to the group. He writes, "The next wave of lesbian and gay activism breaks every rule. Meet Queer Nation. IN YOUR FACE!" (Trebay, 1990, p. 34). Indeed, the term "IN YOUR FACE" sums up the importance of making queer identity known to the group and making one's identity obvious to others through confrontation and direct action. In Queer Nation and in other social movements, however, an analysis of participant identity is complicated by the fact that other identities are also salient to movement participants. For example, an individual may be "queer" but she may also be an African American, a woman, a sister, a youth, and so on.

The issue of members having several important "identities" and how these identities intersect within a movement has become a challenge for social movement theory, which has previously assumed movement actors shared common attributes (race, gender, sexual identities, for example). Contemporary feminist critiques of traditional social movement theory, the most recent being critiques of past work on the black civil rights movement, have argued that gender identity, as well as racial identity, should be examined in analyses of civil rights activism. Several authors have noted that gender, race, and class identities influenced the activist experience and shaped internal dynamics within the movement itself (King, 1987; Evans, 1979). This has also been illustrated by tense intersections of race, gender, and sexual identities within Queer Nation, an issue that will be addressed later in this chapter.

In addition to identity, Queer Nation's protest actions raise important issues regarding movement representation. Representation refers to the image projected by movement members to each other and to the larger society. By challenging stigmatization, Queer Nation attempts to foster gay and lesbian visibility by changing the way that those at the margins are represented by the mainstream. "Widening the margins" is a strategy that has been used in many social movements, including the women's movement, which challenged mainstream gender roles, and the black civil rights movement, which attempted to change the stereotypical misrepresentations of blacks in 1960s America; for example, the expression "black is beautiful" was an effort to change both self-identity and public representations of black Americans. Although the effect of these "widening" strategies on public opinion has been examined by social movement theorists, their effect on movement participants has not, presenting another challenge for contemporary social movement theory.

The role of the media presents challenges to movement representation as media coverage has both positive and negative implications for a movement's portrayal in society (Gitlin, 1980). For Queer Nation, the media are an important vehicle used to get the group's message "out" to mainstream America. A joint action between ACT UP and Queer Nation interrupted the inauguration ceremony of California Governor Pete Wilson and the activists became the focus of the media attention, not the governor (White, 1991a, p. 18). Queer Nation actions are planned for maximum visibility at events where the media are already reporting (e.g., the California demonstration or the Mapplethorpe opening rally at the ICA in Boston.) One member called the type of media attention Queer Nation receives from these events "outreach" (Morrison, in Flowers, 1990): the group is conscious of its use of the media to broadcast its message to both the mainstream (straights) and the margin (queers).

An examination of Queer Nation's ideology and strategy at the local level highlights the way in which representation is an important aspect of the Queer Nation movement. Using observations from Boston, I suggest that several events during the summer of 1990 were important catalysts to Queer Nation Boston's organization.[4] One particular event in New York drew the attention of many Boston gay and lesbian organizers. On June 16, 1990, over 1,000 marchers took to the streets of Greenwich Village to protest anti-gay violence. The march, which rallied to sites of previous queer bashings, was organized by Queer Nation New York. Despite hecklers and two reported physical attacks, the New York march was seen as a success at "reclaiming public space" as gay space (Reyes, 1990a, 1990b; Schwartz, 1990; Trebay, 1990). Word of Queer Nation's formation traveled quickly to Boston, and by the end of July, Queer Nation Boston had organized. A July advertisement in the Boston-based *Gay Community News* read "Where is the Queer Nation?" and announced a meeting place and time. However, the actions in New York were not the only motivation for Queer Nation's formation in Boston.

Also during the summer of 1990, a series of gay bashings took place in the city's South End, which both frightened and angered the Boston lesbian and gay community (Kahn, 1990). The newly formed Queer Nation Boston experienced an urgent sense of militancy, especially for those who resided in the South End. Coupled with the developments in New York and the community's awareness of rising anti-gay violence, the arrival of the Robert Mapplethorpe exhibit at Boston's Institute of Contemporary Art (ICA) over the summer of 1990 also contributed to the development of Queer Nation Boston. The attempt to shut down the Mapplethorpe exhibit by some members of the Boston City Council was interpreted as a direct threat to gay and lesbian expression in the city. Angered by the shut-down attempt, a July 30 meeting evolved into a march to the ICA attended by 125 people, who arrived chanting: "We're here. We're Queer. We're Fabulous. Get Used to it!" (Longcope, 1990, p. 25).

Queer Nation Boston's actions reflect the style and mood of Queer Nation demonstrations in other parts of the country: the Boston march to the ICA after Queer Nation's first meeting is similar to actions in New York and San Francisco. A march held September 29, 1990, in the city's South End was attended by over 200 people and focused on the issue of "bashing back." The march was publicized by posters pasted all over the city, on billboards, traffic lights, and construction walls downtown. Posters picturing state gubernatorial candidates with words like "SHAME" and "QUEER BASHER" imposed over the portrait also appeared in the South End area.

The militant nature of Queer Nation's protests are evident in these and other actions nationwide. "Night Outs"[5] perform local visibility actions in predominantly straight establishments, conveying the message "We [queers] are everywhere." Marches in New York, Philadelphia, Boston, and other cities "take back gay space," and when met with violence, the "bash back" philosophy is often introduced into the conflict. These protest actions are evidence of Queer Nation's attempt to change public perceptions of gays and lesbians: from passive victims to militant defenders of the right to be queer.

QUEER NATION: SOCIAL MOVEMENT THEORY AND BEYOND

The development of the Queer Nation movement required material resources and grassroots assistance in its formative stages, indeed several events occurred during the summer of 1990 that facilitated the development of the movement. After accounting for the material conditions that led to the movement's organization, conventional theory would end the chapter here. But Queer Nation's formation required more than just the antecedent events described. It required a focus on collective "queer" identity, emphasizing a concern for cultural expression and a desire to change the way gays and lesbians are depicted by mainstream society. As Weeks (1985, p. 186) succinctly states, "recent sexual politics have been a politics of identity." However, identity politics cannot be adequately described using existing theories of relative deprivation, mass-society, or resource mobilization commonly used to analyze social movements because the subjective is seen as superfluous and tangential to broader issues of political mobilization. Because Queer Nation's actions and ideologies are so deeply enmeshed in individual and collective statements of queer identity, I argue that conventional theory leaves out important aspects of movement development in its dismissal of subjective aspects of social movement organization.

Participation in Queer Nation is motivated by a number of subjective reasons, one of which is illustrated by a member's statement: "I'm tired of being passive, I feel like I've got to stand up for what I believe in" (in Wutzke, 1990a). What keeps members involved in Queer Nation actions is the group's focus on "queer" visibility or the actions that make the participant's "queer" identity known. An original member of Queer Nation New York states,

We have to be visible. People have to know that we exist and gay youth have to know we are here. Queer is not an orientation we should apologize for. (Morrison, in Flowers, 1990)

and another,

I hope we're going to send a message to all people who think they can harass queer people that they can't do it anymore . . . and also a message to other queer people who might not see the value of visibility. (Forbis, in M. Stein, 1990)

Other members stress that announcing being "queer," and making queer identity uncompromisingly known to the "straight world," is an important part of being in the movement:

For centuries, we have tried through our sense of humor and our politics to have the straight world understand who we are and accept us. I think it's a noble thing, but I don't think things work that way. We have to stand up and say this is who we are and then demand that we be taken seriously. (Velez, in Flowers, 1990)

We want to be in their [straights'] faces. . . . The point is to be different from traditional gay and lesbian groups. We are saying we share this planet with you and don't give a shit if you don't like us, but you had better get used to us. We are not like you and we don't want to be. (Katz, in Kingston, 1990)

Within Queer Nation, queer identity acts as a force that unifies the group and motivates collective action. The gay and lesbian movement, alongside the women's movement and the black civil rights movement of the 1950s and 1960s, developed as a movement based on forwarding positive conceptions of participants' identity within civil society.

The identity issue, again, is complicated by the fact that other identities are also salient among social movement actors. Identities intersect, creating conflict among movement actors, further complicating an analysis of Queer Nation and by extension analyses of other social movement organizations. In an article in *Out/Look,* one Latino member of Queer Nation San Francisco writes:

In the "melting pot" that is our Queer Nation, all difference becomes subsumed under the homogenizing "gay and lesbian" community and important political and philosophical differences get dismissed. (Fernandez, 1991, p. 21)

Because an adherence to "queer ideology" is interpreted as subsuming racial and gender difference by people of color and women in Queer Nation, some members feel separated and isolated from the collective whole and the group's solidarity is weakened. The group's "fixed" (A. Stein, 1992) conception of the primacy of the "queer" experience for all members has begun to be called into question.

Although the questioning of a hegemonic identity may seem inevitable in any movement, it illustrates the way in which collective identity and personal identity intersect and raise problems for movement participants.

Fernandez argues that Queer Nation needs to address issues of race within the group, and adhere to a more "integrated analysis of what is means to be 'gay or lesbian' in this country . . . that recognizes multiple subjects and the necessity to move toward liberations across a greater spectrum of struggles" (Fernandez, 1991, p. 23). A forum held by the Queer Nation San Francisco working group "United Colors" addressed racism within the organization. In the forum, one member stated, "There's been no out-and-out racism . . . but some statements are ignorant, uneducated or misinformed" (Chan Mark in Denny, 1990). Another participant said, "I came out into the lesbian and gay community . . . only to discover that this community—all people involved—were infected with the same diseases [as in her Midwestern home town], racism, sexism and internalized homophobia" (Ramirez in Denny, 1990).

Similar experiences have been noted by women in Queer Nation (Duggan, 1992; A. Stein, 1992; Maggenti, 1991). One woman writes:

I avoided my own late night questions about what it means to be a lesbian in a gay male universe and preferred to believe in the united colors of Queer Nation. But the fact that I could not seem to remember when the meetings were or who to call to find out bespoke my increasing sense of ambivalence. Soon it became apparent that I could not join, I could not participate, I could not sit again in a room filled mostly with men and stand up confidently to argue for a specific proposal. (Maggenti, 1991, p. 20)

Maggenti's hesitance is shared by other female members of Queer Nation. A woman in Boston stated,

Like many women I know who attended the meeting [the first Boston meeting], I had mixed feelings about it . . . gay men are outraged about recent violence that has happened in the gay community. . . . But violence is not a new issue for women and people of color. (Bolinsky, in Briggs, 1990)

Minh-Ha (1991) notes that as the "personal becomes political," new social movements become organizations that "reduce" and "fragment" one identity to a single, hegemonic source of meaning for the group. The reduction and fragmentation of identity results in gay and lesbian identity as the most salient: a homogenized "end-point" (Minh-Ha, 1991) in movement organization rather than a starting point for the "liberation, justice and solidarity" (Fernandez, 1991, p. 23) of all gay and lesbian people. The heterogeneity of movement actors is of crucial analytical importance in our understanding of individual social movement actors and their individual motives for participating in a movement: we must recognize that a movement means a number of different things to different actors (Lilley and Platt, 1994).

CONCLUSION: A "NEWER," "HIPPER" MOVEMENT?

Queer signifies a rebirth of energy, the spirit of activism that happened in the 70s. This is a newer, hipper, generation.[6]

As the Queer Nation member states, this case study posits that the group is "newer," and perhaps "hipper," than many social movements. One of the most important ways in which Queer Nation is "new" has to do with the theoretical nature of identity and the intersection of identities within social movement theory. The importance of queer identity to the group suggests that the development of collective identity is crucial not only for Queer Nation, but for many social movements as well, such as the women's movement; the environmental movement; religious movements; and racial, ethnic, and nationalist movements.

How social movements are presented and represented in larger society is another issue that needs to be addressed by social movement theorists. Few studies have examined the role of the media in social movement organization, and how these media images affect participants' sense of participation and empowerment within a movement. My case study suggests that Queer Nation's messages are broadcast to the public through television, radio, and newspaper reports of its actions and that the group uses this media attention to its advantage.

The idea that group members become empowered through participation is a representation issue that is best described by Gamson's concept of "audience." How participants view a protest as successful without the attendance of spectators raises questions about how society views the movement, and how the movement views itself. Representation also raises questions about how social movements challenge stigmatized notions of their identity held by larger society, and the ways in which a group counters widely held negative opinions about the social movement and participants' identities.

In this chapter, I have used Queer Nation as a case study to emphasize the reflexive, subjective features of movement development. Further examination of these issues is necessary to understand the internal dynamics of social movements. Such an understanding will improve our ability to describe how social movements work, and when and why movements succeed or fail. Important theoretical issues such as identity and representation, heterogeneity and homogenization are those that will make up the substantive theoretical and empirical problems of movement politics in the 1990s. Case studies of contemporary movements bring us closer to understanding how movements fit extant theory, but also challenge theory by going beyond current formulations.

NOTES

I would like to thank Gerald M. Platt, William P. Norris, and Gretchen Steirs as well as the editors of this volume for their insightful comments and criticisms on earlier versions of this chapter.

1. Queer Nation slogan, Boston Institute of Contemporary Art (ICA) demonstration, July 1990.

2. I obtained a copy of "Queers Read This" from a Queer Nation Boston member in the fall of 1990.

3. For the purposes of this paper, I refer to the definition of case study provided by Stenhouse (1982) as research

based on condensed field experience involving observation (rather than the classical participant observer strategy), tape recorded interviews and the collection of documents. (Stenhouse, 1982, in Burgess, 1984:2)

4. The majority of my secondary data collection took place in Boston, while I was on a leave of absence from Oberlin College in the summer and fall of 1990. Most of my informal interviews took place at Oberlin College where I interviewed queer activists who participated in Queer Nation groups in Boston, New York, Washington, and San Francisco.

5. "Night Outs" are a common protest action carried out by Queer Nation groups. A "Night Out" involves a number of group members entering a predominantly heterosexual bar or nightclub and "making their presence known" by dancing in same-sex couples, kissing in public, wearing political tee-shirts, and passing out educational pamphlets at the site. It is this type of expression that illustrates the unique eroticization of protest developed by Queer Nation nationwide. For example, see Wutzke, 1990a through 1990d.

6. Fleck, quoted in Stanley, 1991.

REFERENCES

Anonymous Queers. 1990. "Queers Read This."

Briggs, Laura. 1990. "Birth of a Queer Nation." *Gay Community News* 18:3.

Burgess, Robert G. 1984. *In the Field*. London: George Allen & Unwin.

Denny, Lowell B. 1990. "United Colors Forum on Racism." *QueerWeek*, San Francisco, December 19:1.

Duggan, Lisa. 1992. "Making It Perfectly Queer." *Socialist Review* 92/1:11–31.

Evans, Sara. 1979. *Personal Politics*. New York: Vintage Books.

Fernandez, Charles. 1991. "Undocumented Aliens in the Queer Nation." *Out/Look* 12:20–23.

Flowers, Rich. 1990. "Queer Nation Takes Gay and Lesbian Anger to the Streets." *Outlines (Chicago)* October:1.

Gamson, Josh. 1989. "Silence, Death and the Invisible Enemy: AIDS Activism and Social Movement 'Newness.' " *Social Problems* 36:351–367.

Gitlin, Todd. 1980. *The Whole World is Watching*. Berkeley: University California Press.

Hewitt, John P. 1989. *Dilemmas of the American Self*. Philadelphia: Temple University Press.

Kahn, Ric. 1990. "Fear and Loathing in the South End: Class Conflict Fuels Gay Bashings in Once-Tolerant Neighborhood." *Boston Phoenix,* August 11:6–19.

Kaplan, Esther. 1990. "A Queer Manifesto." *Village Voice,* August 14:36.

King, Mary. 1987. *Freedom Song.* New York: Morrow.

Kingston, Tim. 1990. "In Your Face." *QueerWeek,* San Francisco, December 5:1.

Lilley, Stephen, and Gerald M. Platt. 1994. "Correspondent's Impressions of Martin Luther King, Jr.: An Interpretative Theory of Movement Leadership," in *Constructing the Social,* edited by T. Sarbin and J. Kitsuse, pp. 65–83. London: Sage.

Longcope, Kay. 1990. "Boston Gay Groups Vow New Militancy Against Hate Crimes." *Boston Globe,* August 8:25–31.

Maggenti, Maria. 1991. "Women as Queer Nationals." *Out/Look* 11:20–23.

Minh-Ha, Trinh T. 1991. "Identity Across Difference." Lecture, Oberlin College, Oberlin, OH. Distinguished Lecture Series, March.

Morris, Aldon D., and Carol McClurg-Mueller. 1992. *Frontiers in Social Movement Theory.* New Haven: Yale University Press.

Reyes, Nina. 1990a. "Birth of a Queer Nation" and "On Lookers Attack Anti-Violence Marchers in the Village." *Outweek,* July 4:12–17.

———. 1990b. "Queer Nation Goes to Brooklyn." *Outweek,* August 1:28.

Schwartz, Deborah. 1990. "Queers Bash Back." *Gay Community News,* June 24: 1–15.

Stanley, Alessandra. 1991. "Gay Fades as Militants Pick Queer." *New York Times,* April 6:9.

Stein, Arlene. 1992. "Sisters and Queers: The Decentering of Lesbian Feminism." *Socialist Review* 92/1:33–55.

Stein, Marc. 1990. "Queer Anti-Violence Demo Draws Attack from Cop." *Gay Community News,* 18:3–7.

Trebay, Guy. 1990. "In Your Face." *Village Voice,* August 14:34–39.

Weeks, Jeffrey. 1985. *Sexuality and Its Discontents.* London: Routledge.

White, Allen. 1991a. "Gay Flag Raises Ruckus for New California Governor." *Outweek,* January 23:18–28.

Wutzke, Jeff. 1990a. "Queer Nation Encounters Violence at Stocks & Bonds Club." *Bay Windows,* October 11:3–5.

———. 1990b. "Kiss-In Leads to Violence for Queer Nation Members." *Bay Windows,* August 3:1–10.

———. 1990c. "Queer Nation Bombs Out at Stocks & Bonds." *Bay Windows,* October 25:3–12.

———. 1990d. "Queer Nation: On the March." *Bay Windows,* October 4:1–4.

The Ideological Limits of New Social Movements: The Rise and Fall of the Clamshell Alliance

Stephen Adair

On August 1, 1976, eighteen members of the newly formed Clamshell Alliance were arrested on charges of criminal trespass for occupying the site of a proposed nuclear power plant in Seabrook, New Hampshire. The relatively few participants in this first act of civil disobedience against Seabrook was intentional. Rennie Cushing, one of the eighteen, suggested that each collective action be ten times larger than the one that preceded it.[1] He was not far off the mark. Three weeks later, 180 Clamshell members were arrested following a second occupation. And on the weekend of April 30, 1977, 2,000 Clams set up camp on Seabrook property and stayed for more than twenty-four hours. Most of the 1,414 who were arrested were held for two weeks in makeshift jails in five national guard armories. In a political standoff that drew national media attention, New Hampshire Governor Meldrim Thomson refused to allow them to be released on their own recognizance, and the Clams, exhibiting an intense degree of solidarity, opted not to pay what was deemed unreasonable bail.

In the aftermath of the April-May occupation, the Clamshell's reputation and numbers expanded. Part of the group's allure came from its efforts to create a radically democratic organization based on consensus decision making. Consensus, however, grew difficult. Plans for a fourth occupation were made and scuttled, and made and scuttled again. A legal rally and alternative energy fair in June of 1978 brought nearly 20,000 people, which at the time was the largest antinuclear gathering in U.S. history, but by then, the group was deeply divided. A year later it split. The more assertive faction, Coalition for Direct Action at Seabrook (CDAS), fizzled after two attempts to occupy the site resulted in violent clashes with the state police. By 1981, the Clamshell largely consisted of a mailing address and a skeleton staff.[2]

After its phenomenal rise, the Clamshell seemingly collapsed on the brink of its own success. Since the spring of 1977, a national antinuclear movement had been forming as groups adopted the Clamshell's style and tactics. A partial list of new alliances included the Abalone (California), Crabshell (Washington), Cactus (Southwest), Lone Star (Texas), Bailly (Illinois), Paddlewheel (Kentucky), Palmetto (Carolinas), Catfish (Florida), and the SHAD (New York). In addition, by 1978 public opinion polls showed for the first time that a majority of the population was opposed to the construction of a local nuclear power plant.[3] The nuclear power industry was also showing significant signs of weakness. Several plants were canceled and new orders had slowed to a trickle; 1978 was the last year a U.S. utility ordered a new nuclear reactor. And perhaps most importantly, Robert Harrison, the financial vice president of Public Service Company of New Hampshire, the lead owner of the Seabrook plant, said the decision to cancel the project in the spring of 1978 was "day to day."[4]

Scholars who have reflected on the collapse of the Clamshell have suggested that the Clamshell's participatory style of decision making, and its radical egalitarianism, grew impractical as its numbers grew and as it had to adapt to changing sets of political circumstances.[5] Each, in turn, offers suggestions as to how organizational changes or differing decisions might have altered the group's fate. Yet in important ways, its collapse parallels the trajectory of other recent social movements. The radical women's movement spread rapidly in consciousness-raising groups between 1968 and 1972, but lost much of its initiative once the feminist critique began to be incorporated into the mainstream.[6] Much of the student antiwar movement fell apart as public opinion polls measured that a majority had turned against the war.[7] The Civil Rights Movement waned within months of the passage of the Civil Rights Act of 1964.[8] In recent social movements, it seems as if the mainstream's superficial incorporation of a movement's ideals drains the initiative from radical mobilizations.

In this chapter, I consider the history of the Clamshell to specify the contemporary mechanisms of power that undermine radical social movements. Consistent with other researchers, I argue that the Clamshell participants were caught in a dilemma because they could not simultaneously advance a radical politics while building a majoritarian antinuclear public. This dilemma was not so much indicative of poor organizational choices, as it was representative of the ideological limits of "new social movements." These limits, I argue, are a consequence of the structural changes in recent decades that confine radicalism to the margins of society.

NEW SOCIAL MOVEMENTS AND RELATIONS OF POWER

Over the course of the 20th century in the United States and Western Europe, the dynamic of organized challenges to institutionalized relations of power has fundamentally changed. Power and resistance are engaged less in direct, violent confrontation, and are engaged more through public, discursive maneuvers in an ideological marketplace. Well into this century, labor unionists, socialists, and others often organized in secret for fear of violent reprisals by the state. Direct and violent state repression still persist, but in the postwar era, social movements struggle more against ignorance, callousness, and obscurity, than they do against direct and overt repression.[9]

The shift into ideological terrain occurred alongside the dwindling viability of Marxism. At one time, Marxism not only offered a coherent explanation of the source of antagonism within capitalist societies, but also defined a utopian vision with a relatively clear set of political stakes. By contrast, the "new social movements" that have emerged since the 1960s—the feminist, environmental, multicultural, peace, gay rights, local autonomy, and antinuclear movements—clearly demonstrate that organized resistance is not limited to movements by labor or the dispossessed. In addition, movement activists today rarely espouse socialist visions, and have mobilized in the absence of a comprehensive theoretical vision of alternative possibility.

Academic social theory proved no more able than Marxism to account for the new tactics and the new sources of antagonism. Theories from the early 1960s suggested that collective action would emerge among the most isolated and uprooted segments of society—a prediction clearly belied by the organized quality of contemporary movements. And although more recently, resource mobilization theory considered the organized and rational elements of social movements,[10] it neither attempted to explain the qualitative change in social movements, nor has it tried to present a theory of social transformation.

By the mid-1980s, this theoretical lacuna had been partially filled by the development of new social movement theory. Initially advanced by Western European scholars, new social movement theory associated the emergent qualities of resistance with a fundamental change in the structure of capitalism. Traditional versions of Marxism conceptualized class conflict in the context of the relations of production, yet increasingly the politics of capitalism revolved around sustaining economic growth through the management of markets and consumption. The effort to control consumption required a tremendous expansion in ideological and cultural realms.[11] The overt and repressive use of force that had been instrumental in the control of the wage-labor force could not adequately prepare the citizenry for mass consumption.[12] The commodification of culture resulted in a broadening, deepening, and an irreversibility to the power of capital that broke the barriers that had previously separated public and private spheres.[13]

The breakdown between the public and the private led to what now seems like the inevitable discovery that the "personal is political." That is, if a mass-consumer society led to an "inauthentic" culture, then a radical politics depended on purging both consciousness and popular culture of dominating influences. Beginning in the Civil Rights Movement, but reaching a much fuller expression in the New Left, nonconformity, new experiments in living, and explorations of the self became political acts. For a brief time, it was possible to imagine that revolution could be accomplished by accumulating self-transformations—the margins would overrun the mainstream.

Although this image of revolution no longer seems viable, the political vision that underlies it continues to define the qualities of new movements. New social movements, for example, have effectively identified hidden forms of power that are concealed behind an ideological facade. Melucci argues that the "systemic effects of new social movements are to render visible the power that hides behind the rationality of administrative or organizational procedures or the 'show business' aspects of politics."[14] Likewise, new movements are initiated in the discovery of concealed relations of power, and the heightened sensitivity to ideological distortion within institutionalized practices. Whereas regimes in the past certainly included an ideological apparatus, the fundamental boundaries that limited resistance consisted of building an organization in the face of overt repression. Identifying the source of domination was seldom difficult.

In one form, the radical mistrust of power resulted in the transvaluation of subordinate identities by women, people of color, and gays and lesbians. In another, often overlapping form, this radical mistrust led to the creation of participatory, egalitarian collectives. Beginning with the New Left, hierarchical organizations were perceived not only as concentrating power and privilege, but also as encouraging self-interests to be pursued under the guise of collective goals—the very substance of ideological distortion. Moreover, participatory, egalitarian collectives perform what Breines referred to as a prefigurative politics, which was the task of creating and sustaining within the "practice of the movement, relationships and political forms that 'prefigured' and embodied the desired society."[15]

Realizing a prefigurative politics, however, exists in a delicate balance with the central task of new social movements, which is to build a constituency for social change by exposing, analyzing, and publicizing the subtexts of contemporary consciousness and practice that typify dominant ideological influences. Once the social critique presented by a movement is absorbed into the mainstream, the sense of difference that drives a prefigurative politics seems to abate. The ideological limits of new social movements consist of the apparent inability of contemporary movements to sustain the sense of difference associated with the radical mistrust of power after the movement loses "ownership" of its critique. I describe the history of the Clamshell as a means to consider the boundaries of alternative possibility in a post-Marxist world.

THE DISCOVERY OF POWER

The Early Opposition

New Hampshire, not known for its radical political culture, was seemingly an unlikely place for a left-wing movement to originate. The Clamshell Alliance did not, however, arise from a vacuum. It grew out of the efforts of several citizen groups that challenged the licensing of the Seabrook plant on legal and regulatory grounds. Local opposition and regulatory intervention was not uncommon for nuclear plants proposed in the 1970s, and Seabrook was arguably one of the most vulnerable plants ever proposed.

For example, Public Service Company of New Hampshire (PSNH), the lead owner of the plant, was a small utility that had embarked on a large nuclear project. When PSNH first announced plans to build two 1,150-megawatt generators in 1972, it anticipated both reactors to be on-line by 1981. The estimated cost of $973 million seemingly pushed at the limits of what PSNH could afford.[16] By 1974, two years before construction began, PSNH's financial condition had deteriorated. Its bond rating had been reduced, and it was selling stock at 50 percent of book value.[17] Meanwhile, projected costs continued to escalate; by 1976, it had risen to $2 billion (Unit II was eventually canceled in 1984, and the cost for Unit I, when it came on-line in 1990, was $6.5 billion).

Aside from PSNH's financial weakness, the site posed additional problems for the utilities. The Seabrook plant was situated within two miles of one of the most densely populated beach-front resort communities in New England: Hampton Beach. Effective evacuation from the area was a dubious prospect because of the geography of the region, the population density, and the road network. The plant was also located on a salt marsh in a fertile clamming and fishing region. The original design of the plant required the dumping of some 600,000 gallons per minute of thermal effluent into a tidal estuary. This posed a serious concern for local environmentalists.

Minimizing the environmental impact, locating nuclear plants in remote areas, and ensuring the stability of the owning utilities were central criteria for the Nuclear Regulatory Commission's (NRC) licensing of nuclear power plants. There is insufficient space here to document the complicated and lengthy process by which these matters were adjudicated, but in each area new precedents were promulgated such that the utilities could continue construction.[18]

Discovering Systemic Forms of Power

For many, the NRC rulings left the indelible perception that procedures had been rigged from the start. For some, their frustration "pulled" them toward a more radical politics. Cathy Wolff, who became a Clamshell organizer, thanked the intervenors for documenting "the pronuclear bias of regulatory agencies," but then noted that "legal intervention is time consuming, complex . . . and an exasperating process, usually undertaken before a stacked jury of nuclear advocates."[19] Wolff's perception was compounded by the ideological efforts of the utilities that continued to tout the benefits of clean, safe and cheap nuclear power. Another Clamshell participant explained:

[The utilities and the NRC should] tell the truth about the plant, what it is capable of doing to the public, and what they are capable of doing to protect the public. . . . [But] the more you scratched the surface, the more you realized that there were no truthful answers to be had . . . because the truth is they did not want the public to know about . . . a whole gamut of things. So we realized that the whole thing was just a sham.[20]

The perception of systemic distortion was widespread, as another activist described, "I've always said that you go through stages of involvement with Seabrook, and I've seen it happen with others. You first become aware that there is something wrong here, and then you become informed, and then you come to another level, when you *really realize* that there is something wrong with this whole thing."[21] "Really realizing" connotes a process of critical discovery, where people gained a sense that an illusionary facade had fallen away, and left behind a deeper insight into a concealed reality.

Clearly, not everyone was willing to take the step into a more radical politics. The intervenor groups tended to stay their course. For example, the Society for the Protection of New Hampshire Forests (SPNHF) was a century-old conservation group and one of the largest landholders in the state, most of which had been acquired through substantial contributions. It had joined with the other intervenors because the utilities intended to build transmission lines through a cedar swamp that it owned. The society's participation had caused bitter disagreements among its trustees, and although the group emerged from the struggle a more aggressive defender of environmental values, it did not pursue the Seabrook case after its initial contentions had failed.[22]

For the Seacoast Anti-Pollution League (SAPL), a parallel problem emerged. The group, comprised of local housewives and middle-class professionals, spent most of its meager funds on hiring attorneys for the regulatory fight. SAPL held on to its no-tax status by avoiding political lobbying. When its president, Guy Chichester, began in 1975 to organize for collective action, members forced him to resign. Likewise, the New England Coalition on Nuclear Pollution (NECNP), a Vermont-based group, pulled together scientific experts and legal counsel specializing in environmental law. The group ruled out civil disobedience, viewing it as a threat to its legal and scientific credibility.

The entry of the Clamshell alongside the intervening groups created a division of oppositional labor, and it transformed the meaning of the struggle. The intervenors presumed the legitimacy of rational decision-making procedures, but the Clamshell redefined nuclear energy as a particular manifestation of a deeper structure of power. An activist explained: "The early objective was about the environmental threat that Seabrook posed—and it still presents itself that way—but I think more than that it has come to refer to how we are represented by our government, and the right to personal liberty."[23] In this shift in the perception of power, the Clamshell presented a more radical challenge than was possible using the staid tactics of the legal intervention.

Although the Clamshell grew out of the intervening groups, it drew its energy and strategy from the remnants of the New Left. The discovery of systemic expressions of power resulted in nearly a spontaneous confederating of environmental and leftist groups from across New England.

THE RISE OF THE CLAMSHELL ALLIANCE

The Social Roots of the Clamshell

In 1974, Sam Lovejoy, a veteran of the antiwar movement, tried to inspire the formation of an antinuclear movement. He turned himself over to police after toppling a weather-monitoring tower at a proposed nuclear power plant site in Montague, Massachusetts. In the subsequent, highly publicized trial, he was acquitted on a technicality, while also galvanizing much of the community. The owning utilities seemingly responded to the political pressure and eventually withdrew their intent for the Montague site.[24] At the time, Lovejoy was living on a collective, organic farm, which was subsidized by proceeds from political writings. He and other members of the collective, Harvey Wasserman and Anna Gyorgy in particular, produced a documentary film, *Lovejoy's Nuclear War,* and played key roles in organizing the Clamshell.

Other networks were also mobilized. Members of a local branch of the American Friends Service Committee (AFSC), a Quaker organization, which had actively organized non-violent protests in the 1960s, provided expertise and training for non-violence. Members of the Greenleaf Harvester's Guild, a New Hampshire farming collective devoted to Gandhian pacifist principles, also participated in the group's formation.

The confederation represented a "nexus of the peace and environmental movements, and for a lack of a better term, the movement for community control, which was about challenging powerful political and economic interests."[25] This nexus also suggested a number of angles that the Clamshell could use to attack the utilities and nuclear power. The group maintained that nuclear power "poses a mortal threat to people and the environment . . . [which were being] exploited for private profits."[26] Thermal pollution meant that the "fishing industries of Maine, New Hampshire and Mass. are thus threatened."[27] "The plant would also destroy salt marshes which are invaluable breeding and nesting grounds for fish and birds."[28] Nuclear power creates "fewer jobs than comparable investments in conservation and solar energy."[29] "Basically, nuclear power is a war-like technology . . . [that] have been chosen by the electric industry because they were believed to offer the greatest profit."[30] Thus, opposing nuclear power was also "to promote democratic, public control over energy . . . [and] to promote a pollution-free society in which the means and resources for satisfying basic human needs are controlled cooperatively by local communities."[31]

The rationales were fluid, used to legitimate activity as the context demanded. The movement that the Clamshell tried to capture was, however, more than the sum of these arguments, because it represented a confluence of efforts to challenge the deeper structure of power exposed by the intervenors. The name, "Clamshell," was chosen so as to give symbolic protection and voice to the most humble of creatures threatened by the plant. It denotes activists' sense that they were speaking for the unrepresented.

Organization

The Clamshell was organized with no hierarchy, and little division of labor. Complete democratic participation and unanimity in all decision-making were required in group meetings. Affinity groups served as the basis for intragroup communication and organization as well as coordination and training for non-violent civil disobedience. All potential protesters were expected to attend a six-hour training session on non-violence. These sessions, the affinity group structure, and the process of consensus decision making, led to what was heralded as "incredible solidarity."

The egalitarian style was modeled after the consciousness-raising session used in the women's movement. "Unlike the macho-ridden leadership of the Sixties left, the Clamshell Alliance has had women operating as equals since the formation of the original organizing committee."[32] Or as one affinity group trainer explained, "Direct action evolved out of the personal and collective desire to act for ourselves without the mediation and resulting distortion contributed by representatives, the media, bureaucrats, 'heavies,' or leaders."[33] The organizational structure along with the non-violent forms of civil disobedience were perceived as elements of a Gandhian method, "born out of truth and love."[34]

The organizational structure and the prefigurative politics it embodied were as central to the identity of the alliance as stopping the construction of Seabrook. As one explained, "We are not simply about exposing the evils of things as they are. We are exploring the possibilities of things as they could be."[35]

Periodic meetings of the Alliance Congress were organized to make important decisions, to plan major actions, and to rethink strategies. At meetings of the congress, discussions within affinity groups would lead to various proposals and agenda items. Such issues were brought to the general meeting, which were open to everyone. The meetings were coordinated by a "facilitator," who was charged with ensuring that everyone had an opportunity to speak. When a proposal was presented, objections were sought. Each objection had to be patiently resolved before moving on. Wasserman described the process: "A facilitator—meeting coordinator—would then ask for objections. The group would hold its breath, watching for dissenting hands. When there were none, there was an involuntary cheer, and the decision was made. Thus the Clamshell moved forward by silent consent rather than noisy approval. Somehow, that created a tremendous cohesion and strength."[36] By most accounts, this process worked extraordinarily well through 1976 and into 1977. One referred to this process as working like "magic," remarking, "I listened to other people speak and it was like they were speaking my own thoughts."[37]

THE COLLAPSE OF THE CLAMSHELL

The Organizational Problem

The peak in momentum for the Clamshell developed in the aftermath of the detainment in the New Hampshire state armories in May 1977.

Leading up to the occupation, New Hampshire Governor Meldrim Thomson, and William Loeb, the conservative publisher of the *Manchester Union Leader,* had raised the stakes with some "get-tough" rhetoric. The day before the occupation, Loeb editorialized on the front page, under the headline, "Leftist Groups Hope for Violence:" "It is important for the people of New Hampshire to understand that this is not a Sunday school picnic. This is an act of terrorism and violence." Loeb likened the Clamshell to "Nazi storm troopers under Hitler." Thomson accused the Clamshell of being "a cover for terrorist activity," and a communist organization supported by the Soviet Union.[38] He solicited state police support from all the New England states to manage "the law enforcement crisis."[39] During the detention, Thomson issued a nationwide appeal to pay for the cost of jailing the protesters, arguing that the Clamshell had to be stopped before their influence could spread.[40]

Over the course of the two-week stand-off, Thomson took a heavy hit from the national media. A *New York Times* editorial, for example, criticized him not so much for his undisciplined use of political power, but for the poverty of his strategy: "No one argues that demonstrators who break the law ought not to be punished, but the clear lesson of the 1960s, from Birmingham to Chicago, is that overreaction to protests serves mainly to bring law enforcement into disrepute."[41] The long detention and Thomson's rhetoric may have intimidated some, but the Clamshell appeared to have gotten the upper hand. Front-page coverage in the *New York Times,* as well as articles in *Time* and *Newsweek* brought the Clamshell onto a national stage, and provided a potential model for successful political action. Thomson would not repeat his mistake.

In the subsequent months, the Clamshell became the most salient expression of radical politics in New England. The group's success in mobilizing new constituencies, however, made the process of consensus decision making long and difficult. Meetings of the Alliance Congress grew more strained, and consensus was elusive. The major rift surfaced in 1978 amidst a growing tension between "Hard" and "Soft" Clams. The Soft Clams remained committed to a strict notion of non-violence. Its core membership consisted of most of the initial organizers along the seacoast and the Montague people. The Hard Clams favored more aggressive tactics. Among the "hardest" Clams was an affinity group called Hard Rain, whose members believed that the Clamshell had to be willing to take on the police to gain the support of the American working class.[42]

The split between Soft and Hard Clams was variously referred to as a difference between rural and urban people or in-staters and out-of-staters. One of the original seacoast activists, who hedged, argued:

I guess it was a difference between people. I don't know. I guess it was the difference where in the city there is the anonymity of numbers, in rural areas there is the isolation of recognition. I don't want to stereotype. But in Cambridge there is a demo everyday, people are always carrying pickets for something or other, and it doesn't mean so much, but up here, people know each other, and they weren't used to what was happening at Seabrook.[43]

Although this activist emphasized the need to move cautiously and win the support of local residents, another participant, who became an organizer in CDAS, turned this around, and argued that in-staters unduly dominated the group: "People in New Hampshire [the Soft Clams] really wanted a tone, wanted all of the decisions make on a consensus basis, but then they would make all the public presentations."[44] The emerging dissent reflected the growing tactical problems within the group:

The plan was to decentralize all decision-making, but it was terribly chaotic. With people who you know and who you meet with regularly and [if the group] is small, you can use that model of consensus molding and then reach a decision. In larger groups, it reaches a point where it doesn't work very well. And you had people who essentially wanted to go and meditate the thing away, and you had other people who wanted to drive through the gates with a bazooka in hand. And you had literally that range of opinions. And you had dissent at those meetings.[45]

On the agenda for an Alliance Congress meeting early in 1978 was discussion of the tactics to be used in a fourth occupation scheduled for June. A central issue concerned whether or not the chain-link fences that now surrounded the plant should be cut for the purposes of the occupation. The Hard and Soft Clams came down on their respective sides, with much of the debate focusing on whether or not cutting the fence constituted an act of violence. One member expressed obvious discontent:

We literally sat there for four hours one evening discussing . . . whether or not to cut the fences, or whether to put "A" frame ladders over them so as not to touch their property. And I remember a subtheme was that we should certainly pad the A frames so we don't do damage to their fence. I remember that particular discussion took about an hour. It was about that time that I said, "This is nuts."[46]

The fence-cutting issue, however, was merely a displacement of the more central problem of advancing a radical political agenda, while trying to build widespread public support. The Alliance Congress did eventually arrive at the decision that "no destruction of property would take place," but the meeting left a bitter taste. The "magic" that seemed to be at work in the earlier meetings had faded.

The Rath Proposal

A couple of weeks before the scheduled June occupation, the Attorney General of New Hampshire, Tom Rath, made an offer for a legal rally in place of the planned civil disobedience. Caught between the potentially violent consequences of perhaps 6,000 people attempting an occupation, and the desire to attract the mainstream, the Rath proposal was accepted. The decision was reached by the alliance's coordinating committee of affinity group representatives, which was still most heavily influenced by the original participants—the Soft Clams. Some members charged this violated Clamshell rules of consensus decision making.

Roughly 20,000 people attended the June rally. Yet despite the outpouring of support, the rift had become a breach. The rally did not generate the type of confrontation that some members had expected and hoped. Many had wanted a repeat of the confrontation that had followed events the previous April. Harvey Halpan, of a Boston affinity group, charged that the alliance had "sold out."[47] Another argued that "people felt enraged and cheated over what they believed was a lack of consultation in the decision-making process."[48] Thomson, meanwhile, all but congratulated the group. He said that they were "regenerated and rehabilitated,"[49] and that they "are a well-disciplined group and we give them credit for it. In that sense, we welcome a peaceful demonstration."[50]

We cannot know for sure what motivated the Rath proposal. He might never have expected the Clamshell to accept his offer. In accepting it, Wasserman claimed that the Clamshell had upstaged the state, having "jumped through the eye of the needle," and attracted "a solid mainstream audience."[51] Yet clearly Rath was not interested in a repeat of the 1977 events, and his proposal was, at least in part, a public relations ploy to show the willingness of the state to compromise. It was obvious that the Clamshell could not be threatened out of existence without treading through very troubled political waters. It was equally likely that Rath's proposal was a calculated move to drive a wedge between the Hard and the Soft Clams. As Wasserman himself had commented:

They made us a middle-ground offer that became very hard for us to refuse. If we refused a peaceful solution, we'd appear unreasonable and lose the credibility we gained last year. If we accepted, it would look like we were going soft. It was very well calculated to split the alliance, and it succeeded.[52]

Rath's proposal appears to be a type of win-win situation. If the proposal was not accepted, then the confrontation at the fences might have led to a violent clash, which would likely alienate New Hampshire residents, marginalize the opposition, and intensify the tensions in the group. If the proposal was accepted, then not only might this exacerbate the tensions within the group, but also the sense of political difference necessary to pursue a prefigurative politics would begin to dissolve.

The Ideological Limits of the Clamshell Alliance

Organizational problems clearly developed inside the process of consensus decision making, but the state, the utilities, and pronuclear advocates also had shifted their ideological strategy to marginalize the group. Perhaps learning from Thomson's social-control error in May 1977, the ideological attack centered on undermining the political identity of the group. George Gilder referred to the Clamshell participants as "vegetarians in leather jackets" driving "their imported cars to Seabrook listening to the Grateful Dead on their Japanese tape decks amid a marijuana haze."[53] A Clamshell member described a similar process: "[Utilities] select a couple of more extreme leaders and point the press to those leaders. And they almost always select someone who wears long hair, wears Berkenstock sandals, who spouts a lot of political socialist rhetoric. . . . They are very effective at focusing attention on that person, who may not at all represent the organization."[54] Regardless of the accuracy of this observation, it represents a self-conscious recognition of the pragmatic need for containing the pull toward radicalism. An organizer for Citizens Within the Ten Mile Radius, a local community group mobilized in the mid-1980s to encourage communities to withdraw from evacuation planning, similarly argued: "The role of the Clamshell was double-edged. . . . The demonstrations kept the issue alive not just locally, but nationally. . . . But [nuclear proponents] like to refer to all of their opponents as part of the Clamshell. . . . They just lump 'em all together, as some renegade group of hippies."[55] Whereas the Clamshell was both attracting radicals and creating radical identities, the mobilization process marginalized its own political agenda. The organizational problems were a consequence of being caught in this duality.

The U.S. Council of Energy Awareness, a public relations organization that promotes the nuclear industry, ran an ad on network television in the early 1990s. In the ad, a fortyish, presumably middle-class mom quietly lauds the environmental benefits of nuclear power—no greenhouse gases, and so forth. In a brief phrase in the middle of the ad, she says, "When I was a young, college student I was opposed to nuclear power." She does not provide a "because" for her earlier position, but given the "clues," we are invited to the conclusion that her opposition represented an irrational, naive idealism. The words "young" and "college student" do not account for motive, but they substitute for an inquiry into motive. More importantly, the words bear no relation to their denoted meaning; nevertheless, the intended meaning is understood by all, thereby demonstrating the manner in which the representational terrain has been effectively captured.

In 1977, the force of the opposition had caught elites by surprise, but a systematic campaign began to close the boundaries for the articulation of a radical politics and to marginalize the opposition. The inability to sustain a consensus and the splitting of the group was a function of this representational problem. I am not taking issue with the claim that the style of participatory decision making inside the Clamshell resulted in its collapse. Expecting complete consensus among a large group of people may well be impossible. But the specific issues that resulted in the breakdown were also a consequence of social forces that could not be fully grasped by the participants in the throes of an undertaking.

Within the general evolution of the opposition, activists were simultaneously pushed toward greater radicalism, and pulled back from radicalism. While the CDAS faction adopted more militant tactics than the Clamshell, it also retreated from the radical mistrust of power implicit in the pursuit of a prefigurative politics. The breakdown in consensus was representative of the extent to which the Clamshell's primary commitment ought to be stopping this plant, or whether the political, ideological, and cultural objective ought to have more far-reaching implications. The formation of CDAS indicated that some members opted for the former, where the ideological purity of a prefigurative politics came to be seen as an obstacle in stopping the plant. The choice of more militant means was fostered by the inability to sustain a social space for opposition when protests were coordinated with the state. In the face of such potential "co-optation," seemingly the only possible means for a strategic success was to adopt more radical tactics. Yet, such a step risked marginalization.

For the Soft Clams the transformation into a visible, political force required a "self-editing" process such that tactics and strategies could be devised to counter elite response. The effort to retain the purity of means implicit to a prefigurative politics negated the possibility of adapting to the changed representational environment. In the early days of the Clamshell, the participants were largely free to create their own collective identity and formulate a strategy. Within a couple of years, this was no longer the case. The self-definition of the Clamshell was subsumed by larger, and more pervasive categories within the political culture. The Soft Clams' refusal to abandon their general criticism of technocratic capitalism and their refusal to abandon their prefigurative politics determined their ideological limits.

DISCUSSION: POWER AND NEW SOCIAL MOVEMENTS

The Clamshell created an ideological front against nuclear power and it provided a temporary medium for the expression of a radical politics.

Power relations were momentarily perceived and challenged, yet activists' efforts to challenge and criticize these power relations resulted in marginalization and dissolution. The utilities, by contrast, were able to compress and intensify their efforts to ensure the licensing of the plant, and had merely to diffuse the opposition. The Clamshell had to preserve a social space such that the representational boundaries necessary for the articulation of a radical politics could be retained.

The strategic and political problem for new social movements is a product of building a public opposition in the context of new relations of power. As Melucci argued, contemporary forms of power flow through loosely coupled bureaucratic apparatuses that conceal responsibility through instrumentally rational procedures. In particular sites and moments, the "curtain is pulled back," such that people are able to perceive particular responsibility, objectives, and pervasive ideological distortion. Such moments are limited and brief. The task for elites is to close the curtain, which is primarily accomplished by permitting an appearance of accommodation to oppositional demands. If the opposition resists such an accommodation (as the Clamshell initially did), then it is more or less obligated to articulate more radical objectives, which can be more easily marginalized.

This problem is understood by most participants in new social movements and defines their central strategic problem. The difficult challenge for new social movements is to generate claims and demands that are institutionally negotiable, while expanding a cultural base that cannot be co-opted and subsumed by the political system. Since the late 1970s, many movement groups have "retreated" into single-issue agendas to push at the level of the polity for modest institutional change. Whether this can generate a vision of alternative possibility remains an open question. Other movement groups have resisted accommodation, and therefore emphasized the transformation of personal identities within the relations of everyday life. Whether such groups can avoid becoming a marginalized cliché and generate a bloc for societal transformation is also unclear. What is clear is that both options represent strategies to confront and resist the way in which power is exercised in contemporary societies. The inability of recent radical social movements to transform the mainstream is itself the principal demonstration of the opaque form of contemporary, institutionalized relations of power that confines opposition to the margins of society.

NOTES

I am grateful to Winifred Breines, Michael Blim, Lynn Stephen, Michael Brown and the editors for their comments on earlier drafts of this chapter.

1. Between 1989 and 1991, I conducted interviews with twenty-eight activists who had been involved in groups opposed to the Seabrook nuclear power plant. The data presented in this chapter are taken from those interviews, movement

literature gathered over the course of those interviews, mass media accounts, and secondary literature. This item is taken from my interview with Rennie Cushing, April 1990.

2. The Clamshell surfaced again in the late 1980s to augment the political efforts of the local communities that challenged Seabrook's operating license on the grounds of inadequate evacuation planning. In this chapter, I have limited my focus to the initial history of the Clamshell.

3. Stanley Nealy, Barbara Melber, and William L. Rankin, *Public Opinion and Nuclear Energy* (Ithaca: Cornell University Press, 1983), p. 23.

4. Donald Holt, "The Nuke that Became a Political Weapon," *Fortune* (January 1979): 75.

5. Steven Barkan, "Strategic, Tactical, and Organizational Dilemmas of the Protest Movement Against Nuclear Power," *Social Problems* 27 (1979): 19–37; Gary L. Downey, "Ideology and Clamshell Identity: Organizational Dilemmas in the Anti-Nuclear Movement," *Social Problems* 33 (1986): 357–373; Barbara Epstein, *Political Protest and Cultural Revolution: Nonviolent Direct Action in the 1970s and 1980s* (Berkeley: University of California Press, 1991).

6. See, for example, Jane Mansbridge, *Beyond Adversary Democracy* (Chicago: University of Chicago Press, 1983).

7. Todd Gitlin, *The Whole World is Watching: Mass Media in the Making and the Unmaking of the New Left* (Berkeley: University of California Press, 1980).

8. Frances Fox Piven and Richard Cloward, *Poor People's Movements: Why They Succeed, How They Fail* (New York: Vintage Books, 1979).

9. See, for example, Frances Fox Piven and Richard Cloward, *The New Class War: Reagan's Attack on the Welfare State and Its Consequences* (New York: Pantheon Books, 1985), pp. 121–124, for a discussion on how this change has influenced the political response to the labor movement.

10. J. D. McCarthy and M. Zald, "Resource Mobilization and Social Movements: A Partial Theory," *American Journal of Sociology* 82 (1977): 1212–1241.

11. Herbert Marcuse, *One-Dimensional Man* (Boston: Beacon Press, 1964).

12. Jurgen Habermas, *Legitimation Crisis,* trans. by Thomas McCarthy (Boston: Beacon Press, 1975).

13. Claude Offe, "Challenging the Boundaries of Institutional Politics," *Social Research* 52 (Winter 1985): 817–868.

14. Alberto Melucci, *Nomads of the Present: Social Movements and Individual Needs in Contemporary Society,* edited by John Keane and Paul Mier (Philadelphia: Temple University Press, 1988), p. 76.

15. Winifred Breines, *Community and Organization in the New Left, 1962–1968: The Great Refusal,* with a new preface (New Brunswick: Rutgers University Press, 1989), p. 6.

16. Donald Stever, *Seabrook and the Nuclear Regulatory Commission: The Licensing of a Nuclear Power Plant* (Hanover, N.H.: University Press of New England, 1980).

17. Robert Bedford, *Seabrook Station: Citizen Politics and Nuclear Power* (Amherst: University of Massachusetts Press, 1990), p. 96.

18. Documents on the legal and regulatory history of Seabrook, which now spans hundreds of thousands of pages, are located in the Exeter Public Library,

Exeter, New Hampshire. Stever's and Bedford's books are essentially summaries of this history.

19. Cathy Wolff, "Roots of the Antinuclear Movement," pp. 289–296 in *Accidents Will Happen: The Case Against Nuclear Power* (New York: Harper and Row, 1979), p. 292.

20. Confidential interview, August 1989.

21. Confidential interview, August 1989.

22. Stever, *Seabrook*, p. 16.

23. Interview with Barry Connell, May 1990.

24. Harvey Wasserman, *Energy Wars: Reports from the Front* (Westport: Lawrence Hill and Co., 1979), pp. 27–40.

25. Confidential interview, April 1990.

26. Clamshell Alliance, "Founding Statement," pamphlet, 1976.

27. Clamshell Alliance, "It's a Fact," leaflet. No date (1977?).

28. Clamshell Alliance, "It's a Fact," leaflet, 1977.

29. Clamshell Alliance, "Declaration of Nuclear Resistance," leaflet, 1977.

30. Clamshell Alliance, "It's a Fact," leaflet, 1977.

31. Quoted in Downey, "Ideology," p. 367.

32. *The Real Paper,* May 17, 1977, p. 17.

33. Quoted in Downey, "Ideology," p. 369.

34. Clamshell Alliance, "Civil Disobedience," pamphlet, 1978.

35. *The Real Paper,* May 17, 1977, p. 25.

36. Wasserman, *Energy Wars,* p. 109.

37. Confidential interview, December 1989.

38. *Manchester Union Leader,* April 30, 1977, p. 1.

39. Of the New England states, only Massachusetts, under Governor Michael Dukakis, refused to send state police to New Hampshire. Loeb editorialized on May 2, 1977: "Massachusetts, governed by the bleeding-heart, left-wing liberal Dukakis, refused to send any. This was not unexpected because most of the protesters came from Governor Dukakis' kooky and almost bankrupt state."

40. *New York Times,* May 7, 1977, p. 8.

41. *New York Times,* May 7, 1977, p. 24.

42. Epstein, *Political Protest and Cultural Revolution,* pp. 73–74.

43. Confidential interview, April 1990.

44. Confidential interview, June 1990.

45. Confidential interview, May 1990.

46. Confidential interview, November 1989.

47. *Boston Sunday Globe,* June 25, 1978, p. 38.

48. *New York Times,* June 25, 1978, p. 18.

49. *New York Times,* June 26, 1978, p. 14.

50. *Boston Globe,* June 25, 1978, p. 38.

51. Wasserman, *Energy Wars,* p. 115.

52. *New York Times,* June 25, 1978, p. 18.

53. Quoted in Bedford, *Seabrook,* p. 82.

54. Confidential interview, May 1990.

55. Interview with Thomas Moughan, August 1989.

The United Colors of Multiculturalism: Rereading Composition Textbooks in the 90s

Sandra Jamieson

The Conference on College Composition and Communication's 1989 resolution to "adopt a curriculum policy that *represents the inclusion* of women and people of color in the curriculum at all levels" (my emphasis) is typical of the gestures made in response to the "celebration of diversity" on U.S. campuses. Although some conservative commentators condemn such policies, accusing them of being motivated by "political correctness" rather than genuine desire for reform, I believe that the real problem is not that they promote quotas or discriminate against middle-class white male students, but that they encourage faculty with the best intentions to believe that "diversity" is simply a matter of "inclusion" of the "Other" in a curriculum remaining steadfastly Eurocentric. Such an assimilationist understanding of "diversity" has long been held by textbook publishers in this country, and unfortunately, also by many involved in the current debate over multiculturalism and school textbooks; even most of those who argue that textbooks should provide models for students to emulate seem to ignore the importance of what those models *say* and in what *context* they are placed. More important, they seem also to ignore the complexities of identity construction and the role of language and ideology in that process. Nowhere does such an oversight subvert radical intentions more thoroughly than when it occurs in texts designed to teach literacy.

Because the debate concerning the pedagogical and cognitive effects of simple inclusion has centered on school textbooks rather than college-level texts, few people have discussed the identities being constructed for the next generation of academics and college-educated professionals at the site of advanced language acquisition in college composition classes. This absence of analysis has encouraged a flood of so-called "multicultural" textbooks to follow the tentative titles produced in the mid-1980s, and even revised versions of traditional composition anthologies (collectively known as "Readers") emphasize their increased "diversity" and inclusiveness. A consideration of whether the apparent revolution in composition texts has been as radical as it might appear is long overdue. And an appropriate place to begin seems to be with the issue of what model of the relationship between the cultural "mainstream" and its "margins" is represented in textbooks adopting this new politics of inclusion, what model seems to motivate them, and what impact this might have on students reading them.

I situate my consideration of these questions within three broad assumptions: (1) Althusser's (1971) thesis that mature capitalist social formations install education as the *dominant* ideological state apparatus where it becomes both the stake and the site of class struggle; (2) Foucault's (1972, p. 227) argument that education "follows the well-trodden battle-lines of social conflict [where] every educational system is a political means of maintaining or of modifying the appropriation of discourse, with the knowledge and the power it carries with it"; and (3) Adorno and Horkheimer's (1979) analysis of how the "culture industry" incorporates challenges and sets limits on the nature of the possible resistance. My findings suggest that although the collections of essays used to teach composition appear to have been radically transformed in recent years, the changes are largely superficial because the same mainstream/margin model is operative in them as in earlier texts. Although appearing (and in some cases claiming) to represent a resistance to hegemonic culture with its traditional mainstream/margin structure, many of the current wave of "multicultural" projects and texts in fact simply replicate that structure.

The last twenty years has seen a rapid rise in the number of students entering American colleges without the necessary reading and writing skills, and composition theorists led by Bruffee (1986), Bizzell (1986), and Brodkey (1987) have responded by exploring the complex social factors influencing literacy acquisition and membership in discourse communities. Bartholomae (1985) describes students having to "reinvent" the university every time they write for it, and Rose (1985) finds a language of exclusion that ensures that "under-prepared" students remain on the margins of the academy. These theorists, which Faigley (1986) termed "Social Commentators," have found many supporters anxious to find ways to teach literacy skills and at the same time compensate for some of the inequalities that produce under-prepared writers. "Multicultural" texts appear to satisfy both needs. A combination of increasing class size and the widespread use of untrained teaching assistants and adjuncts to teach writing have made composition Readers the most popular way to teach writing because Readers, written by compositionists, contain both a variety of texts and the apparatus to teach them, and are designed, in fact, to teach the class all by themselves. "Readers" are collections of pieces of writing (from 50 to 200), with each piece generally followed by comprehension questions, issues to stimulate class discussion, and topics for writing in response to, or in imitation of, the piece. Some, like their forebears the *McGuffey's Readers* of the 1870s, include definitions of words, although modern Readers have replaced the instructions for reading aloud with brief descriptions of purpose, audience, style, and structure.

Although textbook Readers include many extracts from works of fiction, students in a composition class have a different relationship to them than they might if they read those works in a different context; the instructional nature of the class (which students are often required to "pass" in order to remain in the academy) forces them into a more thoroughly passive relationship to the text than that often claimed to exist in other encoder/decoder relationships (most notably in the work of Fiske [1986, 1988], who criticizes studies that assume a passive audience and a simple interaction between audience and text). The nature of the textbook, its inclusions, juxtapositions, and pedagogical equipment including comprehension questions and topics for discussion and writing, essentially precludes the possibility of the multiple interpretations Condit (1989) terms "polyvalent" readings by carefully determining how the texts are read and what is to be considered "important." The texts provide students with the cultural codes and discourses necessary to "correctly decode" the essays they contain; therefore, the kinds of decodings described by Radway (1984), Fiske (1986, 1987), and Steiner (1988), who find audiences resisting the hegemonic values and messages of the text, can only take the form of resistance to literacy instruction itself, which translates into (among other things) punitive grades. If we find that composition texts that appear to resist hegemonic culture actually reinscribe the hierarchical mainstream/margin model of that culture, we must ask what impact this message has on the mostly "marginal" students required to take composition classes on their entrance to colleges and universities, and, in turn, on the "multicultural" aims of the university and larger educational goals of society.

It is my contention that these texts reinforce the ideology of "mainstream" white American male supremacy over "marginal" white women who are represented as primarily concerned with "women's issues" and American women and men of color who appear as non-academic, "self-involved" victims unable to change their fate. Thus, I believe that just like their predecessors, these revised textbook Readers might benefit white male students, especially those from the working class who may not have been able to imagine themselves as "insiders" before they used these texts, and they might also benefit white women who we see theorizing gender issues rather than simply describing them, and recent immigrants who may not have believed that they had anything to contribute before they used these texts; but they do this at the expense of reinscribing the "programmed failure" of women and men of color, teaching them that people like them do not, and by implication cannot, write academic essays at the very moment when it would appear to be teaching them the skills to do so. Obviously, this subverts the stated national agenda of increasing representation of these groups in higher education and the professions it provides access to. Perhaps most troubling is that at the same time it inscribes the notion that the failure of these programs is "natural."

Because the essential model of diversity that motivated them remains unexplored, textbook Readers have this effect in spite of the best intentions of most of the editors and publishers involved. Indeed, these liberal good intentions have betrayed composition textbook producers for this same reason since their large scale return to the field in the 1960s. The emphasis on inclusion and the selection of material intended to "provoke thought" and "stimulate discussion" about "important issues" reveal a clear understanding of the role textbooks play as inscribers of values; however, the actual pieces selected and the juxtapositions in which they are placed indicate less of an understanding of the complex ways in which ideology reproduces subjects through texts. Althusser (1971, pp. 132–133) argues that for capitalist systems of production to function smoothly they must have built into them the means for both the literal and the mental reproduction of labor: "a reproduction of submission to the ruling ideology for the workers, and a reproduction of the ability to manipulate the ruling ideology correctly for the agents of exploitation and repression, so that they, too, will provide for the domination of the ruling class 'in words.' " Again, one of the major agents in this reproduction is the education system, and as the domination is to be achieved "in words," literacy education becomes crucial. Prior to the 1960s policy of Open Admission and more recent efforts to increase college enrollment by appealing to "traditionally under-represented groups," colleges of higher education focused on training those who would, in Althusser's terms, "manipulate the ruling ideology," but as a result of these policies they must now also reproduce those college-educated white-collar workers who must "submit to the ruling ideology." Composition Readers become a tool in this process by teaching not only concrete skills but also what Althusser terms "know-how": "rules of morality, civic and professional conscience" and other social values. It is, again, this ability to teach skills *and* values that attracts many progressive educators to textbooks, but if they simply include "other" writers while retaining the original structure of the texts, they will not challenge the social order because that structure was designed to teach literacy skills "in forms which ensure subjection to the ruling ideology *or* the mastery of its practice." Thus contemporary textbooks that would duplicate the stated functions of early Readers inadvertently also perform the work of ideology that was their other function.

A BRIEF GENEALOGY

The first Composition Readers in 15th-century England taught English and French mercantile traders how to write for business purposes, but in the process they inscribed appropriate attitudes and values *about* that business and, by informing, *re*formed those who participated in it. The tradition of selecting literature for literacy education, which also reproduced the values of the ruling ideology, continued through texts designed for Huguenot immigrants, colonized Bengali, and English "scholarship" students. Readers in use in 19th-century America actually stressed their dual agenda as part of their self-descriptions. Porter's *Rhetorical Reader* of 1841 explains (p. v) that in selecting readings "regard [was] paid first to the moral sentiment of the pieces, as suited to make a safe and useful impression on the young." Similarly, the revised *Mc-Guffey's Sixth Eclectic Reader* of 1880 promises (p. iv) that new inclusions "present the same instructive merit and healthful moral tone which gave the preceding edition its high reputation." Sanders' *Union Fifth Reader* of 1876 goes even further, claiming (p. iii) that its pieces "breath forth the sentiments of loyalty, and tend to *inspire* the spirit of patriotism, and a deeper devotion to the cause of our republican institutions, and to the welfare of our whole country," and in 1929 *The Elson Reader, Book Six,* continued this pattern offering (p. vi): "patriotic literature, rich in the ideals of home and country, loyalty, service, thrift, cooperation and citizenship—ideals of which American children gained a new conception during the World War and which the school Reader should *perpetuate.*"

The need to construct "Americans" who were "useful," "patriotic," "devoted to the cause of republican institutions," and so forth, was considered so fundamental that all texts stressed their ability to mold character, whereas few even commented on the applicability of their selections as exemplars of the rhetorical "know-how" outlined in the text. The 1939 Modern Language Association "Statement of the Committee of Twenty Four" also presented such an emphasis, arguing that literature fosters "good citizens" more effectively than any other aspect of education and calling for the re-establishment of literature-based composition courses, not because they are an effective way to teach writing, but because through them a student's

feelings are *purged* and *disciplined* by an application of the familiar psychological doctrine of empathy. He feels his impulses toward unruly and subversive emotions to be at once released and *controlled* by adopting for the moment the career of the fictional characters swayed by the same emotions. *In this way his brute instincts are transmitted into civilized values.* (Berlin, 1987 p. 111, italics added)

In their most recent forms, textbook prefaces have ceased to directly state the ideological aspects of their instruction, but they still seem committed to the construction of "citizens safe for democracy," and they still adopt almost identical structures and strategies as their forebears, dropping only the lengthy chapters on pronunciation and principles and rules of grammar. Much too often, although their overt agenda is recognized, their underlying ideology, because it is hegemonic, remains invisible.

Traditional Readers, such as Decker's *Patterns of Exposition* (1990) and Eastman et al.'s *Norton Reader* (1992), are still the most popular. This kind of text follows essentially the same design as its 16th-century ancestors: apparently unconnected readings are organized by rhetorical strategy (narration, description, persuasion, exposition, etc.) and surrounded by a teaching apparatus which ensures that students learn the "lesson" of the piece and can imitate its style. These texts have responded to calls for "inclusion" by increasing the number of pieces written by people of color and white women, creating an alternative canon of writings "from the margins." Publicity materials proclaim this numerical increase, but stress that the structure and principles remain unchanged. So, unfortunately, does the ideology that they inscribe because the new inclusions remain consistent with the older model in which white men are the producers of academic or "correct" writing in the terms set out by the text, whereas white women write less-academic prose about women and "women's issues," and people of color write, largely from a child's perspective, narratives about racial victimization.

The apparently more radical response to the issue of inclusion has been the birth of the "multicultural Reader" organized by theme and featuring what many prefaces describe as "a wide spectrum of writers" who narrate or describe non-Western/non-white experiences and practices. The first "multicultural" Reader, *Crossing Cultures,* was published in 1983, but the popularity of such texts escalated in the late 1980s to the point that today every publishing house in the composition textbook market has at least one, and most have several. They include many of the pieces canonized by traditional texts such as Richard Rodriguez' "Aria," Langston Hughes' "Salvation," and Maxine Hong Kingston's "Girlhood Among Ghosts," and they offer these pieces to both "educate" their readers from the "mainstream" and "empower" their readers from the margins; however, because they adopt this traditional mainstream/margin model, they undercut any radical pedagogy within which they are used and, so, serve to perpetuate structures of dominance even as they would appear to challenge them.

THE MAINSTREAM/MARGIN MODEL

"Multicultural" readers can be grouped according to focus, target audience, or specific agenda. With respect to content and focus, one group presents cultures of the world where "American" is the monolithic "mainstream" culture and the rest of the world is the "other," whereas a second group focuses on "multicultural America" where representatives of mainstream "American culture" are contrasted with "talented emerging writers" from marginal American "sub-cultures." They all offer a different ratio of insider accounts and anthropological pieces about this "other," and they all offer a slightly different relationship between the mainstream and the margin, but none reject this model as an organizing principle or even call it into question.

As Nancy Shapiro points out (1991), some of these texts seem targeted to English as a Second Language students whose difference they seek to appropriate, while others (perhaps the vast majority) are intended to raise the consciousness of European-American students with little or no cross-cultural experience. Some even refer to their student readers as "we" Americans and speak of "our" culture when discussing aspects of European-American/mainstream culture (although most avoid the term "they" to refer to other U.S. and foreign cultures).

Perhaps the more revealing grouping occurs along the lines of ideology and the mainstream/margin model from which the editors appear to operate. In this aspect, the division does not fall between "world" and "U.S." identities but among attitudes towards diversity. The four competing pedagogical responses to diversity outlined by Sciachitano (1991) help us to think about the ideologies informing these texts. Her taxonomy ranges from what I shall call the "color blind" to the "locational," and describes general attitudes and strategies that we see reflected in pedagogies, policies, and texts throughout American colleges. Although, as Sciachitano points out, there are other responses and these categories are necessarily broad, Readers on the market today can be seen to fall quite neatly into the first three, which we can identify by their emphasis on promoting "color blindness," identifying cultural uniqueness, and confronting the conflicts. Reading composition Readers in light of these categories help us to see the mainstream/margin models on which they rest.

The first and most conservative of Sciachitano's categories, she claims, has developed in response to the fear that "diversity . . . will inevitably lead to divisiveness" and that this is necessarily bad. Instead of focusing our attention on "difference," proponents of this school of thought propose that we all learn to be "unaware" of it. Such an ideology is evidenced in a pedagogy which emphasizes "the 'unifying,' 'common' themes underlying diversity," stressing the "universal voice" and promoting "a 'color-blind' and 'gender-blind' society" (p. 1). In this model the "Otherness" of the margins is domesticated by the center in order for the mainstream to retain its position. Marginal cultures are not incorporated into the mainstream, but rather are made to seem to be basically the same as it and thus not entitled to the claim of difference on which calls for curricula and social change are grounded. For some, this move could appear to also reduce racial discrimination; however, in fact it simply obscures the power relations underlying it and emphasizes physical racial difference by denying cultural heritage. By reconstructing the Other as "really like" the "normal" Western subject, this position also achieves what Said (1979, p. 3) claims Orientalism did for Europe whose "culture gained in strength and identity by setting itself off against the Orient as a sort of surrogate and even underground self."

Hirschberg's *One World, Many Cultures* and Repp's *How We Live Now* are examples of texts that fall into this category. Hirschberg (1992, p. vii) promises essays that "challenge readers to see similarities between their own experiences and the experiences of others in radically different cultural circumstances," whereas Repp (1992, p. v) explains that the thematic organization of his text is "designed to reflect universal experiences" and render cultures which "may seem unfamiliar at first . . . accessible to students." These texts are designed to make the Other feel "at home." Hirschberg (1992, p. vii) claims that his text will "reflect the cultural and ethnic heritage of many students," whereas Repp offers a text that will "allow students from traditionally marginalized groups to recognize expressions of their culture." Thus difference is reduced. Hirschberg's preface and the writing assignments following the readings direct students toward what they identify as shared emotions and our common humanity rather than our different cultural formations although, as I will show later, its content totally belies this aim. This is not surprising according to Sciachitano's taxonomy, which describes this position developing from a common failure of its proponents "to recognize their own race, gender, and class-privileges" and inability to "see their relation to the struggles for power."

Although this position is marked by its denial of the fundamental importance of difference, Sciachitano's second position is occupied by those who recognize its structural role and so focus exclusively on individual difference. They tend to "privilege cultural 'uniqueness' " and the often "romantic, nostalgic, or exotic" personal narrative. Unfortunately, as Sciachitano explains, such actions have the effect of making "racial, gender, class and culture-specific difference" appear to determine identity, while mystifying the sociohistorical contexts in which these features became important (Sciachitano, 1991, p. 1). The "mainstream" can thus identify itself in relation to the Other and even celebrate the "margins" as the place from which vision of the "center" is clearest. This double move ensures that the mainstream/margin model remains intact and that the power relations that depend on it are obscured.

Texts and teachers with the most radical aims can be undone by this "underlying ideology of individualism and cultural imperialism," as is the case with Columbo et al.'s *Rereading America: Cultural Contexts for Critical Thinking and Writing* (1992) and Layton's *Intercultural Journeys through Reading and Writing* (1991). The first edition of *Rereading America* had the highest percentage of personal narratives of all of the multicultural texts surveyed by Shapiro (1992), whereas *Intercultural Journeys* ranked third. Both texts work from the premise that "through knowing others we come to know ourselves more fully" (Layton, 1991, p. xxiii) although the nationalities of those "others" differs between the two texts.

The narratives in *Rereading America* are a little more sophisticated than those described in Sciachitano's model, tending toward anger and frustration rather than romanticism; however, racial and ethnic factors still determine the identities of people such as Studs Terkel's "Stephen Cruz" and George Wolfe's Man/Kid. Moreover, although their description of problems may be accurate, the rhetorical forms adopted (first-person narrative and drama) allow little room for historical detail. If students reading Wolfe's piece need footnotes explaining "Murray's pomade" and "Stokely Carmichael," they are unlikely to know what "SNCC" or the "Black Panther Party" were or what roles they played, nor, one assumes, are they qualified to discuss what would be "appropriate symbols of African American culture" as the questions at the end invite them to do (without providing this additional information). Furthermore, the issue in the piece is not *which* symbols, but that assimilation allows *no* symbols: "Man" feels he must reject the *personal* symbols of his past, but the questions following the piece recast them as the uniform symbols of all African Americans. Thus this text first constructs an individual based on racial symbols and then colonizes him into a representative position for students to occupy and from which they can view the world.

A text like *Rereading America* which promises (1992, p. vi) to challenge cultural myths is very appealing to many liberal and radical teachers. But, by "ask[ing] students to explore the influence of *our* culture's dominant myths—*our* national beliefs" to help them "break through conventional assumptions and patterns of thought" by allowing them to "stand outside [our] culture" (1992, p. 8) in the shoes of men like Cruz and Wolfe, it becomes problematic on several levels. The "we" of the text is the American of European descent. The student of the mainstream. And *he* may find this text very enlightening. But the Other in whose position he is invited to stand must remain marginal for his convenience; indeed, her Otherness is emphasized to allow "us" to explore "our" culture. Thus the reader of this text is forced to occupy the univocal subject position of the white, American male, the only subject position from which the text can be interpreted. This might explain the apparently illogical fact that most of the analysis in the collection is written by European Americans rather than drawing on the double-consciousness that W.E.B. Du Bois demonstrated those already "outside" dominant culture must develop to survive. By celebrating diverse voices from the margins, and presenting analysis of the mainstream by the mainstream or from the perspective of the mainstream, this and other texts in this category maintain their emphasis on the individual by mystifying the power relations that determine "dominant myths" and thus denying that "institutionalized sexism, racism, classism, and other forms of oppression exist and are continually sanctioned in our society" (Sciachitano, 1991, p. 2).

Sciachitano's third position, which she says is "advocated by many liberal educators who are sincerely and seriously concerned about social issues," challenges such mystification by "teaching the conflicts." Although this pedagogy may be conscious of the impact of vertical structures of power, and include collaborative projects and class debate to "empower" students, it tends not to see power as relational. The result, she claims (1991, p. 2), is that "there is little, if any, recognition or discussion of the differences in power relations between different groups of people" and thus, I would add, educators occupying this position also fail to locate themselves (and in this case, their texts) and different groups of students within the complex power structure of a multicultural classroom or society.

Many of the more "radical" texts fall into this category. For example, McLeod et al.'s *Writing About the World* (1991, p. v) identifies the CCCC resolution as its starting point, and explains to students that the text is intended to increase their "understanding of the complexity and richness of other cultures" which "is important given Americans' lack of knowledge about the rest of the world in a time of increasing global interdependence." Similarly, Verburg's *Ourselves Among Others: Cross Cultural Readings for Writers* (1991, p. iii) aims to give "readers in this country information to use in writing about the larger world," stressing the urgency of college students becoming "better informed about our 'global village' " because of how "interdependent we in the United States are with our worldwide neighbors." Both texts stress the importance of "Americans" understanding "other" cultures but fall back on the euphemistic term "interdependence" to describe the relationship between "first world" and "third world" and thus avoid discussing the unequal nature of that "interdependence," and the demands of monopoly capitalism that cause it.

They also ignore the role of education and the issue of the power at work in the notion of "understanding" the Other. It is the notion that somehow liberal educators have reached a level of objectivity that does not implicate them in the colonization of the Other, which allows editors of texts in this category to adopt Western anthropological positions even as they include maps like that in Verburg's *Ourselves,* which decenter the Americas. Thus Verburg (1991, p. 40) can quote Shiva Naipaul: "to blandly subsume, say, Ethiopia, India and Brazil under the one banner of Third Worldhood is as absurd and as denigrating as the old assertion that all Chinese look alike," but then dismiss this criticism with the assertion that the "concept of the Third World" can be useful to examine "certain tendencies shared by nations that are otherwise dissimilar," and follow this with an essay about the "Third World" by British writer Paul Harrison. The message here is clear: we must be aware of what "the Other" has to say about Western projects, but "respecting their opinion" does not require us to abandon those projects. Harrison's essay ignores Naipaul's condemnation of the term "Third World" and (1991, p. 42) explains how "Cultural Imperialism began its conquest of the Third World." It thus fits the liberal agenda of educating mainstream students about their collective guilt and responsibility; however, according to Naipaul, its terminology also "denigrates" the very "Third World" scholars and students it appears to be concerned about and, so, the text ultimately demonstrates the cultural imperialism it decries.

We have yet to see texts fitting Sciachitano's fourth category, which (1991, p. 2) requires teachers to locate instruction within what Adrienne Rich calls the " 'politics' of location—a location which recognizes that writing and teaching writing are political acts," and calls for composition instructors to "recognize, name, legitimize the complex, and in many cases, contradictory locations which have always existed" and then trace their impact on the writing process. This would force teachers to become hyperconscious of the power relations of the classroom and the textbook, and also their own place within this matrix: the ways they confirm or resist dominant ideology and the implications that has for their students learning to "write their way" into the academy. Many composition theorists and teachers doubt that any really revolutionary texts could be produced by mainstream publishers within the current system; certainly it would require a more radical politics than that currently dominating the field of composition.

CONSTRUCTING THE NATIONAL AND GENDERED SUBJECT

Despite the writings of Foucault on this subject, composition Readers precede each essay with a brief biography of "The Author." In the preface to the revised *Sixth Eclectic Reader,* McGuffey (1880, p. iv) promises that such "biographical notices, if properly used, are hardly of less value than lessons themselves," and in this case he was right. It is through an examination of these biographies that we see the mainstream/margin model most effectively demonstrated and the radical intentions most clearly deconstructed. Although we are given information such as that Andrew Carnegie "immigrated to the United States from Scotland" (Columbo et al., 1992, p. 20), we are only told the *race* of the author if she is American but *not* Caucasian. Further, Americans of color tend to be described by their racial group *rather than* their nationality, whereas foreigners are described by their nationality but not their race—"English" and "French," like "American," mean Caucasian, only those who are not the norm must have their race identified. Those given national identity thus appear to speak on behalf of a nation of people "just like them," whereas American people of color speak only for their race. White Americans are never described as offering the white/Caucasian/Anglo-Saxon perspective on issues or explaining what it means to be a white American, whereas Americans of color are *only* called on to describe their Otherness. The implication, then, is that white American (and English) writers speak for "humanity." And, once again, they speak to a white American male reader, either inviting him to discuss their shared humanity or explaining to him what it means to be "other."

In *One World* (Hirschberg, 1992) the unspecified "American," such as Joan Didion and Mark Salzman, has no racial grouping whereas "other" Americans are identified *only* by their racial group or heritage and not their current nationality. Thus, Amy Tan is described as a "second-generation *Chinese* girl" (1992, p. xiv), Cha Ok Kim is "a Korean *immigrant*" (1992, p. xiv), and Nicholasa Mohr's characters have "left [their home] in Puerto Rico" (1992, p. xx). Similarly, Toi Derricotte is "black," and Robert Santos is "Hispanic" but neither appears to have any nationality and no people of color are described as "American." In *Writing About the World* (McLeod et al., 1991) U.S. Caucasians can be identified *only* from the fact that neither their ethnic/racial heritage nor their nationality are mentioned, in contrast to: "Gloria Anzaldúa, who describes herself as a Tejana (native Texan) Chicana" (1991, p. 316), Paul Laurence Dunbar who "was one of the most well-known African-American writers of his century" (1991, p. 369), or Wole Soyinka "a Nigerian poet" (1991, p. 354). The same pattern is repeated in *Ourselves Among Others* (Verberg, 1991) where the fictionalized "Argentine girl," the "!Kung tribeswoman" in an anthropological study, and the "Native of Antigua," join the "Hispanic Army lieutenant," the "black girl," and the "poet of Onondaga Micmac, and French Canadian heritage" as representatives of the generic Other juxtaposed against the unmarked norm of the white American.

The "world" constructed by these texts is one in which the Caucasian American is the normative subject and the position from which we gaze. As Said (1979, p. 25) explains in relation to Orientalism, this position allows the subject-as-scholar to both establish an identity in contrast to what it is not, and assert control over the Other by "interpreting" it and representing it back to itself from the perspective of the scholar. In each of these texts "Other" cultures are not meaningfully represented so much as "glimpsed"—as if from a moving tour bus or a series of *National Geographic* photographs. At best we gain a sense of competing cultures, which the assignments for further writing tacitly require students to rate and evaluate—even those in texts such as *One World* that stress the agenda of tracing "similarities." What we also get, however, is a discourse of the Other that, like the discourse of Orientalism, both manages and produces a "Third World"/Of Color identity for the object of our study, while at the same time "obliterating him as a human being" (Said, 1979, p. 27).

Those texts seeking to represent as many cultures as possible in under 700 pages can rarely avoid simply presenting stereotypes, especially when they decide to include anthropological pieces by people outside of the culture in question, as Shapiro (1991) demonstrates in the case of Sheena Gillespie's *Across Cultures*. As Shapiro (1991) observes, this "reach for a goal of geographic diversity risk[s] trading depth for breadth" both in the limited number of representatives of each culture and the lack of sufficient background information. And this, added to the types of narratives, stories, and descriptions included, render the Other impenetrable and exotic rather than encouraging any real cultural exchange or understanding.

Shapiro (1992, p. 4) reveals that the fact that 18 percent of the readings in *Across Cultures* and 25 percent of *Crossing Cultures* are texts by "Western observers" was "intentional [the publishers said, because] . . . Anthropologists . . . bring insights to the cultures that they study that students would otherwise miss. The best anthropologists are consummate observers and story-tellers. And even more to the point, these authors wrote in English, which mooted the translation problem." Of course, it simply presents a *different* translation problem, but it places the onus onto the anthropologist rather than the publisher. One might expect multicultural texts to spend considerable time discussing the issue of translation and observer bias given the extensive scholarship on both, but they do not. Nor do any that I have seen discuss the fact that anthropological studies tend to emphasize cultural difference because their agenda is to isolate and *know* that difference and thus "understand" the culture. Undiscussed inclusion of such pieces undermines efforts to break down the mainstream/margin barrier.

Perhaps the best example of how content can conflict with stated purpose to reveal the underlying ideology driving the text is to be found in *One World* (Hirschberg, 1992), which includes exotic anthropological descriptions of "Haiti's Living Dead," Quiché birth ceremonies, a !Kung tribeswoman's marriage, Balinese cockfighting, initiation into an Iban "tribe of headhunters" and Maasai Warrior status, and female circumcision, with only the last two being insider accounts and none seeming "similar" to any experiences in the United States as the preface promises they will. One wonders how many students of Haitian ancestry have been asked to explain the "whole complex social world" of voodoo by their peers and even teachers who have read in this text that "the vast majority of Haitian peasants practice" it (1992, p. 592). One wonders, too, just how empowering such an experience would be, and how much those students would feel that the European-American botanist author had reflected what they valued about their cultural and ethnic heritage. Finally, one wonders what impact it has to see themselves as the "written of" rather than the writers of academic texts.

The issue of empowerment goes much deeper than simply feeling good about images one sees of oneself. Althusser shows that in presenting these images, texts also construct and reconstruct the identities of their readers. He argues (1971, p. 165) that ideology interpellates or calls into being "concrete individuals as subjects" and represents to them "an *imaginary* relation . . . to the *real* relations in which they live." Thus it determines how they perceive themselves and how they understand and act in their everyday lives and these things, in turn, serve to reinforce the fairly consistent representations of themselves reflected by the dominant ideology. Thus, images presented in textbooks speak to us as if we held specific identities and perceived the world in a certain way, and to make sense of the text, we must answer *as* those identities and with that perception. We can only respond if we "recognize" ourselves as the person to whom the text speaks. So the text literally calls into being the reader it needs to make sense of it, making those readers unwittingly adopt that subject position. Because that position is also demanded by other (ISA) Ideological State Apparatus (other areas of education, the press, radio and television, the church, literature, cinema, the arts, sports, and so on), we come to recognize it as "natural." Indeed, it is "so integrated into our everyday 'consciousness' that it is extremely hard, not to say almost impossible" to extricate oneself from it. Because it is the only subject position from which things "make sense," and because it is the identity reflected as "ours" by so many cultural mirrors, we come to see ourselves as "obviously" the person ideology interpellates us to be. Once we have "freely accepted" this identity we tend to "act according to" its world view, then, Althusser says (1971, p. 182), ideology is working "all by itself." That is, ideology replicates itself in our behavior and determines how we perceive everything else. I believe it is this structure that has caused radical educators to replicate the mainstream/margin model even as they would challenge hegemony.

To see how this works we must look at the identity positions being offered in these texts. As I have already argued, the selections in these texts still demand that the reader adopt a white, middle-class reading subject position, which is also still generally male. They then proceed to either address "him" as an equal in the mainstream and present a universal theory to "him," or carefully explain and narrate a personal event which will enhance "his" (mainstream) understanding of "their" (marginal) world. By adopting these two different positions in relation to their interpellated *reading* subject, the "Authors" make themselves available to, and thus hail, a variety of different *writing* subjects. However, the subject positions offered for writers are as clearly defined and delineated as the univocal reading subjects. Rather than being forced to "be" a white, middle-class, American male in order to write, students using these texts are "invited" to adopt the subject position that most corresponds to the gender, race, class, and ethnic identity they "recognize" to be their own and write from there. The essays become more than just "models" of writing then, because the writing subjects presented in the texts also "model" (and inscribe) their relation to the "mainstream" reading subject.

Shapiro (1991) is correct when she observes that multicultural texts offer a broader set of possibilities for white women than traditional Readers, which rarely present white women writing about topics unconnected with the condition of their gender. Certainly *Writing About the World* (McLeod et al., 1991) is the most impressive on this note, offering as Shapiro (1992) put it: "essays by women scientists and philosophers such as Rachel Carson and Susanne K. Langer on topics other than gender and feminism." Given McLeod's scholarly concerns it is not surprising to find an emphasis on academic texts in her Reader, but even when compared with Writing Across the Curriculum texts that do not also adopt a "multicultural" stance, this one is to be praised for the range of academic writing subjects it offers to white women (Cynthia Eagle Russett on Darwin, Margaret Mead on warfare, Suzanne H. Sankowsky on "World History," Patricia J. Sethi interviewing Augusto Pinochet, and many more).

Most other multicultural Readers also include white women addressing issues traditionally reserved exclusively for white men, but not to the same extent. *Rereading America* (Columbo et al., 1992) gives us broadly theoretical pieces by Elayne Rapping on local news media, and Patricia Nelson Limerick on the westward migration, but most of the other analytical pieces by white women address "women's issues," albeit more seriously than their predecessors (Judy Safire's once canonized "I want a wife" is replaced with Susan Griffin on ecofeminism, Janet Saltzman Chafetz on gender role conformity, and Arlene Skolnick on stereotypical families). In this text, such analyses outnumber personal narratives in which white women relate and explain their experiences as women ("I want my fingernails long and clean"), marking what is, perhaps, the most significant development from the ideology of traditional Readers. *One World* (Hirschberg, 1992) also follows this trend. Although it does not contain white women discussing "universal" issues, it does contain pieces in which they adopt the (albeit dubious) anthropological position formerly reserved for white men (Gretel Ehrlich describes the Kiowa Sun Dance, and Joan Didion discusses the Cubans in Miami). In addition, Francine du Plessix Gray, Simone de Beauvoir, Marilyn French, and Gloria Steinem theorize about gender roles, and Margaret Atwood offers humorous analysis of literary endings. Once again these vaguely analytical pieces outnumber simple narratives by white women. Like earlier multicultural Readers, *Ourselves Among Others* (Verburg, 1991) offers a greater overall percentage of narrative essays than the other texts considered here, and the pieces by white women are no exception. There are no analytical pieces about "universal issues," but du Plessix Gray and de Beauvoir are included in addition to Jill Gay offering commentary on prostitution in Southeast Asia. These essays allow white female students to answer to the call of a vaguely academic writing subject who is able to distance herself from the narrative of details of her life if not from issues directly related to her gender.

This marks a significant advance from earlier texts were women were only offered narrative and humor as positions from which to write. Some of this undoubtedly reflects the Writing Across the Curriculum movement's call for composition classes to teach academic writing that will help composition students in their other classes, but I suspect there is more to it than that. As women have become more numerically noticeable in the academy (despite the overwhelming majority remaining untenured), their work has gradually been accepted by at least some of their male colleagues, and thus they have been incorporated into the system, albeit in a somewhat circumscribed position. If this newly accepted academic is to recognize herself as a subject in ideology and thus not be a challenge to it, she must be interpellated as such. Thus the modified ideology both addresses her as an academic and mediates the way she recognizes herself by constructing a subject position for her that is subtly different than that created for white men. This trend bodes well for white composition students, because, despite its limitations it allows these texts to assist *these* students in their quest to succeed in the academy.

Writers identified as "foreign" offer a similar form of "interested analysis" as that written by most of the white women in these collections. Octavio Paz analyzes the Mexican national psyche, Nawal El Saadawi summarizes and analyzes her interviews with Egyptian women about female circumcision (Hirschberg, 1992), Shigeru Nakayama compares Eastern and Western education, S. Ogbuagu analyzes the use of Depo Provera in Africa (McLeod et al., 1991), and so on. However, by far the majority of the pieces are written in narrative form. Narrative is not in and of itself "bad"; indeed, it is the simplest and most accessible rhetorical form and as such can be a good place to begin literacy education. It is also the most powerful form of writing and thus serves the agenda of cultural education well. The problem is that it is almost never an appropriate writing form for the academy, so if it is the only model offered to students who are placed in composition classes to increase their academic writing skills, those students are ill-served. Too often students at the academic margins resort to narrative prose in response to every writing assignment, and few non-composition faculty accept it. A textbook that suggests and teaches other possibilities as well plays an important part in their efforts to resist the writing subjects represented to them in larger society and construct themselves as the writing subject demanded by the academy.

Texts that offer national and gendered writing subjects that students find it easier to recognize themselves in, and thus be interpellated by, obviously do the work of ideology very effectively. If women and foreigners are to move into positions of some responsibility in this country or power in relation to it, they must be interpellated appropriately and allowed to recognize themselves as subjects able to produce academic discourse. The white male students who might once have expected to grow into unlimited power must also be reinterpellated into subject positions that affirm their own superiority at the same time as they accept that the Other will have some limited power in the new world order. The new multicultural Readers invite these changes, confirming the white male writing subject as possessor of the academic voice of theory and power, but also establishing white female and foreign male and female writing subjects as secondary possessors of that voice, albeit usually an interested rather than entirely "objective" version.

THE "VICTIMS" ON THE MARGINS

The flip side of this is, of course, that that possibility is rarely offered by these texts to American students of color. In a mainstream/margin model, someone must remain on the margins. As Althusser (1971, p. 131)

puts it, "labor power has to be (diversely) skilled and therefore reproduced as such. Diversely: according to the requirements of the socio-
technical division of labor, its different 'jobs' and 'posts.' " It may be a
simplification to observe that increasing the diversity of American colleges
increases the numbers of diversely skilled workers they can produce. Indeed this would deny the fact that the impetus for diversification came
from the Civil Rights movement rather than from higher education or the
state. But a self-perpetuating system can adjust to such monumental
changes because it can appropriate as well as apportion power. As Carragee (this volume) reminds us, we must think of the character of hegemonic ideology as "complex, contradictory and evolving" in response
to what Williams (1977, p. 112) describes as "pressures not at all its
own." As the composition class became increasingly diversified, so, too,
did the composition textbook. But the nature of the new inclusions differs significantly from the pieces they were added to and thus they interpellate very different writing subjects.

Although the texts selected are by well-known and respected authors,
it would appear that little thought is given to which pieces are included
or how they interact with other pieces in the text. I have not found one
piece by a writer identified as an African American or a Latino/Latina,
which does not deal in some way with racist victimization.[1] It may conclude with an overcoming of sorts as do Maya Angelou's "Graduation"
and "Momma, the Dentist and Me," or an assertion of identity like that
in Toni Cade Bambara's "The Lesson" or Martin Luther King, Jr.'s "I Have
a Dream," but the writing subject is still presented as a victim. Moreover,
that subject is overwhelmingly often a child (as in three of the four preceding examples). And that child is frequently a victim of language or
linguistic complexities (as are Langston Hughes in one of the most popular essays, "Salvation"; Richard Rodriguez in another frequently anthol-
ogized piece, "Aria"; Maxine Hong Kingston in "Girlhood Among
Ghosts"; Ernesto Galarza in "Growing into Manhood"; and Dick Gregory
in "Shame"), and is thus powerless to prevent the problem, protect him-
or herself against it, or even, for that matter, understand it with the comprehension of an adult. These pieces were all canonized in the traditional
Readers and have been widely adopted by the new ones. But in at least
a dozen of the 1992 texts there was a new inclusion whose appearance
makes its author the most rapidly canonized to date. This newly em-
braced author is Shelby Steele, and the extracts are taken from his controversial 1990 book *The Content of Our Character.*

The extracts are all narratives of incidents in Steele's life interspersed
with his conclusions about them and sweeping generalizations about
Black duplicity in systems of white racism. They might make some white
students question the *status quo* as one assumes the editors hope, but I
suspect few Black students would be comfortable discussing them in a

mixed class (even if they were not asked to verify the experiences), and any attempts to mimic the style would not be granted acceptable in social science papers, which require more than anecdotal "evidence."

Although formulating theories based on personal experience is one way to introduce students to the rhetorical strategies required in academic papers, if they are not then encouraged to research other articles on the same subject, cite documented studies, and test their theories against other statistical, sociological or psychological analysis, they are left unprepared for the real requirements of the academy. None of the texts I have seen comment on Steele's lack of supporting evidence, although some editors (such as Columbo et al., 1992, p. 358) ask whether "bargaining [is] an available and acceptable alternative for all African Americans." If the content remains unquestioned, students will do what they have been taught to do all of their lives: they will read to learn. And what they will learn is that African Americans "have a hidden investment in victimization and poverty" and do not "advance" because they depend for power on their collective status as victims rather than bargaining individually with white society, "granting . . . its innocence in exchange for entry into the mainstream" (Steele, 1990, reproduced in Columbo et al., 1992, p. 353). Like Bill Cosby, they learn, students of color must not "assault [white] innocence with racial guilt" if "the race" is to "advance." Instead they should assimilate, or, as Steele puts it, "compromise." They must accept their place on the margins because at least that is a place "in" the system, and by individual will some of them can slip unnoticed into the mainstream.

This lesson may have been designed to provoke discussion, but it so matches the beliefs presented in the Reagan-Bush ideology (under which most of our students have lived most of their lives) that many will see nothing to discuss. The fact that Richard Rodriguez is also included in most of these texts and appears to echo Steele's position on affirmative action and the need for a strident individualism to counter the damage done by "liberal" social programs, seems to support this lesson further. Steele's assertion overwhelmingly corroborates the image of the "victim of color" presented in these texts and the ideology on race increasingly presented by other ISAs. His theory that "there is an unconscious sort of gravitation toward them, a complaining celebration of them" is also implicitly supported by the editorial decisions (whether or not they are motivated by what Steele calls "white guilt," 1990, p. 80) to select other extracts by people of color narrating their victimization. Thus, Steele's lack of supporting data can be ignored because the Readers themselves appear to provide that data and support his assertions.

These victim narratives also allow white students to ignore what Peggy McIntosh calls "white privilege." She argues (1988, p. 1) that white Americans have been taught "about racism as something which puts others at a disadvantage, but . . . not . . . its corollary aspects, white privilege, which puts [whites] at an advantage." Essays like these allow us to continue to avoid the painful reality that white students and faculty benefit from being white even if we strive to overcome the racism that our culture has inscribed in our attitudes and practices. These essays therefore support the dominant ideology that racism is the problem of "others" (who have tended to make themselves into victims) as well as the more liberal ideology that they have been rendered victims by a corrupt system, but can be "helped" by good whites who are somehow above that system. Both of these ideologies reinscribe the traditional mainstream/margin model. The supremacy and innocence of those of Anglo-Saxon ancestry is reaffirmed, justifying both our position at the center and the notion of people of color as helplessly balanced on the margins.

Although Steele's argument is seriously flawed by his failure to consider ideology or structures of power, his description of the paralysis resulting from "misrecognizing" and thus allowing oneself to be interpellated as "victim" is compelling. Martin Luther King, Jr. (1964, p. 65) also described the depowering influence of this structure when he explained that many African Americans were reluctant to join the non-violent protest movement in Birmingham in 1963 because they had "accepted the white man's theory that . . . [they were] inferior . . . [and were unable to] resist the influences that had conditioned [them] to take the line of least resistance." These subjects, constructed as "inferior" "individuals" by a combination of ISAs were literally rendered unable to take any kind of action that would challenge their subjugation. It is therefore doubly ironic that so many multicultural and traditional Readers have decided to include Steele as the only "theoretical" voice in their collection of victim narratives by people of color. His discussion confirms the subject position interpellated in the rest of the text helping to construct the very "victims" that he would save. Once these new powerless and marginalized writing subjects have been created, the extracts from Steele's book tell students to "blame the victim" for this state of affairs, and allows responsibility to be shifted from the hegemonic structures governing these texts to people of color themselves. Not only is the mainstream/margin model reinforced, but those who benefit from it are absolved of all guilt.

Like all other textbooks, composition Readers are produced in response to market demand. These new multicultural Readers developed because many composition teachers rejected the traditional model and called for texts that are theme based and more inclusive. And they do represent a significant improvement over the old model in these areas (although traditional Readers are responding to the same pressures in creative and productive ways). However, the writing subjects created for our multicultural society still ensure a mainstream/margin model. In addition, the majority of these texts fail to teach the range of rhetorical skills necessary for survival in college. Although they may produce some more *confident* writers, they do not produce *academic* writers so the question of confidence may be a moot point. They do produce writing subjects who "naturally" fit into a system demanding "diversely skilled" workers and thus, like their predecessors, they also produce "citizens safe for democracy" as we know it. The irony of this is that multiculturalism, and especially multicultural writing texts, *could* represent the challenge to dominant culture that those on the political right fear. By challenging the apparently "natural" hierarchy on which advanced capitalism rests, and as Sciachitano proposes, replacing the univocal reading subject with a multitude of subject positions for readers and writers that are not determined by that hierarchy, composition texts *could* provide students with the means to engage in oppositional readings of culture and the academy and thus, perhaps, reshape them. That conservative academics understand multiculturalism's power and potential more fully than those on the left reflects, I believe, their rejection of *any* change rather than a more developed understanding of how ideology actually works. But it does underscore the importance of a careful analysis of ideology and cultural theory by those who call for "increased diversity" and engage in the practice of producing multicultural curricula and textbooks.

NOTE

1. This is also the case for traditional inclusions by Asian Americans such as Maxine Hong Kingston, although an interesting development recently is the "model minority" text—both essays about it and narratives demonstrating it. Extracts from Amy Tan's novel *The Joy Luck Club,* for example, show the child victimized by her mother's faith in the "American Dream" and its assertion that in America she can do and be anything her mother dreams for her. Similarly, Cha Ok Kim, the "Korean immigrant" tells the story of making it in America as a result of his hard work and determination. This trend is not as fully developed as the other, and seems to reflect our ambiguous relationship to the success of Asian Americans and the economy of Japan. It will be interesting to see whether the image of the "Asian" victimized by her own ability and success will gain in popularity in the next editions of these texts.

REFERENCES

Adorno, T. & Horkheimer, M. (1979). The Culture Industry: Enlightenment as Mass Deception. In J. Curran, M. Gurevitch, & J. Woollocott (Eds.), *Mass Communication and Society* (pp. 349–383). Beverly Hills, CA: Sage.

Althusser, L. (1971). Ideology and Ideological State Apparatuses (Notes Towards an Investigation). In *Lenin and Philosophy and Other Essays.* (Ben Brewster, Trans.). New York: Monthly Review.

Bartholomae, D. (1985). Inventing the University. *When a Writer Can't Write: Studies in Writer's Block and Other Composing-Process Problems.* New York: Guilford, pp. 134–165.

Berlin, J. (1987). *Rhetoric and Reality: Writing Instruction in American Colleges, 1900–1985.* Carbondale and Edwardsville: Southern Illinois University.

Bizzell, P. (1986). What Happens When Basic Writers Come to College? *College Composition and Communication, 37,* pp. 294–301.

Brodkey, L. (1987). *Academic Writing as Social Practice.* Philadelphia: Temple University Press.

Bruffee, K. (1986). Social Construction, Language, and the Authority of Knowledge: A Bibliographical Essay. *College English, 48,* pp. 773–790.

Carragee, K. (1996). Critical Ethnographics and the Concept of Resistance. (This volume).

Columbo, G., Cullen, R., & Lisle, B. (1992). *Rereading America: Cultural Contexts for Critical Thinking and Writing* (2nd ed.). Boston: Bedford.

Condit, C. (1989). The Rhetorical Limits of Polysemy. *Critical Studies in Mass Communication, 6,* pp. 103–122.

Decker, R. (1990). *Patterns of Exposition, 12.* Glenview, Ill.: Scott, Foresman.

Eastman, A., Blake, C., English, H. Jr., Hartman, J., Howes, A., Lenaghan, R., McNamara, L., Patterson, L., & Rosier, J. (1992). *The Norton Reader* (8th ed.). New York: Norton.

Elson, W. & Keck, C. (1929). *The Elson Reader, Book Six.* New York: Scott, Foresman.

Faigley, L. (1986). Competing Theories of Process: A Critique and a Proposal. *College English, 48,* pp. 527–539.

Fiske, J. (1986). Television: Polysemy and Popularity. *Critical Studies in Mass Communication, 3,* pp. 391–408.

———. (1987). *Television Culture.* London: Methuen.

———. (1988). Critical Response: Meaningful Moments. *Critical Studies in Mass Communication, 5,* pp. 246–251.

Foucault, M. (1972). *The Archaeology of Knowledge and The Discourse on Language.* (A. M. Sheridan Smith, Trans.). New York: Pantheon Books.

———. (1977). What is an Author? In *Language, Counter-memory, Practice.* Ithaca: Cornell University Press.

Gillespie, S. & Singleton, R. (1991). *Across Cultures: A Reader for Writers.* Boston: Allyn & Bacon.

Hirschberg, S. (1992). *One World, Many Cultures.* New York: Macmillan.

Hall, S. (1980). Encoding/Decoding. In S. Hall, D. Hobson, A. Lowe, & P. Willis (Eds.), *Culture, Media, Language* (pp. 128–138). London: Hutchinson.

King, M. L. K. (1964). *Why We Can't Wait.* New York: Mentor.

Layton, M. (1991). *Intercultural Journeys Through Reading and Writing.* New York: Harper Collins.

McGuffey, C. (1880). *McGuffey's Sixth Eclectic Reader, Revised Edition.* New York, Cincinnati, & Chicago: The American Book Company.

McIntosh, P. (1988). *White Privilege and Male Privilege.* (Working Paper #189). Wellesley College Research on Women.

McLeod, S., Bates, S., Hunt, A., Jarvis, J., & Spear, S. (1991). *Writing About the World.* San Diego: Harcourt Brace Jovanovich.

Nietz, J. (1961). *Old Textbooks*. Pittsburgh: University of Pittsburgh Press.

Porter, E. (1841). *The Rhetorical Reader; Consisting of Instructions for Regulating the Voice, with a Rhetorical Notation, Illustrating Inflection, Emphasis, and Modulation; and a Course of Rhetorical Exercises* (75th ed.). Andover: Gould & Newman; New York: Leavitt, Lord & Co.

Radway, J. (1984). *Reading the Romance*. Chapel Hill: University of North Carolina Press.

Repp, J. (1992). *How We Live Now: Contemporary Multicultural Literature*. Boston: Bedford.

Rose, M. (1985). The Language of Exclusion: Writing Instruction at the University. *College English, 47,* pp. 341–359.

Said, E. (1979). *Orientalism*. New York: Vintage.

Sanders, C. (1876). *Union Fifth Reader: Embracing a Full Exposition of the Principles of Rhetorical Reading; with Numerous Exercises for Practice, Both in Prose and Poetry from the Best Writers; and with Literary and Biographical Notes*. New York & Chicago: Ivison, Blakeman, Taylor.

Sciachitano, M. (1991). Diversity or Division in First Year Composition?: Four Competing Positions. Presented at the *Penn State Conference on Rhetoric and Composition*. (Unpublished mss. from the author.)

Shapiro, Nancy. (1991). Review Essay: Multicultural Readers. *College Composition and Communication, 42,* pp. 524–530.

———. (1992, March). Rereading Multicultural Readers: What Definition of "Multicultural" are We Buying? Presented at the *Conference on College Composition and Communication,* Cincinnati, OH. ERIC ED 346 472.

Steele, S. (1990). *The Content of Our Character: A New Vision of Race in America*. New York: St. Martin's.

Steiner, L. (1988). Oppositional Decoding as a Form of Resistance. *Critical Studies in Mass Communication, 5,* pp. 1–15.

Verburg, C. (1991). *Ourselves Among Others: Cross Cultural Readings for Writers* (2nd ed.). Boston: Bedford.

Williams, R. (1977). *Marxism and Literature*. Oxford: Oxford University Press.

The Writings of Women Prisoners: Voices from the Margins

Susan Ross

In the last fifteen years, the percentage of women prisoners has risen dramatically. In 1980, there were approximately 10,000 women imprisoned in the United States; by 1989, that number had risen to 40,000.[1] Although explanations for these statistics vary,[2] the issue of women's incarceration is meriting increased attention. Women present a special challenge as prisoners because their needs and interests are different from men's. An often-circulated story among prison workers tells how men who arrive in prison ask for their lawyers, whereas women ask about their children. The separation from their children increases the sense of isolation and restriction that prisoners feel anyway. This is a relevant issue, given that two thirds of the women in prison in this country are mothers of one or more children under the age of eighteen (Baunach, 1985). The psychological conflict between the responsibility of motherhood and the subordinate dependence in prison exacerbates the sense of guilt, ambivalence, and imprisonment even further.

Women prisoners face further constraints unique to their gender. Women's prisons are less numerous than men's, and tend to be located in geographically distant areas that make family visitations logistically cumbersome. Women feel the lack of privacy in prison acutely, interpret prison edicts in dress code as identity incursions, and respond to the excessively controlled environment with a compliance that counteracts their need to develop self-responsibility and control (Beirne and Messerschmidt, 1991; Goodstein, 1979; Goodstein et al., 1984; Mandaraka-Sheppard, 1986; Sobel, 1982). Particularly humiliating are rulings, such as what happened recently in a women's prison in Pennsylvania, that prohibit demonstration of physical affection. The loss of personal items that women have treasured—a special item of clothing, jewelry, or even knitting supplies, as Jean Harris (1986) describes in her autobiography, *Stranger in Two Worlds,* devastates women and deprives them of meaningful identity props or activities.

But besides these kinds of indignities, the very presence of women in prisons is a phenomenon fraught with contradiction. Behind the statistics lie stories of women, particularly those with life sentences, who have little criminal history or whose crimes stem from economic necessity or unfortunate circumstance.[3] Of the pool of writers in this study, for instance, more than half landed in prison with life sentences due to the influence of a male co-defendant. The women's presence in prison, therefore, corresponds to their inability to frame decisions in their own self-interest. Do prisons provide an environment that "rehabilitates" these kinds of people? Does the prison environment address social issues inherent in the gender, race, and class of most women inmates? Since most correctional research in the past few decades has focused on the male offender (DeCostanzo and Scholes, 1988), much about women offenders, including treatment options and appropriate sentencing guidelines, has yet to be explored. Little is known about the background and life experiences of the female offender.[4] Women in prison are a truly "marginal" population, in terms of their geographical location, but also in terms of their exposure in scholarly studies.

This chapter, a rhetorical analysis of some women prisoners' writings, is an attempt to explore the answers to questions about inmates and language use, as well as to unearth women prisoners' voices from the depths of their invisibility. By examining how the woman prisoner negotiates a sense of self within an environment primarily defined by a criminal act, this study hopes to shed light on the role prisons play in the lives of life-sentenced women inmates. Is language a useful tool to empower people in hardship?

RHETORICAL ANALYSIS

One way to analyze how language functions for its users is rhetorical analysis. "Our experiences of our world derive from the nature of the symbols we use to describe them," is how Foss et al. (1991) describe the underlying assumption of rhetorical analysis. Language is seen to create and sustain a reality among and for its users, and to generate a response from the audience, or reader. Rhetorical analysis looks for the symbolic underpinnings of language usage, and describes how audiences are inclined to respond based on the meanings inscribed through and in the chosen symbols of a speaker's or writer's language. Words are viewed as symbolic tools to convey not just a denotative meaning, but a whole worldview and cultural construct. Hence, rhetorical analysis often includes a discussion of contextual, historical, biographical, and social issues surrounding the communicative event that may influence the choice and nature of chosen symbols.

The word *rhetoric* implies a suasory view of language. Our attempts to send messages to other communicators are laden with cues and clues that provide openings for certain kinds of feedback. Communication is audience-bound, which means that audiences can affect, construct, or simply receive our messages, depending on the type of communicative model one embraces. Hence, this study is looking at how the writings of women prisoners necessitate a response, both from the readers and from the writers themselves.

Since this study focuses on a body of writings that emerge from a particularly peculiar context, a women's prison, it is helpful to discuss how cultures are constituted in and through language. In his book, *When Words Lose Their Meaning*, James Boyd White (1984) says that "we literally are the language that we speak, for the particular culture that makes us a 'we'—that defines and connects us, that differentiates us from others—is enacted and embedded in our language" (p. 20). The image of culture that underlies this view of language is that of Clifford Geertz (1973), who describes culture as consisting of "the webs of significance man has spun," which makes any analysis of culture "an interpretive one in search of meaning" (p. 5). Language is seen as a force that both reflects cultural mores, values, and priorities and creates them.

Prisons are one place to study this dynamic. Prisons as cultures generate and define modes of thought and language usage that in themselves contain information about how the members of the culture view themselves and their social milieu. Combining the issues of prison life with issues surrounding women's use of language, rhetorical analysis of the writings of women prisoners can reveal how women function discursively in this setting to maintain and establish relationships, to define an audience, to position themselves as authors and authorities, to effect judgments and make claims, and to develop community.

One woman whose writings have been studied exemplifies the dynamic of world-building through her prison writings. Agnes Smedley, says Judith Scheffler (1988), used prison to "find her voice, to develop the confidence and determination that her message had to be communicated, and to recognize that writing was her proper medium" (p. 200). Smedley also began her lifelong crusade for social equality while in prison, where she found a subject in women's welfare, the rights of oppressed people, and revolution.

Smedley represents an ideal use of writing in prison, a use of situation to find and develop a voice. Smedley, however, had more education, political savvy, and social privilege than the women of this study. In the interest of giving voice to a more prosaic population, I chose to visit a state correctional institution and examine the writings of a select group of women there.

THE WOMEN OF THE STUDY

The women of this study are twelve life-sentenced inmates from a state correctional institution in Pennsylvania. The women in this group range in age from twenty-six to fifty-nine. Out of twelve women, four are white. All of the rest are African American. The shortest time spent in prison by any of these women is seven years. The longest is twenty-three years. All are from Pennsylvania, although not all originally. Nine out of the twelve have children. Most of the children do not visit regularly. The reasons for this are often unclear; all of the women except one claim to have extremely supportive families.

These are women who have the ability to reflect on themselves and their circumstances in a more sophisticated manner than newly arrived, trouble-burdened inmates. Imprisoned for an average of thirteen years, these women have had time and opportunity to contemplate their existence. And, due to the nature of a life sentence in Pennsylvania,[5] the women have been forced to resign themselves to the thought of a life in prison and what that means to them. Also, "lifers," as they are called, have a reputation for providing a calming, stable influence in prisons, since the prison is their home and they have a stake in creating a tolerable environment.

The demographic profile of these twelve women matches the national profile of the "typical" American prisoner.[6] Within the last ten years, the number of women behind bars in the United States has increased from just over 10,000 to 40,000. Women represent about 6 percent of the entire prison population in this country. The number of female inmates is growing at a rate of 15 percent annually, which is approximately twice the rate of men's incarceration. This trend has been evident since 1960. An estimated 75 percent of these women are mothers. As recently as January 1991 the racial composition of Pennsylvania prisons matched the national trends mentioned in the popular press: about 65 percent are of color (of those, about 35 percent are Hispanic), 35 percent are white, and very few are Asian.

Most have a sporadic employment history (73.8 percent of women are jobless at the time of their arrest), have less than a high school education (the median prisoner tests at approximately eighth grade level and almost a third are functionally illiterate), and come from low-income backgrounds. Most prisoners are under the age of thirty, have a sporadic employment record, and had personal income of less than $10,000 in the year prior to their arrest.

Most female prisoners come from abusive childhoods or marriages.[7] Property crimes such as check forgery and illegal credit card use are the most typical violations that lead to imprisonment of women. One increasing crime by women is the possession and/or sale of drugs. One warden estimates that as many as 90 percent of her female inmates have a chemical dependency. Very few women commit violent crimes. Non-violent property offenses are the most common.

THE WRITINGS

The analysis in this study is concentrated on writings primarily from 1989 to 1991, and includes mostly journal entries and writing done in occasional workshops held by visiting professors. The writings from the workshops include answers to specific questions, such as, "What does it mean to be a life-sentenced prisoner in the state of Pennsylvania?" or "Who am I?" In addition, some short excerpts written by the women for an art exhibit in the summer of 1991 that featured portraits of and by men and women serving life sentences in Pennsylvania are included in the body of texts analyzed here. Some of the pieces stem from writing done in therapy groups for victims of abuse. And some are excerpts from letters to editors, letters to family members, and letters to an imagined public. Each inmate has provided a different amount of writing and a different kind of writing to be analyzed.

Language and Empowerment

How does this writing by these life-sentenced inmates grapple with issues of identity and community? Can writing like this serve to create an alternate realm where the women can almost remake themselves as characters, creating a new social identity in the process? One model that helps tap into the possible power of writing for these women is Hannah Arendt's Communications Concept of Power. Arendt links communication and power through her emphasis on communication as an act. Power becomes a "potency that is actualized in actions" (Habermas, 1977, p. 3) rather than some absolute, immobile quality that resides within a dominant group. Power is enacted through communication and its relational nature:

Power corresponds to the human ability not just to act but to act in concert. Power is never the property of an individual; it belongs to a group and remains in existence only so long as the group keeps together. When we say of somebody that he is "in power" we actually refer to his being empowered by a certain number of people to act in their name. (Arendt, 1970, p. 44)

For the prisoner who is steeped in isolation of a physical, social, and emotional nature (Goffman 1961), acting in concert, even if only via *expression* of communal attachment, is a crucial remedy.

Hannah Arendt's emphasis on the element of human commonality inherent in communication provides a framework from which to view women's prison writings as discursive maneuvering to establish rules for relationships and to act in concert. Empowerment becomes a kind of community-building through language. Hence, language in women's prison writings that seeks a new communal space *devoid* of prison-enforced language, identity, or constraints points the rhetorical critic to expressions of power. Arendt's model of communication invites a concept of rhetorical expression that creates social relationships founded on strategic community-building. Language that invites the audience to share in constructive (as opposed to denial or blame-laden) resistance of prison-imposed edicts is an act of empowerment; language that curls into itself in self-absorbed pity or obsession would represent the opposite.

Two elements guide the search for such linguistic expressions: audience and intentionality. Judith Scheffler, in her exploration of the genre of women's prison writings, tells us that women inmates generally write to reach out to a community of imagined listeners, and that the writings are strategically engineered: "Most works are very specific, conceived in terms of a concrete audience, form, purpose, content, and point of view" (1986, p. 58). Although this may seem to be true of all writing, this is no small matter for lifers whose contact with the "outside world" has been limited physically, materially, and psychologically. As mentioned before, a sense of audience, a sense of ability to intentionally address an imagined audience, or even a sense of ability to embrace the opportunity inherent in communication to connect and enact community—all of these are foreign concepts to the isolated lifer. The very act of negotiating connection with other humans is an act of empowerment often unobtainable and unimaginable to lifers. How the writer negotiates and molds her message with an imagined audience is symptomatic of the power dynamic in her expressions. Rhetoric asks for a response, generates relationships, and creates shared meanings; all elements of what Arendt considers to be acts of power and, ultimately, freedom. For the population being studied here, this is primarily a psychic freedom, an ability to transcend the immediate community and its standards and reach out communicatively to establish a new community. Obviously, the opportunity literally to create a new community does not exist, but the chance to reconfigure relationships through writing might. The female inmate who does not embrace this opportunity is, according to Arendt, imprisoned in a private realm of isolation.

One goal of this study is to tease out the possibilities of "re-making" identity through writing, and to ascertain whether the writers use writing to heal "assaults on personal identity." Of interest here is how the women writers define themselves, whether they see themselves as viable, active players in the discursive realm, whether they view themselves independently or seek external crutches to construct a self, and what that particular self-construct has in common with the real issues these women face, both in prison and in their larger lives. The question here is whether language within women's prison writings could invoke a sense of self, and what that would look like.

According to psychologist Polly Young-Eisendrath, in her book, *Female Authority* (Young-Eisendrath and Wiedemann, 1987), the expression of "authentic self" would extricate itself from the social/institutional milieu and would exude a reflexive sense of worth, values, wishes, and experiences entirely unique to the individual. This expression of self is easier to identify by what it is *not:* it is not defensive retreat from institutional demands, it is not adaptation to expectations from the "outside world," and it is not conflict with authority (p. 101). Goaded by her own curiosity about the self within her that may have been sublimated in response to parental or institutional pressures, a woman's expression of self would have the guiding energy of a creative need to establish a sense of being that is autonomous, strong, non-self-rejecting, and steeped in a belief in the existence of choice (as opposed to a helpless acquiescence to an other-determined fate) (Mandaraka-Sheppard, 1986, p. 149).

THE WRITINGS OF WOMEN PRISONERS

To get a sense of how the women's writings work to create a strong sense of both self and community, it is valuable to note, first of all, simply what is there. What kinds of words do the women use to describe themselves and their situations? How do they position themselves? Do they retain a seemingly prison-based identity of a victimized individual, or do they position themselves beyond that limitation, working toward Arendt's vision of an empowered communication? Even more interesting, what is missing? What parts of themselves do they veil, evade, or blatantly neglect?

One woman's expressed sense of self points to a tendency among the lifers to separate themselves in their writings from the prison environment by an emphasis on non-criminal aspects of the self. The word "murderer" never appears.[8]

One writer writes about her childhood and prison experience, in response to the question "Who Am I?", but never elaborates on the life-altering occasion that seemed to have changed her destiny, although the man she describes may have been an instigating factor:

> I really began living when I had been in prison for about six years or so. I'm still learning all about myself—and at times I'm so amazed at what I can accomplish. As I was growing up I was told repeatedly that I couldn't do anything right. Well, after awhile I was a believer—I was worthless, I couldn't do anything right!— What good am I?!!? A man came into my life when I was sixteen. I was young, but I had my whole life figured out—I was to be alone and to take care of my family as I had been doing. This man turned my whole life around! He made me feel like a being with worth. He caused me to look at myself and to accept myself as being more than what I thought of myself. He caused me to appreciate the beauty in nature that was all around me. What I once saw as scary—and a sort of prison, suddenly I saw as peace and life. Through my years of prison, I've been learning a lot of things. I'm learning about people, and living, and myself. I'm learning all the things I feel I should've learned as a little girl.

What happened between "peace and life" and prison? What happened between the last two paragraphs? The gap between the two is "unsayable," as Michel Foucault (1972) describes it, and communicates a vast silence of experience (p. 41). The experience never reaches the level of language. It remains nonexistent, and inaccessible to the reader. Perhaps it is also inaccessible to the writer.

An extension of this negation of self is the fantasy of possible non-prison identities. One published poet envisions herself as an eccentric motorcycle mama:

When I Grow Old

When I grow old and
My skin sprouts valleys
As if too long in bathwater,
And brown spots colonize my hands,
I shall let my tinted hair grow long
And wear a pink tam
Cocked impertinently to the side
Matching the Yamaha that I'll ride.
People will call me disgraceful,
And my grandchildren's friends
Will hang out at my house,
Swapping youth for sixties dialogue
And snappy answers.
I'll be pushy at check-out lines,
And swear at impatient drivers,
And know all the words to the Top Forty.
I'll offend the sensibilities
Of every prim and proper twit,

And people who know me now will say,
God, she hasn't changed a bit.

This tendency to fantasize is an extension of the writers' emphasis on what they are *not*. For one poet "somewhere joy is hiding," but it is not readily available. She is "Missing Inaction" says the title of one poem. "Freedom shall come like the winter." Happiness is postponed to another time, another realm. Prison is "a constant maybe later." The deflection of the here-and-now represents a vision of the world that offers limited choices.

Postponement of joy and fulfillment is a necessary part of prison life, yet the fact that the writings also express that same necessity of postponement is perhaps an indication of the depth of despair the inmates feel. One area where that despair does not permeate the writers' expressed worldview is in their descriptions of nature, some of which are crafted to envelop themselves in an almost nurturing fashion. One writer describes leaves:

Leaves gently fall from the trees
like tears gently fall from my eyes.
They reach the earth to comfort,
to nourish and to protect.
It is the same with my tears.
For they reach my heart to comfort,
to cleanse, and to protect.
The leaves comfort the earth
with a soft blanket of themselves.
They nourish with their lives.
And they protect in this same way.
My tears, in fact, comfort me too.
Tears cleanse not only my mourning eyes,
but also my heavy laden heart.
Tears do protect—like the leaves—
from outside forces that would hurt
and even kill the heart of man
or the heart of the tree.
Leaves.
They are so like my tears.

One possible reason for the predominance of nature images is the setting of the prison, which is located in a rural, hilly part of central Pennsylvania where the seasons can be experienced in intensity.

But the beauty doesn't counteract the women's status: criminal offender. Especially for life-sentenced women, "lifers," the decades of time spent here aren't about care-free living in quiet country splendor. Some of these women have spent their most formative years contemplating what for many was a first offense, often the result of a lifetime of poverty, danger, and abuse. Some women even describe prison as a haven from drugs, forced sex, and humiliation. There is an irresolvable tension between the benefits of a life apart from hostile influences and the disadvantages of life in a punitive, restricted environment.

The prison's power over the women's fate threads its way through many of the writings. One woman couches a plea to the "public" in terms she hopes will be convincing:

Check into us and let us give something back to you for a change. If I'm no longer a risk to your society then your money is being wasted on me. If I'm to be punished for the rest of my life on earth for what is my first mistake, then so be it, but the Commutation Board you're paying for says that some of us have changed, and all I ask of you is to check into those of us who have changed.

The writer defers to what she knows to be a prominent aspect of discussions about corrections in this country: money. By using economic incentives to bargain with her imagined readers, she retains discursively the very hierarchal structures that keep her "imprisoned," particularly when she attributes so much power to others' decisions about her fate:

The next question you'd probably ask is "well then what, you're criminals, so perhaps we should cut down on what we pay to incarcerate you and let you make do with what we spend on you the best way you can!" My response to that is, if you do this, your politicians will panic, the keepers of your prisons will panic, and when the systems get together to find out what to do, the answer will be to introduce bills that will reduce the amount of time in prison people not serving life will do, and aren't those people the ones out there now terrorizing your streets?

Her language leaves her no recourse if the public rejects her. Her fate *does* lie in the hands of others, and her written plea makes no attempt to reframe that issue in her readers' minds. The tone of her passage is that of a victim.

Deference to others' opinions is a common theme. So much of the writing describes efforts to deflect away from one's self and let others' opinions and needs dictate their identity. One inmate writes about making masks, "I hope the other lifers are having more fun than I am." This woman's deference to others' opinions is common and is more subtly expressed by one inmate whose whole self image is inextricably tied to her father's opinion of her. This woman is an actress who "stages" herself. "It's me" is a statement of struggle toward an identity that hasn't ever solidified. In trying to negotiate an identity separate from her father, she enmeshes herself further with him and his spell over her:

I only wanted to be Daddy's Little Girl. Why? Because she was good and perfect and you loved her more than anything in the world. Well, it's time for the truth to be told. . . . If I am to become the person that I want to be, then I must rid myself of this yoke of guilt and pain that I've been carrying around with me. I can no longer be the am that I am not. I cannot be real to you and unreal to myself. . . . If I am a rainbow, then *you* [emphasis mine] will have to add the colors of black and gray to the spectrum, because to everything beautiful there is ugliness.

Not only does she solicit her father's approval for this new self she seeks to find, but she later couches her crimes in terms of the "me" for whom she seeks love: "When I finally did take charge of my life, I made a mess of it. I admit that I did everything the wrong way, but at least it was my way." She grants her father the ultimate judgment for her actions. The bad girl is her father's image of bad, and this woman provides images of ugliness and hopelessness to describe this "real" self of hers: "The apple of your eye is rotten Daddy; it had a worm in it," and "How can I be your pie in the sky, when the baker left out so many important ingredients?"

The writings of the women lifers show an almost uniform tendency to deny, through over-simplicity or through descriptions of modes of escape, their own complexity and individuality. This urge speaks not of a desire to reconstruct a sense of authority in one's life, but to simply walk away from it:

This is not an ending for me, but a bright new beginning. I must get off of this sea of misery and guilty, for I am drowning in it. It is time for me to let my wounds heal, because if I continue to let them fester, they will swallow me and I may be lost forever. It is time for my yesteryears to find their own time and space; for I can no longer be their keeper. I can no longer be the jailor of myself.

Highly poetic, idealized images dominate her writings:

New seeds have been planted. I now have started to grow into a strong, beautiful oak tree and my branches are filled with fresh green leaves. And if I continue to strive one day I may be a giant redwood.

The beauty of this writer's images is hard to resist, yet, as with other writers, it creates gaps. That is, the development described with her metaphors is either a good/ugly bipolarity, like the burlap that is scratchy and irritating to the touch versus the silk, or it describes a linear growth process that fails to acknowledge the bumpiness and perhaps ugliness of remaking one's life. Pain and hardship are referenced: "The experience has been harsh and cruel," and "the winds of winter had raped it [her] and left it barren." But quickly on the heels of these allusions to a darker side come the images of blossoming nature, "bright new beginning," the woman who will be "durable and strong enough to endure." She sees herself as "drowning in misery and guilt" that must be left behind and abandoned.

Other writers reject idealism and dwell, instead, on the haunting hopelessness of the prison environment.

Tapwater Coffee

They took away our coffee pots;
You know the type:
Big forty-cup, with chrome,
Black plastic spigot and feet;
The kind you'd never use at home.
They said a weapon
Potentially lurked there,
Were it heaved or water thrown.
Now in the land of synthetic dreams,
Of cup-a-soup and instant tea,
Another compromise
Slips in to burden me.
I may suck caffeine
Of paper packets and sleepless nights
And write endless narratives
Of wasted years and trampled rights,
But, try as I may, as I burn midnight oil,
And heat up my verses, and curse my toil,
My thirst is room temperature—
My water won't boil
Ah, what emotional masturbation
Brews in the grounds of this pleasure dome;
Drinking tapwater coffee,
And thinking of home.

This poem points to the limitations of the prison context on empowered expression. The relationships and meanings the writers can create within their writing are ensconced in an inherently disempowering context. The linguistic strategies must be devised within that context, strategies that automatically negate any chance of negotiating with a community outside of that realm.

One writer, however, does reach out, tragically, to effect connection in the wake of one of the more horrific scourges of prison life, AIDS:

> While in the shower a place where you can cry and people will assume
> you got soap in your eyes.

> While in the shower a place where you can punch the wall and people
> will think that that thump they heard must have been you falling.
> While in the shower contemplating if I will be granted a reprieve, my
> thoughts were interrupted when a woman with AIDS said, "Oh, thank
> God for this hot shower. Sometimes my bones ache like I have arthritis.
> It's one of the side-effects of my AZT."
> While she was drying off she said, ". . . but otherwise I feel fine, and I try
> to keep myself looking good even though I am sick."
> She looked up at me and smiled. Then she said, "You deal with what you
> get in life and that's the way it is."
> While in the shower contemplating what the woman with AIDS had said
> to me, I realized that in addition to me she also had a life-sentence. I
> asked myself, other than health factors, what was the difference be-
> tween the two? I realized the answer to that question was very simple
> and matter-of-fact. She has a life-sentence for which she will be granted
> no reprieve.

The image this passage evokes, of a woman on the margins watching a woman even more marginalized, is heartrending and begins to hint at the reasons why examining women's prison writing is so necessary. The issues this writer confronts, and the empathy of her reaction, pull the hidden life of prison existence out from the geographical and physical margins of experience. While this writer does not have the physical re-sources to engage actively in Arendt's coming-togetherness of commu-nicative power, her ability to reflect on her own situation, miserable as it is, and empathize with someone even worse off shows a yearning for the kind of connectedness Arendt describes.

CONCLUSION

Criminologists and sociologists interested in language have discovered the possibility of writing as a vehicle for women (and men) to develop a sense of alternative authority in the midst of the presence of the daunting, seemingly overpowering authority that surrounds them (Fiske, 1989; Gel-fand, 1981; Harlow, 1986; O'Neil, 1990; Parker, 1990). Gelfand and Har-low both examine the act of writing by women prisoners as an act of political empowerment. Fiske, O'Neil, and Parker are interested in a very different aspect of writing for the prisoner, the promising possibility that increased literacy leads to better decision making, and thereby less recid-ivism, or maybe even reduced crime overall. Both approaches show the promise of writing as an activity for inmates, and both approaches hint at the necessity of continued studies of the effects of writing for inmates' development and well-being.

From examination of the small body of writings presented here, it is evident that writing in prison provides a means of expressing frustrations and thoughts about life in prison. Writing also serves an empowerment function; as Carolyn Heilbrun writes in her treatise on writing women's lives (1988, p. 18): "Power is the ability to take one's place in whatever discourse is essential to action and the right to have one's part matter." Women prisoners' inherently marginal status makes it difficult to "have one's part matter," unless we begin to focus more on their voices, both for their benefit and for ours as researchers. As one prison writer, Luke Janusz, put it succinctly in the *New York Times* recently: "When the inmate press is censored, everyone loses" (November 20, 1993, p. 15).

NOTES

1. All of the statistical information presented here is compiled from Flanagan and Maguire (1989) and Zawitz (1988), unless otherwise stated.

2. The debate centers more on the nature of the crime and the criminal behavior patterns of women offenders before they get to prison, rather than on the nature of women prisoners once they are incarcerated. For an example of two opposing explanations for the escalation in female crime, see Adler (1975) and Steffensmeier and Steffensmeier (1980).

3. Nanci Koser Wilson says in "Feminist Pedagogy in Criminology" (1991, p. 82) that "feminist researchers have been vitally interested in the question of women's lesser violence and criminality, but this research has rarely entered mainstream criminological debate."

4. Carol Burke's (1992) fascinating study of women prisoners' narratives is one recent, notable exception that, like this study, examines women's expressions from a qualitative perspective.

5. There is no parole for lifers in the state of Pennsylvania, although there is a commutation process where a panel of legislative, criminological, and psychological experts assess the potential of an inmate to be released on permanent parole. The decision of the panel is subject to a vote by the governor of Pennsylvania, and the number of commuted lifers tends to vary according to the political climate.

6. All of the demographic information here comes from the U.S. government publications from the Department of Justice by Flanagan and Maguire (1989) and Zawitz (1988), and from DeCostanzo and Scholes' (1988) study, unless otherwise noted.

7. Only two of the women in this study mentioned that their crime was related to a spousal abuse situation. Only one woman openly discussed how her murder conviction was a retaliation against such abuse. More than half of these women described how abusive situations, either as children or as prostitutes, existed prior to their arrest.

8. It is interesting to note, also, that as a researcher, I felt an implicit expectation to avoid discussing the crime for which the woman had been convicted. Mention of the crime seemed to interject an immediate barrier and decrease the inmate's trust toward me.

BIBLIOGRAPHY

Adler, F. (1975). *Sisters in crime.* New York: McGraw-Hill.

Alpert, G. P., & Hawkins, R. (1989). Women in prison. In Geoffrey Alpert & Richard Hawkins (Eds.), *American prison systems: punishment and justice* (pp. 300–333). Englewood Cliffs, NJ: Prentice-Hall.

Arendt, H. (1970). *On Violence.* New York: Harcourt, Brace, and World.

Baunach, P. J. (1985). *Mothers in prison.* New Brunswick, NJ: Transaction Books.

Beirne, P., & Messerschmidt, J. (1991). Feminist criminology. In P. Beirne & J. Messerschmidt (Eds.), *Criminology* (pp. 507–526). New York: Harcourt Brace Javonovich.

Burke, C. (1992). *Vision narratives of women in prison.* Knoxville: University of Tennessee Press.

Carlen, Pat (Ed.) (1985). *Criminal women: autobiographical accounts.* Polity Press.

DeCostanzo, E., & Scholes, H. (June 1988). Women behind bars: their numbers increase. *Corrections Today, 104*–108.

Fiske, E. B. (1989, September 27). About education. *New York Times,* p. B8.

Flanagan, T. J., & Maguire, K. (1989). (Eds.) *Sourcebook of Criminal Justice Statistics 1989.* Washington: US Department of Justice, Bureau of Justice Statistics.

Foss, S. K., Foss, K. A., & Trapp, R. (1991). *Contemporary perspectives on rhetoric* (2nd ed.). Prospect Heights, IL: Waveland.

Foucault, M. (1972). The formation of objects. In M. Foucault, *The archaeology of knowledge* (pp. 40–49). New York: Tavistock.

Geertz, C. (1973). *The interpretation of cultures, selected essays.* New York: Basic Books.

Gelfand, E. (1981). Imprisoned women: toward a socio-literary feminist analysis. *Yale French Studies, 62,* 185–203.

Goffman, E. (1961). *Asylums.* New York: Anchor.

Goodstein, Lynne. (1979). Inmate adjustment to prison and transition to community life. *Journal of Research in Crime and Delinquency, 3,* 246–272.

Goodstein, L., MacKenzie, D. L., & Schotland, R. L. (1984). Personal control and inmate adjustment to prison. *Criminology, 22,* 343–369.

Habermas, J. (1977). Hannah Arendt's communication concept of power. *Social Research, 44,* 3–24.

Harlow, B. (1986). From the women's prison: third world women's narratives of prison. *Feminist Studies, 12*(3), 501–524.

Harris, J. (1986). *Stranger in two worlds.* New York: Macmillan.

Harris, J. (1988). *They always call us ladies: stories from prison.* New York: Scribner's.

Heilbrun, C. (1988). *Writing a woman's life.* New York: Ballantine.

Janusz, Luke. (1993, November 20). Captive writers. *New York Times,* p. 15.

Lundstrom, F. (1987). Research design in total institutions: problems, pitfalls, and possible solutions. *Quality and Quantity, 21,* 209–218.

Mandaraka-Sheppard, A. (1986). Coping with the self in prison: inmates' self image and its relations with behaviour in prison. In *The dynamics of aggres-*

sion in women's prisons in England (pp. 144–160). Brookfield, VT: Gower.

Naffine, N. (1987). *Female crime: the construction of women in criminology.* London: Allen & Unwin.

O'Neil, M. (1990). Correctional higher education: reduced recidivism? *Journal of Correctional Education, 41,* 28–31.

Parker, E. A. (1990). The social-psychological impact of a college education on the prison inmate. *Journal of Correctional Education, 41,* 140–146.

Pollock-Byrne, J. M. (1990). *Women, prison, and crime.* Pacific Grove, CA: Brooks/ Cole.

Scheffler, J. A. (Ed.). (1986). *Wall tappings: an anthology of writings by women prisoners.* Boston: Northeastern University Press.

Scheffler, J. A. (1988). Agnes Smedley's "cell mates": a writer's discovery of voice, form, and subject in prison. In A. Kessler-Harris & W. McBrien (Eds.), *Faith of a (woman) writer* (pp. 197–207). Westport, CT: Greenwood Press.

Sobel, S. B. (1982). Difficulties experienced by women in prison. *Psychology of Women Quarterly, 72,* 107–118.

Steffensmeier, D. J., & Steffensmeier, R. H. (1980). Trends in female delinquency: an examination of arrest, juvenile court, self-report, and field data. *Criminology 18,* 62–85.

White, J. B. (1984). *When words lose their meaning: constitutions and reconstitutions of language, character, and community.* Chicago: University of Chicago Press.

Wilson, Nanci Koser. (1991). Feminist pedagogy in criminology. *Journal of Criminal Justice Education, 2,* 81–93.

Young-Eisendrath, P., & Wiedemann, F. L. (1987). *Female authority: empowering women through psychotherapy.* New York: Guilford.

Zawitz, M. W. (1988). (Ed.) *Report to the Nation on Crime and Justice* (2nd ed.). Washington: US Department of Justice, Bureau of Justice Statistics.

Part II

Audiences, Ideology, and Cultural Representation

Liberal Television: Property and the Politics of Commercial Broadcasting

Thomas Streeter

INTRODUCTION: TELEVISION AS LEGAL INSCRIPTION

In a society of private property, much of our experience involves bounded objects. We walk down a residential street and, by way of walls, driveways, and picket fences, are made instantly aware of the boundaries that separate homes into finite, ownable things. We walk through a grocery store, and are surrounded by thousands of packaged objects, each distinct, each with a price.

When we watch television or listen to the radio, however, ownership boundaries are not at all obvious. To be sure, most of us have at times, in a late night stupor, watched the closing credits scroll by all the way to that final moment when the copyright notice—the textual equivalent of a picket fence—levitates onto the screen. But to most viewers, this is just a bit of legal flotsam, the debris of complex machinations that have taken place elsewhere. The broadcast media provide us less with discrete objects than with an unending rush of images, sounds, and messages, with the complex stream of juxtaposed texts that Raymond Williams (1977) dubbed "flow."

One of the peculiarities of commercial broadcast media is that ownership boundaries are similarly obscure and fluid from the other side of the camera, from the point of view of those for whom copyright notices matter greatly. Even to those who care, the copyright notice that punctuates a program's closing credits hardly begins to chart the labyrinthine and often systematically blurred "boundaries" that delineate the exchange relations embodied in that program and its distribution.

This chapter is about the role of the category of property in the social construction of commercial broadcasting in the United States. Property is important to broadcasting for a number of reasons. First, property is constitutive of commercial broadcasting as we know it. Commercial broadcasting, if it is to be commercial, involves taking a set of activities— the reproduction of disembodied sounds and pictures for dissemination to vast unseen audiences—and somehow constituting those activities as things that can be bought, owned, and sold, as property. Second, the way in which this is done is fundamental to the distribution of power over broadcasting. The particular ways in which property is legally constructed and enforced largely determines who gets what, under what conditions— who owns TV stations, who owns the creation and distribution of programs, and what powers are generated by the conditions of ownership.

Third, property is a work of collective imagination, in particular, the liberal imagination, by which I mean it is enacted by way of a political discourse of rights, individualism, and markets (Unger, 1975). One could speak of commodification instead of property, and might thereby gain some theoretical precision. But the word property is useful in this context because it helps accentuate the *ideological* character of the process of commodification in which commercial broadcasting is constituted. Property is one of the principle official ways that our social and legal systems try to address the values of difference and diversity ("to each his own") and, in view of its limitations, it thus plays a key ideological role. To call property ideological is not to suggest it is illusory (property relations are hardly an illusory element of contemporary capitalist societies), but rather to emphasize the way it is *both* very real and profoundly imaginary at the same time. Property relations are created and shaped by the way people imagine them. Their reality is conditioned on (although not simply reflected in) their imaginary quality.[1]

Take, for example, a television set. Television is not a thing, it is a practice, it is something that people do. The box in our living rooms wouldn't be much more than an oversized doorstop without the fact of a number of very complex, organized, ongoing, collective activities: internationally coordinated systems for designing, manufacturing, and distributing equipment, for example, or people devoting their lives to making programs, and the institutional networks for distributing those programs. The box itself is made practical, made into a practice, by its internal organization in concert with the socially determined technical specifications, spectrum allocations, and so forth that make broadcasting possible. A television is thus a collection of tubes, wires, and microchips whose organization is determined by, or inscribed with, the social structures that constitute broadcasting.

Of course, all this involves law and politics, that is, lawyers, judges, and legislators making, changing, and enforcing laws and regulations that enable and shape both the equipment of broadcasting and the institutions that make the equipment come alive. The tools of broadcasting, in other words, even the boxes in our living rooms, are to a large degree legal constructs. A television is not just a technology, then, but a kind of legal inscription on technology.

Much of that inscription, this chapter will show, involves the discourse of property law. Even on a popular level, part of the practice of television in U.S. culture is that we imagine it as a thing, not a practice; you go to the store, buy a box, put it in your living room, and by right it belongs to you, not to someone else, not to the state; it is a commodity, a device, in any case an object. In the United States, we still tend to imagine property this way, in a kind of folk version of the 17th-century Lockeian framework, wherein property is understood as a natural right of individuals over things. But property also is important to debates about media law and media structure around the globe. The formula of "free markets," of free speech attained through private property and competition, is more prominent today than ever before, and underwrites the contemporary expansion of the transnational media system.

The U.S. case suggests that private property is both a linchpin and weak point in the legal discourse that constitutes commercial broadcasting. On the one hand, property serves as the principle and paradigmatic device for defining rights and freedoms as limits to state intervention, and thus underwrites the liberal dream of transcending politics. Property plays a key role, in other words, in imagining the practices that are radios and televisions as things instead of practices.

The political implications of this, in turn, are crucial: the supposedly mathematical clarity, neutrality, and private character of property, we are told, guarantees freedom by shielding individuals from the arbitrary winds of politics associated with government intervention. Thereby is "private" broadcasting defined as "free," and freedom of speech becomes the legal protection of the power of media owners against political intervention or responsibility.

On the other hand, property in commercial broadcasting is highly political in all the ways the private property supposedly is not. The commodification of broadcasting, this chapter will show, is a political activity on several levels. It is political both in the conventional sense of requiring ongoing government activity and in that it involves value choices and the enactment of belief systems. In particular, it embodies an uneasy mix of classical liberalism, based in notions of formal, natural rights, with corporate liberalism, in which rights become functional standards subject to qualification by the procedures of administration and bureaucracy. Property, as a result, is a weak link in the political legitimacy of commercial broadcasting. The highly political, collective character of broadcast property conflicts with the broad, classical liberal vision that helps legitimate it. This suggests, in turn, an opening for potential political interventions in broadcast policy.

Beginning with a discussion of the nature of property, this chapter goes on to explore the commodification of broadcasting in three key areas: the creation of marketable broadcast stations, the extension of copyright to broadcast programs, and the construction of marketable "audiences" that broadcasters sell to advertisers.

WHAT IS PROPERTY? THE POLITICAL CHARACTER OF COMMODIFICATION

It is often thought that there is something uniquely peculiar about property in electronic intangibles. Broadcast programs, computer software, and the like are ephemeral. Unlike beans, ball bearings, or real estate, they have no physical presence. From this it is often concluded that software and other intangible goods of the information age present challenges to legal systems of ownership quite unlike the blunt and obvious material forms of property characteristic of the nineteenth century.

Property in information is unique, however, only if property is about physical things. As political scientist C. B. Macpherson (1978) has pointed out, the belief that property is about physical things indeed remains the commonsense view in our time and has important roots in our legal and philosophical tradition. It is still common to assume that property is an obvious, "natural" right of ownership over physical things. However, as the legal realists first demonstrated early in this century, this view of property is neither philosophically coherent nor empirically accurate (Cohen, 1928). Property of any sort is neither blunt nor obvious. Ownership of a stock, for example, merely confers a narrow set of rights to income under certain circumstances, not exclusive control over anything physical. Similarly, the right to private property, subject to shifting interpretations and based as it is on state enforcement, is logically indistinguishable from a government-granted privilege.

Property, the legal realists concluded, is neither a thing nor a natural condition of human existence, but is rather a shifting, flexible bundle of rights, a set of contingent political decisions about who gets what in what circumstances. As Macpherson puts it, property is an "institution which creates and maintains certain relations between people," and the relations created and maintained, and thus the meaning of the word property itself, are not constant but rather constantly changing from context to context (Macpherson, 1978).

Of course, the argument that the meaning of property is never constant need not be taken to mean that property is meaningless, that it is *merely* a bundle of rights, that as a concept it is "disintegrating" (Grey, 1980). Far from being meaningless, any definition or assertion of property rights involves a particular vision of how society is or ought to be. According to Macpherson, property changes in ways "related to changes in the purposes which society or the dominant classes in society expect the institution of property to serve." It also involves social struggle and power: property is an attempt to get social organizations (typically the state) to enforce and legitimize particular claims embodying particular social relations. Property is thus foremost "a political relation among persons" (Macpherson, 1978). The historian Martin Sklar (1988, p. 7) summarized the scope of property nicely:

Property . . . is not simply a thing, nor simply an economic category, but is a complex social relation—of an intro- and inter-class character—that involves a system of authority inextricably interwoven with the legal and political order as well as with the broader system of legitimacy, the prevailing norms of emulative morality and behavior, and the hierarchy of power.

The fact that information, the radio spectrum, the broadcast audience, or electronic software are resources, therefore, should not be conflated with the treatment of these resources as commodities. As Dan Schiller (1988, p. 3) has remarked, "A resource is anything of use, anytime, anywhere, to anyone; but a commodity . . . bears the stamp of society and of history in its very core."

ENCLOSING THE SPECTRUM: THE PECULIAR PROPERTY STATUS OF THE BROADCAST LICENSE

Government involvement in broadcast stations is not necessary for broadcasting per se (as successful pirate radio stations demonstrate). But government involvement is necessary for commercial broadcasting as we know it. Historically, the foundation for commercial broadcasting in the United States was laid by the creation of the legal requirement of a broadcast license and with it, the marketable broadcast station. The principle organizational unit in American broadcasting is the station, and a station is something that is owned, bought, and sold; the principle way to gain access to the broadcast airwaves is to buy a station.

The broadcast "station," however, is not a self-evident thing but a legally constituted and protected combination of a particular frequency with a particular transmitting facility, linked with a federally issued license. There is nothing natural or technologically necessary about the broadcast station. Theoretically, frequencies, transmitters, and licenses to transmit can vary independently of one another. The station is thus an arbitrary creation of the state. And yet it is that act of creation that makes it possible for the station to become a commodity, an "object" available for purchase and sale on a for-profit basis.

The commodified broadcast station is premised on several determining acts of government intervention. The most fundamental (and today, least questioned) involves the simple assertion of government power over radio frequencies. Spectrum regulation typically also involves the legal designation of particular frequencies for particular uses (e.g., commercial broadcasting as distinguished from amateur communications), an act that can not only create entire industries, but can profoundly structure the behavior, interests, and communicative product of those industries. The government plays a constitutive role, in other words, not only in creating the thing sold, but in creating the motive to sell it.

Next, government regulations must sanction and be coordinated with the general process of buying and selling; as spectrum regulation adopts to technological progress and institutional innovations, considerable government effort goes into coordinating the developing system of regulation with the ongoing marketplace in stations. And last but not least, all this elaborate government activity on behalf of private enterprise must be legitimated. State action on behalf of business must be rendered acceptable in a political environment in which private and public actions are supposed to be held separate.

The first step toward commodification, the assertion of government power over the spectrum, did not originally seem to be the obvious necessity it is taken to be today. Both the entrepreneur-inventors and amateurs who collectively pioneered much of both radio technology and the practice of broadcasting were at best indifferent to government regulation, and in some cases actively opposed to it (Douglas, 1987). Radio interference was approached the same way we approach the problems generated by incompatible computers and computer programs today: it was a technical problem that came with the territory, a by-product of the technology and competition that could be dealt with informally.

The idea of a commodified spectrum entered the field of radio, not through the actions of free individuals of Lockeian fable, but in a process of interaction between military, corporate, and government interests, particularly on an international level. Because radio promised both to revolutionize naval warfare and, as a potential successor to undersea cables, facilitate communication with and control of colonial outposts, it excited the ambitions and concerns of the governments and militaries of the European powers and the United States. Pressure from international forces, from the Navy, and from concerns about maritime safety combined to goad Congress into passing the Wireless Ship Act of 1910 and the Radio Act of 1912.

The immediate concern motivating both pieces of legislation was public safety at sea—the 1912 Act was passed less than six months after the Titanic disaster. But the 1910 and the 1912 Acts also firmly established in U.S. law the general principle that the radio spectrum was properly subject to legal restraints on access; all radio operators were required to obtain licenses from the secretary of Commerce and Labor. The Act divided useful portions of the spectrum between the Navy and "commercial operators," while amateurs were relegated to shortwave, a realm then thought to be of no practical value. Those given privileged access to the spectrum were not simply "private" interests—the amateurs were certainly private, but were banished to a spectrum wasteland—but were large, bureaucratic institutions interested in the extension of bureaucratic hierarchies across space, in this case the Navy and the Marconi Company, by then a burgeoning transnational corporation. Beginning in 1912, therefore, state action wrested control over a new communications medium from a mixed group of small entrepreneurs and hobbyists and turned it over to large corporations and the military. The possibility of a spectrum without boundaries or with informal regulations was thus eliminated; all further disputes would involve the legal technicalities of the system, but not the question of legal restraint itself. The enclosure of the spectrum had begun.

How was massive government intervention in the service of impersonal bureaucracies reconciled with the individualist vision of free enterprise and its associated understanding of private property? Why was this not a departure from property, perhaps an unjust government interference with property?

The 1912 Act was legitimated to a large degree by the logic of expertise and administrative procedure characteristic of what some call "revisionist" or "corporate" liberalism (Hawley, 1978; Streeter, forthcoming, 1996).[2] The Act was framed, not as a matter of formal rights, but as a response to technical problems amenable to solution by experts: safety of ships at sea, the needs of the Navy, effective coordination and maintenance of radio service, and the like. The restraints were legitimated, therefore, not by the courts in the name of common law property rights, but by agencies of the federal government, in the name of the public good. Access would be described more as a contingent, technologically justified privilege than as a formal right.

Although the 1912 Act had little explicit to say about the property character of the airwaves, therefore, it contained implicit answers to property-related questions in its corporate liberal logic. Was it legitimate to eject the amateurs from their established places in the airwaves? Was it fair to grant Marconi such a large protected chunk of the spectrum free of cost?

Yes, according to the logic of the Act: these actions were legitimate and fair because of the complexities of radio, public safety, and the national interest as determined by the experts, that is, by Marconi, engineers, and Navy officers. Were not some questions still left unresolved? For example, was Marconi accruing private property rights in the spectrum by dint of his investments after 1912? Many questions were left unresolved: this is inevitable in complex, evolving technologies, which is why the Act established a mechanism for dealing with such contingencies, the administrative power of the secretary of Commerce and Labor.

The 1912 Act, in sum, did not resolve the property question by affirming the existence of a natural right in the airwaves, or by precisely specifying the contents of the rights associated with broadcast licenses. Instead it set up an intellectual and institutional framework for responding to still nascent questions of property whenever they might arise: intellectually, property would be conceived in corporate liberal fashion as a flexible standard instead of a formal rule. Institutionally, an administrative system would be established to handle unresolved questions as matters of fact and efficiency to be dealt with in context. The Act thus established a system that *transformed* the property question from one of rights and fairness into a technical question of efficiency as determined by experts and administrators. The outer framework was still one of free enterprise; the inner structure was one of contingency, administration, and expertise.

Full-fledged commodification of stations would have to wait for broadcasting to appear on the scene in the early 1920s. The marketable broadcast station is a direct product of the legal and policy regime worked out between 1920 and 1926, involving a permanent system of federal licensing that allows for both limited government intervention and the development of broadcasting on a private, for-profit basis. The basic patterns of regulation and behavior were established informally, under the loosely defined legal powers of the 1912 Act.

In the first years of the 1920s, as consumers discovered the wonders of listening to broadcast entertainment and news, and as manufacturers discovered the profits to be made in the new phenomenon, the number of transmitters in the United States mushroomed. Then Secretary of Commerce Herbert Hoover responded with the established practice of subdividing the spectrum into divisions designated by use. Arguably, Hoover's most momentous act was the separation of broadcasters from point-to-point operators and the designation of broadcasting as a "commercial," non-amateur activity.[3] Hoover's Act, at the time, quietly treated as a simple administrative procedure necessary for the maintenance of "order" in the spectrum, laid the legal foundation for commercial broadcasting and effectively cut off the development of alternative institutional possibilities, such as non-profit amateur broadcasting and the possibility of a form of popular radio that freely mixed two-way point-to-point communications with one-way broadcasting (a form common amongst amateurs in the 1910s).

In the midst of this period of aggressive government intervention, the practice of buying and selling broadcast stations and, along with them, their licenses, began. Having done much through allocations to establish the profit motive as the dominant organizing principle in broadcasting, the government then channeled that motive in the direction of speculation in stations: because the government, through military reservations and related regulations, had restricted broadcasting to a narrow band (roughly today's AM band), the broadcast band began filling up. As congestion grew, broadcast licenses were turned into potentially valuable commodities. This process was accelerated when, in 1925, the Department of Commerce ceased issuing new licenses altogether. Not surprisingly, some of the businesses involved in broadcasting thought it would be useful to be able to buy and sell their licenses along with their stations. Because the station was integral with a government-issued license, the sale of a station required permission from the Commerce Department, to which it readily acquiesced (Barnouw, 1966, p. 174). The American market in broadcast stations has been brisk ever since.

Again, this final step in the commodification of broadcast stations was legitimated by corporate liberal logic. Although the larger framework was one of support for the principles of "free enterprise," the specific decisions were presented as involving technical, administrative details, not formal rights. To Hoover and other corporate liberals, the positive value of encouraging the commercial development of broadcasting was just as obvious as was using government regulation to provide such encouragement.

What may have seemed obvious to Hoover, however, was less so to the polity at large. As the broadcast industry solidified, more elaborate measures were needed to legitimate the system established in the early 1920s. This was accomplished in the 1927 Radio Act, which basically codified existing practices into law.[4] In particular, the Act sanctioned the practice of buying and selling stations along with their licenses, thus privileging capital in access to the airwaves and ensuring the property-like character of the broadcast station.

The tenuous ideological nature of the practices underwritten by the 1927 Act, however, is underscored by a tension within the regulatory system it established. The paradox here is an old one: the effort to pursue the principle of private property in broadcasting involves the use of elaborate political intervention to achieve the goal of the liberal ideal of private property, namely, limiting political intervention. To maintain political legitimacy, the ideological trick is to maintain the coherence of the boundary between private property and government in the face of the government's helpful reach across that boundary when it creates a broadcast station.

The 1927 Act dealt with this problem by directing the Federal Radio Commission (FRC) to regulate the airwaves according to the criteria of "the public interest, convenience, and necessity," declaring that a license provided "for the use of such channels, but not the ownership thereof." This clause has played an important role in American broadcast law. Without it, government regulators might have lacked the legitimacy and legal power to undertake the many tasks necessary to maintain a commercial broadcast system. The public interest and nonownership language of the 1927 Act framed the licensing system as an exception to the rule of private property, necessitated by the peculiarities of radio. The language thus helped maintain the meaningfulness of the idea of property itself by suggesting a difference between the licensing system and "true" private property.

The practice of regulating the airwaves in "the public interest," then, was itself less a decision to limit to private ownership in broadcasting overall than it was a way to justify and make sense of the use of government powers to aid private ownership. By explicitly forbidding private property in the spectrum while inviting the buying and selling of the stations that licenses create, elaborate government intervention on behalf of particular corporate interests could be legitimatized without undermining the basic idea of the separateness of free enterprise and property from government.

The system is indeed odd. The law seems to simultaneously designate licenses as both property and not property. It is thus not surprising that it is nearly impossible to find an article about U.S. broadcast licensing in the law journals that doesn't criticize the system from one or another point of view (e.g., Coase, 1959; Reich, 1964). In part, the tenuousness of the system has been dealt with in American law largely by making an imaginary distinction between broadcast licenses and broadcast stations: in theory, you can sell the station, but not the government-granted license. The weak point in this construct is that the license is inseparable from the station. Overall, it's as if the government hands out some very valuable pieces of paper and then tells people that you can't sell the front side of the paper, the license, but you can and should sell the back side of the paper, the station.

So another part of the response has been a tendency on the part of regulators to be extremely timid in invoking the powers vested in them by the non-ownership and public interest clauses. Since the 1927 Act, the regulatory system has demonstrated an extreme reluctance to interfere with the possession and exchange of broadcast licenses. Broadcast stations have changed hands by sale more than 6,000 times, and in most cases the amount paid clearly includes a substantial sum for the economic value of the license itself. The Federal Communications Commission (FCC) renews more than 3,000 licenses every year, and has used its power to revoke licenses without compensation less than 150 times in its sixty-four years of existence—only twice in the case of the more valuable television licenses (Ellmore, 1982, pp. 114–115; Sterling, 1984, p. 45). Licenses may not be property, but the regulatory system treats them for the most part as if they were property.

Perhaps because the contradiction is buried inside a labyrinth of legal jargon and technology, however, it has sat there unchanged for most of this century. The quiet commodification of the airwaves, in sum, appears to have been accomplished with little resistance.

ENCLOSING BROADCAST CULTURE: COPYRIGHT, BLANKET LICENSING, AND FEDERAL REGULATION

Commodification of the spectrum ensured corporate mastery of access to the spectrum, but it left unresolved the question of control over what was broadcast. Commercial broadcasting could not be what it is without copyright law. Copyright is a classical liberal legal construct; its treatment in broadcasting clearly illustrates the character of liberalism's revision in the corporate era. In a construct dating back to the 18th century, authors are generally thought of as individuals who are solely responsible for originating unique works (Woodmansee, 1984). The figure of the romantic author-genius was to an extent an offshoot of the figure of the free, property-holding, individual capitalist entrepreneur (even if the figure of the romantic author also contained a critique of the entrepreneur's calculating rationality). Even when the individuality of the author seems obscured by commercial concerns, as is the case with Anglo-American law, the categories associated with copyright, such as originality and the distinction between an idea and its expression, are derived from the romantic image of authorship as an act of original creation whose uniqueness springs from and is defined in terms of the irreducible individuality of the writer (Frow, 1988).

Whatever one's opinion of the content of American television and radio, the terms "uniqueness" and "individuality" are not likely to come to mind. Reconciling the collective, industrial nature of broadcasting with the individualist romanticism of copyright has been a central problem for the institution of commercial broadcasting and the electronic media generally. Space prohibits a full review of the question of copyright and electronic technologies here, but three developments are particularly important to this reconciliation. First, the legal fiction of the corporate individual has turned industrial bureaucracies into legal stand-ins for the individual author. Second, property has been what I call "bureaucratized" in the statistical formulas of blanket licensing organizations. Third, ownership boundaries have been attenuated by the construction of an elaborate labyrinth of industry-inspired federal regulations that shape and channel the production and distribution of television programs.

The key role of the fiction of the corporate individual in the production of broadcasting is fairly obvious. Giving corporations the status of persons under law grants them the ability to stand in for "authors" in the framework of copyright, thus transferring the bulk of control over media "works" from individual creators to large bureaucratic institutions. Programs are thus created, produced, owned, and exchanged by corporate bureaucracies. The television industry's notorious penchant for crassly formulaic thinking in broadcast programming is largely the product of this bureaucratic organization. To a large degree the bureaucratization of intellectual property in broadcasting is a product of the simple fact that large industrial bureaucracies have taken the place of individuals both in law and in the process of cultural production.

As a rule, therefore, programs are created, produced, owned, and exchanged by corporate bureaucracies, not entrepreneurial individuals. This does much to alleviate problems that broadcasting, with its collective production and indiscriminate, ephemeral mass distribution, would otherwise present to a traditional legal regime framed in terms of individual creativity and ownership of discrete objects. If, as was common in the early days and still occurs today, a corporation produces programs, broadcasts those programs, and sells the receivers that pick them up, perplexing questions of where one person's ownership leaves off and another's begin are circumvented.

There are, however, many corporations involved in broadcasting, which leaves some boundary questions unresolved. One principle means of resolving them has been the administrative technique of the blanket license. The blanket license predates broadcasting by a few years: it originated when ASCAP (the American Society of Composers, Authors, and Publishers) sought to collect from huge numbers of often small and casual "performances" of copyrighted works in nightclubs, restaurants, and other commercial establishments across the nation in 1917. Actually collecting payments for each individual performance of copyrighted works from, for instance, every piano player in every bar in the United States was thoroughly impractical. Instead, ASCAP granted licenses, for which each establishment would pay a fee more or less like an annual subscription, determined by things like the size of the establishment but not by the specific content of the performances. The money thus collected would then be distributed to copyright holders according to a statistical formula designed to approximate the actual but unknown number of performances of each work.

Over the years, blanket licensing has been elaborated and extended. In the 1920s, ASCAP successfully forced a blanket license system on the newborn broadcast industry for radio performances of music. The relation between copyright holders and broadcasters, however, was a bureaucratic stand-in for market exchange, not an actual market. In a classical market, when people raise their prices too high, competition either forces them to lower prices or causes them to go out of business. In the case of ASCAP's blanket license, market regulation was absent. What was to prevent ASCAP from raising its prices? The problem was not one of monopoly: there were plenty of potential "buyers" and "sellers" of programs—in a sense, too many of them. The problem was that prices were being set by a bureaucracy according to a theoretical model of an imaginary market, not by a market itself.

It thus could have been predicted that ASCAP would begin to raise its fees in the late 1930s. When ASCAP in 1937 announced yet another increase of 70 percent to be implemented in 1939, the National Association of Broadcasters (NAB) responded by organizing a competing licensing organization, Broadcast Music Incorporated (BMI). BMI's library of licensed music remained slim at first. Between January and October of 1941, BMI's first year, broadcast listeners were treated to the unending repetition of the few available BMI and public domain songs, during which the BMI-licensed "I Dream of Jeannie with the Light Brown Hair" was forever engraved on American popular memory (Sterling and Kittross, 1990, p. 193). Instability ensued as listeners grew weary and various broadcast organizations considered defecting to ASCAP. To further complicate matters, the Department of Justice filed suit against both ASCAP and the broadcast networks for antitrust violations. Stability did not return until a compromise with ASCAP was reached in conjunction with an antitrust consent decree that caused license fees to return to old rates and allowed BMI to remain in existence and share the business of blanket licensing with ASCAP. With small modifications, the arrangement reached in 1941 has survived to this day.

The blanket licensing technique as a means of simulating property relations continues to be invoked. When Congress rewrote the Copyright Act in 1976, they created the Copyright Royalty Tribunal (CRT), one of whose functions is to operate a blanket licensing system for cable television. The CRT, a part of the Library of Congress, collects money from cable operators, puts that money in a "pot," and then redistributes it to program copyright holders. Cable operators pay an amount set by a formula based on their subscriber rate, and program copyright holders receive payments according to a similar formula.

What has happened to the categories of property and copyright in this process? At first glance, it seems that copyright was enforced, property rights in broadcast content created, and broadcast programs were successfully commodified. To some extent, this is true; money flows from users of copyrighted works to copyright holders, and works—broadcast programs—flow the other way.

At second glance, however, the situation appears more complicated. Goods, even of an ephemeral kind, are not actually exchanged. Copyright holders do not get paid and users of those works do not pay for individual performances of works. Both parties deal first of all with a bureaucracy. On a day-to-day basis, both copyright holders and users experience the process as being more like paying taxes or procuring welfare: amounts are determined by formulas and bureaucratic procedure.

For example, the struggles between ASCAP and the NAB were not, technically speaking, manifestations of straightforward marketplace competition. Rather, they were more like the political struggles that often occur within or between rival bureaucratic institutions: the rivalry was expressed in terms of statistical formulas, membership lists, and general legitimacy. Costs and payments are set, not by supply and demand, but by bureaucratic formulas established in a process more akin to political lobbying than marketplace bargaining. Entry into these particular "markets" involves having the appropriate qualifications and filling out the appropriate forms, not offering to buy or sell a product. In the case of cable television, increasing one's profit is sometimes a matter of lobbying Congress and the CRT, not of buying more cheaply or selling more dearly.

Blanket licensing organizations, furthermore, have numerous "side effects" uncharacteristic of markets but characteristic of bureaucracies. Non-market rationales often play a crucial role in the process. In a frank if modest redistributive effort, for example, Congress allocated an extra-large percentage of the CRT "pot" to the Public Broadcasting Service (PBS), and none to the three networks. Even when "market criteria" are used to make decisions, the formulas used to calculate payments inevitably favor some at the expense of others and thus become matters for intraindustry political disputes, as was the case with ASCAP's attempts to raise fees in the 1930s. Profits are certainly at stake in these struggles, but profit is determined by the relative political strength of the institutions in question, not by buying more cheaply or selling more dearly. The blanket licensing organizations are bureaucratic, political entities, and they behave as such.

Copyright, in this light, can be said to have taken on a new role in relation to the process of cultural production. In classical liberal legal practice, property's role was formal. In theory at least it was used to draw boundaries in a marketplace: one person's property rights began and ended at a certain specific point. The common sense view of private property suggests that ownership confers a kind of sovereignty, the right to do whatever one wishes with the thing owned. This notion was reflected in 19th-century industrial disputes, which were most often treated as a matter of locating the formal boundary between the property rights of the parties involved. If the effluent from a coal mine spilled into a neighboring farmer's field, for example, the courts would set out to find the line between the farmer's and the mine's property rights. Were the farmer's property rights being violated by the spill or would forcing the mine to limit operations violate its property rights?

In the technique of blanket licensing, copyright's role is exemplary of corporate liberal practice. It is less formal and more like a functional standard: copyright acts as a general bureaucratic guideline, signifying the general goals of the system (capitalist profitability and expansion) to those inside it. The specific implementation of those goals depends less on the classical liberal concern for boundary-setting than on bureaucratic arrangements that keep the system running, even if boundaries are allowed to grow quite blurry in the process. The question of who in the final instance "authored" a broadcast program or song, or more importantly who owes whom what for it, is often left vague, but this is unproblematic as long as the general goals of the system are being served, as long as the industries involved are profitable, expanding, and relatively stable.

A second transformation in the role of intellectual property is evident in the elaborate role of federal broadcast regulation in shaping the control and ownership of broadcast programs. Administrative agencies are a hallmark of corporate liberalism, and they are central to commercial broadcasting. Television corporations face an elaborate labyrinth of administrative regulations that shape and channel the production and distribution of program "property." TV stations, for example, could not broadcast network entertainment programs between 7:30 and 8:00 P.M.; networks cannot contractually obligate their affiliates to broadcast network programs; program producers and distributors could not grant networks distribution rights for program reruns; cable operators must blank out certain cablecast programs that duplicate local over-the-air offerings. All of these rules have generated vociferous debate over the rules' fairness and efficiency, yet few object to them on the grounds that they violate property rights.

Officially, these rules are justified by the philosophy of antitrust: government intervention is intended to enhance the competitive, marketplace nature of the industry. In practice, however, competition has tended to come largely from new institutional structures like cable and PBS. FCC regulation of program and profit flows between established industry segments, on the other hand, has largely been a matter of the arbitration of pie-sharing struggles. Industry leaders and lobbyists for broadcast industry factions have become accustomed to using the FCC as a terrain for settling factional disputes. In the late 1950s, for example, squabbles between Hollywood program producers and the networks set off hearings and rulemakings that eventually led to a series of regulations governing ownership and distribution of programs. The producers' complaint was basically that the networks, as sole buyers of prime time programming, exploited their power unfairly. To redress this perceived imbalance, in 1970 the FCC forbade networks from syndicating independently produced programs (the syndication rule), and from obtaining any financial or proprietary rights in independently produced programming beyond the right for first-run network broadcast (the financial interest rule). That same year, networks were prohibited from broadcasting more than three hours of entertainment programming during prime time (the prime time access rule), which effectively created a half-hour slot between 7:30 and 8:00 P.M. reserved for non-network, syndicated programs (FCC, 1980, p. 451). (Both rules were dropped in 1995.)

The rise in this century of the use of federal administrative bodies as interindustry dispute resolution mechanisms is a long and elaborate story. What is significant here is the transformed role of copyright. In blanket licensing, intellectual property is approximated by bureaucratic structures. In FCC regulation of program flows among industry subdivisions, on the other hand, the question of property is very nearly abandoned and replaced by the goal of a smoothly functioning and profitable system for program production and distribution, measured by standards such as efficiency and the "public interest." In each case, large institutional structures based in the administrative apparatus of the state work to undergird and profoundly shape the structure of private industry.

VIEWERSHIP AS PROPERTY: IDEOLOGY AND THE AUDIENCE COMMODITY

The successful commodification of broadcast programs allowed for relatively predictable exchange relations in programming, but it left one crucial set of relations unresolved: what were the programs going to be exchanged *for*? The solution is encapsulated in one of the favorite phrases of American broadcast executives: broadcasters don't sell programs to audiences, they sell audiences to advertisers.

The literature on the economic character of broadcasting's main economic engine is large and complex (Smythe, 1977; Jhally, 1990; Maxwell, 1991). Here I can only add to the discussion a suggestion derived from the character of licenses and copyright: commodification of intangibles can be a messy, paradoxical affair driven by political and ideological, as well as economic, concerns. Some of the peculiarities of the commodity audience, therefore, might be illuminated by considering internal and external pressures of political legitimacy faced by the broadcast industry.

Internally, the problem is that, before business can proceed, something must be bought and sold. Before the game of economic competition can begin, agreement must be reached about the terms of competition among the players. Given the absence of ticket booths in broadcasting, that something has become an abstract, statistical representation in the audience. The language of money is numbers; by transforming the elusive audience into apparently unequivocal numbers, the ratings provide an industry consensus, a basis for bargaining over the dollar value of air time.

This consensus need not be understood as a conscious conspiracy. Even from the point of view of a self-interested advertising executive, ratings are rhetorically useful because, accurate or not, they "secrete the aura of reason": a bad decision based on ratings is safe for one's career, but one based on intuition would be dangerously impolitic (Gitlin, 1985, p. 45). In the words of J. Walter Thompson executive Alice Sylvester, "The Nielsen ratings right now represent an agreement between the buyers and sellers to use them as the currency of negotiation . . . for what we're doing with the ratings and the way we plan, buy, and execute, it works just fine" (*Nova*, 1992).

Externally, the ratings also help to ward off threats: they ground the television industry's claim to be democratically "giving the audience what it wants." The industry may use ratings, in sum, in a way that does more to ensure industry stability in the face of internal and external threats than a clear understanding of its audience.

The possibility that the commodity audience is as much a product of political and institutional pressures as economic ones may help account for an otherwise puzzling characteristic of the system: the surprising indifference of industry executives to the accuracy of the ratings. As Meehan (1990) and others have pointed out, audience ratings are notoriously inaccurate: there is little dispute, for example, that the Nielsens overrepresent middle-class white families at the expense of minorities, the poor, and the elderly. Survey methodologist Peter Miller has said, "Strictly speaking, from a survey research point of view, those numbers are fragile and the agreement that the advertisers and broadcasters have struck in some ways stretches those numbers beyond their tolerance limits, particularly at the local level" (*Nova*, 1992). Even within the industry, furthermore, there is a widespread suspicion that millions of dollars regularly change hands based on numbers that are well under the range of measurement error (Gitlin, 1985, pp. 47–55; Chagall, 1981).

Yet industry members rarely express much concern about this chronic inaccuracy. One ABC executive said, "you can't really take into consideration everyday, 'boy do I have confidence in that number or not?' . . . It wouldn't really be practical to think about whether these numbers are right or not" (*Nova*, 1992). In the late 1980s the industry was faced with the appearance of two or three different and inconsistent ratings reports that accompanied the introduction of competitors to Nielsen, particularly

Audits of Great Britain (AGB). Industry members invariably complained, not about the chronic inaccuracy made evident by the disparities, but about the difficulty of doing business when more than one number is available because of the uncertainty this introduces into the buying and selling of advertising time. The issue was not confusion about the audience, but confusion in the day-to-day affairs of the corporate system. Uncertainty about the audience is acceptable, it seems, but uncertainty in dealings *within* the corporate system is not.

CONCLUSION: COMMERCIAL BROADCASTING, THE IDEOLOGY OF FREE ENTERPRISE, AND THE POLITICS OF PROPERTY

Although the definition of private property and its place in liberal theoretical systems has varied considerably, property's centrality to the liberal vision as a whole cannot be denied. In direct contrast to the arbitrary hierarchy and inequalities inherent to statist regimes, the system of property supposedly provides a form of social life characterized by a mathematical clarity, political neutrality, fairness, and freedom from government intervention. The idea that private property serves as the principle and paradigmatic device for defining rights as limits to state action is central to American political thought (Nedelsky, 1990).

If it weren't for all the government involvement, the bureaucratic infighting, and talk about the public interest that infuses the practice of broadcasting in the United States, the fact that commercial broadcasting is both the product of and an ideological flagship for the American popular philosophy of free enterprise would hardly bear repeating. But it needs be said: the U.S. system of radio and television is largely the outcome of a sustained, deliberate social and political effort to put the principles of the marketplace and private property into practice in the field of mass communication.

At the moment of its founding in the 1920s, the government and corporate architects of the commercial system—the same people that introduced the concept of the public interest to broadcast law—justified their actions by proudly drawing a contrast between European government controlled systems such as the British Broadcasting Corporation (BBC) and the "free" and "competitive" system they understood themselves to be constructing (U.S. Senate, 1926, p. 50). Ever since, it has been a commonplace of broadcast law that the Communications Act "recognizes that the field of broadcasting is one of free competition" (*FCC* v. *Sanders Brothers*, 309 U.S. 470, March 25, 1940). Even most attacks on commercial broadcasting are framed within the philosophy of free enterprise. In 1941, when an aggressive New Deal era FCC staffed by Roosevelt appointees successfully broke the National Broadcasting Company's

(NBC's) near monopoly of network radio, it justified its actions by declaring that the free market was "the essence of the American system of broadcasting" (FCC, 1941, p. 95). In what was probably the most famous verbal assault on the commercial broadcast establishment, Newton Minow's "Vast Wasteland" speech, the Kennedy-era FCC chair felt compelled to add to his stinging attack on the low quality of broadcast television, "I believe in the free enterprise system. I believe that most of television's problems stem from lack of competition" (Minow, 1961). Any discussion of broadcasting in the United States must accept the classical liberal faith in markets, competition, and private property if it is to be taken seriously by the law and policy establishment.

That faith involves more than rhetorical gestures, moreover. It has played a central role in concrete decisions affecting the institution of broadcasting in profound ways. Most obviously, the policy decision to operate broadcasting on an advertising-supported, commercial basis that was first made in the 1920s was enabled by the marketplace faith. That decision has been reaffirmed at several critical junctures since, including the writing of the Communications Act of 1934, the shift from radio to television in the late 1940s, and the introduction of cable as a major electronic medium in the 1970s and 1980s. In each case, completely new technologies and/or legal regimes were introduced in ways that wholeheartedly reproduced commercial legal and institutional structures on new terrain. The pressures of the classical liberal scenario are felt in numerous small ways as well. Numerous small regulatory decisions such as license renewals stop short of logical extensions because of the shadow cast by the faith of markets and property. Classical liberal marketplace principles, in sum, form the broad outlines of broadcast policy, the outer shell, from its origins in the early part of this century to today.

This rather obvious point is worth making because so much of what we associate with radio and television appears to conflict with marketplace principles. The outer shell is classically liberal, it would seem, but the inner workings are not.

The contrast between the liberal vision and the details of commercial broadcasting is dramatic. The creation of property in broadcasting is a story of highly politicized, conceptually indeterminate, ongoing collective actions and government interventions that systematically favor some groups and individuals over others. The creation of marketable, privately owned broadcast stations has involved a permanent system of federal licensing, systematic government elimination of small private entities from broadcasting in favor of large corporate and government institutions without compensation to the former or payment from the latter, and a glaringly contradictory legal regime that simultaneously forbids ownership of the airwaves and invites their treatment as private property. Ownership of broadcast programs is approximated by statistical abstractions, blurred by elaborate webs of contractual relations between program suppliers and distributors that are in turn heavily contorted by fluctuating government regulations, and in general subject to constant political wrangling between industry factions. And the economic success of the system rests on a bizarre and methodologically tenuous construction wherein the majority of the people involved, the listeners and viewers, are understood not as the free, active, rational individuals of liberal anthropology but as themselves a form of property, as audiences that are sold to advertisers. The commodities that make up the daily business of commercial broadcasting are not inevitable artifacts of a laissez-faire world. They are created and maintained as commodities through extensive political and social effort; their contorted character reflects the strains of that effort.

Although constructed in the name of the classical ideal of property, in sum, American commercial broadcasting calls that ideal into question. The commodification of broadcasting has been highly political. It has required ongoing government activity and all the concerns that go along with it: shifting struggles and alliances among interest groups, contingent moral and value judgments, and concerns for political legitimacy. It has involved a series of extra-market decisions about who gets what, on what terms, thus using government to allocate power and control on the most fundamental level. These phenomena, furthermore, need not be understood as the inevitable product of impersonal forces such as the market, the logic of capital, or autonomous technology. They are the result of a collective effort of imagination, an effort to square deep liberal political values of individual freedom and autonomy with the bureaucratic, collective, technological world of modern electronic communications. Broadcast property is thus political in that it involves the enactment of value choices, of a particular vision of how the world is and ought to be.

The case of commercial broadcasting raises the possibility that similar conflicts may emerge elsewhere as the American system is duplicated abroad and the role of electronic intangibles in the economy and everyday life continues to grow. As institutions turn more and more to privatization and the "market approach," conflicts and dilemmas will arise in courts, legislatures, and industry trade organizations concerning ownership boundaries, industry stability, and institutional organization.

One possible response to those dilemmas will be to echo the response of U.S. broadcasting: to speak in the language of the marketplace, competition, and private ownership. This strategy, based in the mythology of absolute property rights existing naturally outside the purview of the state, will lead at first to discussions of phantasms like perfect competition and to debates over whether or not to engage in after-the-fact regulation of privately-owned information industries. Eventually, this strategy will lead to a highly contradictory pattern of political discourse:

information industries will one moment speak the language of rights and minimal government interference and the next moment invite elaborate state intervention to maintain industry stability and growth.

An alternative strategy would be to begin with an acknowledgment of the deeply political character of property in an "information society." If property in electronic intangibles is reframed in political discourse as as much a privilege as a right, if the creation of ephemeral commodities is understood as a political choice instead of as the product of reifications like the market and technological progress, then political interventions of a relatively profound type might become ideologically, and thus politically, acceptable. Instead of trying to engage in after-the-fact regulation of the behavior of private owners of information properties, it might be feasible to try to politicize their ownership. And then the question of organizing information technologies might be framed, not as a pointless search for ways to limit government interference in the private rights of corporations, but as a matter of broad political choice in the service of democracy.

NOTES

This chapter is condensed, with a few additions and changes, from "Selling the Air: Property and the Politics of U.S. Commercial Broadcasting," *Media, Culture, and Society,* Vol. 16, No. 1, pp. 91–116; thanks to the editors for permission to republish.

1. By ideology, I do not mean false consciousness, but something like Althusser's shopworn but still useful definition of ideology as "systems of representation in which men [sic] live their imaginary relation to the real conditions of existence" (1977, p. 233).

2. Corporate liberalism understands liberal values such as private property not as hard rules but as general standards to be flexibly applied according to questions of efficiency and fact, as interpreted by expert bodies such as independent regulatory agencies. Moderate deviations from liberal norms are thus justified in terms of technical contingencies and the advice of corporate and government experts. What to the classical liberal appears as blurring and confusion is thus justified as a practical, expertly informed response to technical complexities (Streeter, forthcoming 1996).

3. On January 11, 1921, the secretary of Commerce prohibited amateurs from "broadcast[ing] weather reports, market reports, music, concerts, speeches, news or similar information" (Bensman, 1975, pp. 547–548).

4. The 1927 Act is often portrayed as a product of a "crisis of the airwaves" precipitated by legal uncertainty in the 1920s. Although the legal complications of the period certainly helped to goad Congress into action, the 1927 Act had been in process for several years, and most certainly would have been passed even without the famous "crisis" period.

REFERENCES

Althusser, L. (1977). *For Marx* (Ben Brewster, trans.). London: New Left Books.

Barnouw, E. (1966). *A Tower in Babel: A History of Broadcasting in the United States to 1933.* New York: Oxford.

Barnouw, E. (1968). *The Golden Web: A History of Broadcasting in the United States, Vol. II—1933 to 1953.* New York: Oxford University Press.

Bensman, M. R. (1975). "Regulation of Broadcasting by the Department of Commerce, 1921–1927," in L. W. Lichty and M. C. Topping (eds.), *American Broadcasting: A Sourcebook for the History of Radio and Television.* New York: Hastings House.

Chagall, D. (1981). "Can You Believe the Ratings?" pp. 197–209 in B. Cole (ed.), *Television Today.* New York: Oxford University Press.

Coase, R. H. (1959). "The Federal Communications Commission," *Journal of Law and Economics,* 11: 1–40.

Cohen, M. R. (1928). "Property and Sovereignty," *Cornell Law Quarterly,* 13: 8–30.

Douglas, S. J. (1987). *Inventing American Broadcasting 1899–1922.* Baltimore: Johns Hopkins University Press.

Ellmore, R. T. (1982). *Broadcasting Law and Regulation.* Blue Ridge Summit, Pa.: Tab Books, Inc.

FCC. (1941). *Report on Chain Broadcasting,* Docket No. 5060.

FCC. (October, 1980). "Evolution of Rules Regarding Network Practices," in *Final Report, New Television Networks: Entry, Jurisdiction, Ownership, and Regulation.*

Frow, J. (Winter 1988). "Repetition and Limitation: Computer Software and Copyright Law," *Screen,* 29, no. 1: 4–20.

Gitlin, T. (1985). *Inside Prime Time.* New York: Pantheon.

Grey, T. C. (1980). "The Disintegration of Property," pp. 69–70 in J. R. Pennock and J. W. Chapman (eds.) *Property: Nomos XXII.* New York: New York University Press.

Hawley, E. W. (1978). "The Discovery and Study of a 'Corporate Liberalism,'" *Business History Review,* LII, no. 3: 309–320.

Jhally, S. (1990). *The Codes of Advertising: Fetishism and the Political Economy of Meaning in the Consumer Society.* New York: Routledge.

Macpherson, C. B. (1978). "Introduction," pp. 1–14 in C. B. Macpherson (ed.), *Property: Mainstream and Critical Positions.* Toronto: University of Toronto Press.

Maxwell, R. (Spring-Summer 1991). "The Image is Gold: Value, the Audience Commodity, and Fetishism," *Journal of Film and Video,* 43, no. 1–2: 29–45.

Meehan, Eileen. (1990). "Why We Don't Count: The Commodity Audience," pp. 117–137 in Patricia Mellencamp (ed.), *Logics of Television: Essays in Cultural Criticism.* Bloomington: Indiana University Press.

Minow, N. (1961). Address to the National Association of Broadcasters, Washington D.C., May 9, reprinted p. 215 in F. J. Kahn (ed., 1984), *Documents of American Broadcasting,* 4th ed. Englewood Cliffs, N.J.: Prentice-Hall.

Nedelsky, J. (1990). *Private Property and the Limits of American Constitutionalism: The Madisonian Framework and Its Legacy.* Chicago: University of Chicago Press.

Nova (1992). "Can You Believe the Ratings?" (broadcast in the U.S. on the Public Broadcasting Service, February 19).

Reich, C. (1964). "The New Property," *Yale Law Journal,* LXXIII, no. 3: 733–787.

Schiller, Dan (1988). "How to Think About Information," pp. 27–43 in V. Mosco and J. Wasko (eds.), *The Political Economy of Information,* Madison: University of Wisconsin Press.

Sklar, M. J. (1988). *The Corporate Reconstruction of American Capitalism, 1890–1916: The Market, the Law, and Politics.* Cambridge: Cambridge University Press.

Smythe, D. (1977). "Communications: Blindspot of Western Marxism," *Canadian Journal of Political and Social Theory,* 1, no. 3: 1–27.

Sterling, C. H. (1984). *Electronic Media: A Guide to Trends in Broadcasting and Newer Technologies, 1920–1983.* New York: Praeger.

Sterling, C. H., and J. M. Kittross (1990). *Stay Tuned: A Concise History of American Broadcasting,* 2nd ed. Belmont, Calif.: Wadsworth.

Streeter, T. (forthcoming, 1996). *Selling the Air: A Critique of the Policy of Commercial Broadcasting in the U.S.* Chicago: University of Chicago Press.

Unger, R. (1975). *Knowledge and Politics,* New York: The Free Press.

U.S. Senate. (1926). *Radio Control,* Hearings before the Committee on Interstate Commerce, Sixty-Ninth Congress, First Session, at 42 (Hearings on S. 1 and S. 1754), Jan. 8 and 9.

Williams, Raymond. (1977). *Television: Technology and Cultural Form.* New York: Schocken.

Woodmansee, M. (Summer 1984). "The Genius and the Copyright: Economic and Legal Conditions of the Emergence of the 'Author,' " *Eighteenth-Century Studies,* 17:425–448.

Critical Ethnographies and the Concept of Resistance

Kevin M. Carragee

The study of the interaction between media audiences and media texts has become an increasingly significant part of a broader cultural studies tradition in communication research. Critical ethnographies of the ways in which audience members construct the meanings of media messages have challenged the mainstream "effects" tradition that has long dominated research (see, for example, Lewis, 1991; Morley, 1986, 1980; Press, 1989). In turn, these studies have received critical scrutiny (Carragee, 1990; Curran, 1990; Evans, 1990).

These developments have underscored the complexity of text-audience interaction; they also have produced a challenging environment for researchers concerned with the mass media's role in contemporary societies. This chapter attempts to contribute to this dynamic environment by providing a critical assessment of recent research on the interpretations of media texts by readers or viewers. In particular, this analysis provides an evaluation of current definitions of oppositional decoding or cultural resistance.

The concept of cultural resistance has become increasingly significant within critical audience research. It is directly related to the central themes of cultural studies scholarship: culture, ideology, and hegemony. The recurring emphasis on cultural resistance also provides a definition of text-audience interaction that celebrates the ability of readers and viewers to challenge the ideological meanings embedded within mainstream media texts.

In an effort to provide an appropriate context for this critical assessment, the analysis begins by assessing the central themes and concepts in critical research on audience reception of media texts. Often influenced by the encoding/decoding model outlined by Hall (1980a) and employed by Morley (1980), these studies have examined the interpretive processes employed by audience members in their decoding of media texts. Accusing past neo-Marxist research of ignoring audience activity (for example, the contributions of the Frankfurt School), these analyses view meaning as a product of the interaction between media messages and the multiple interpretive strategies utilized by readers or viewers.

The effort here is not to provide an exhaustive review of a rapidly expanding literature in media research; rather, an attempt is made to point out significant similarities within critical studies on audience interpretations of media texts. The focus on similarities should not indicate that these approaches share a completely integrated perspective. It does indicate, however, that these studies share a number of significant conceptual features.

Although properly avoiding perspectives that define readers and viewers as passive recipients of media messages, some studies within this tradition have a number of significant theoretical and conceptual problems.

These problems include difficulties associated with the encoding/decoding model. Specific studies within this tradition also advance problematic definitions of the following central concepts: polysemy, hegemony, and interpretive communities. The problematic definitions of polysemy and hegemony contribute to conceptual problems in the articulation of oppositional decoding or cultural resistance.

Current generalized definitions of cultural resistance frequently ignore the amount of cultural work necessary to construct an oppositional reading, while simultaneously failing to trace the degree to which these critical readings are representative of wider patterns of interpretation. Importantly, studies often have failed to distinguish between significant forms of resistance and trivial forms of "oppositional" decoding that are divorced from or remote to questions of political power. This failure has produced a depoliticized definition of cultural resistance. Finally, there is a growing tendency to romanticize audience members by emphasizing the degree to which they consistently construct oppositional readings of hegemonic media texts.

The chapter concludes by advancing a revised perspective on cultural hegemony and by providing a more precise and useful definition of cultural resistance or oppositional decoding. By critically examining this tradition of research, complex issues related to the mass media, culture, hegemony, and the interaction between media texts and marginalized subcultures can be confronted.

COMMON ASSUMPTIONS AND CONCEPTS IN CRITICAL RESEARCH ON AUDIENCE RECEPTION

The Encoding/Decoding Model and its Influence: Signification, Hegemony, the Active Audience, and the Polysemic Text

The encoding/decoding model developed by Hall (1980a) and employed by Morley (1980) was an effort to produce a comprehensive framework for an examination of the interaction between media texts and audience members. Influenced by the insights of the British cultural studies tradition, symbolic interactionism, phenomenology, semiotics, and structuralism (see Hall, 1980b), this model sought to avoid the reductionism of past approaches to this interaction by emphasizing the historical and cultural contexts that shape the production and interpretation of media texts.

Hall's and Morley's initial articulation of this model and studies influenced by their work stress the mass media role in the signification process; that is, these studies affirm the media's decisive contribution to the construction of meanings and values within a society (see, for example, Dahlgren, 1988, 1985; Hall, 1979; Morley, 1986; Sigman & Fry, 1985; Press, 1989). As storytelling institutions, media organizations provide their audiences with definitions of social and political realities. By underscoring the media's role in the signification process, critical research on audience reception avoids the theoretical difficulties of approaches to cultural works and practices that assume that these artifacts and social processes are simply reflections of an existing social order. The integration of sociological and semiological approaches to mass mediated discourse was an important contribution of the encoding/decoding model and the studies informed by it.

Although varied approaches have acknowledged the mass media's contribution to the construction of meaning (see, for example, Carey, 1975; Newcomb & Hirsch, 1984), critical media research in general and critical studies on audience reception in particular have relied on Gramsci's (1971) concept of hegemony as a central theoretical construct in assessing the nature of the media's cultural production. Hegemony refers to the complex processes by which ruling classes or groups shape popular consent through the production and diffusion of meanings and values. By focusing on the significance of cultural production, the concept of hegemony reminds us that the "struggle for economic or political power . . . takes place alongside the struggle for meaning" (Lewis, 1991, p. 41). Given the centralization of symbolic processes within the media, these institutions play a significant role in hegemonic processes that serve to maintain the existing social order. Varied researchers have noted the complex, contradictory, and evolving character of hegemonic ideology. Williams (1977, p. 112), for example, writes that hegemony "has continually to be renewed, recreated, defended and modified. It is also continually resisted, limited, altered, challenged by pressures not at all its own." The continuing struggle for meaning concerning social and political issues produces hegemonic ideology characterized by contradiction, not consistency. The attention given to the hegemonic role of the mass media within critical media research links moments of reception to issues of political and cultural power.

The encoding/decoding model and critical studies on audience reception attempt to recognize the media's hegemonic role in a number of ways. These studies often emphasize that the encoding processes within media institutions produce texts that primarily express preferred or dominant ideological meanings. However, given the contradictory and evolving character of hegemony, these texts do not articulate a seamless and univocal dominant ideology. Ideological gaps and contradictions exist within media messages, and cultural forms become sites of struggle over hegemonic meanings and values (see, for example, Dahlgren, 1988; Gitlin, 1980; Hall, 1979; Lewis, 1991; Morley, 1986, 1980).

Critical research on audience reception frequently has focused on the degree to which audience members accept or resist the hegemonic or preferred meanings and values embedded in media texts (see Fiske, 1987; Morley, 1980; Press, 1989; Sigman & Fry, 1985; Steiner, 1988). This emphasis was evident in Hall's (1980a) definition of the encoding/decoding model; he pointed to three primary decoding positions: dominant, negotiated, and oppositional, all defined in relation to the degree to which audience members accept the preferred or dominant meanings within media texts. Although this definition of decoding positions suffers from a number of shortcomings, it did serve as a useful heuristic device, stimulating a range of studies on audience interpretations of media texts. Ang (1985, p. 251) emphasizes that research has defined television viewers "as more than just passive receivers of already fixed 'messages' . . . opening up the possibility of thinking about television as an area of cultural struggle." The attention given to the varied forms of resistance to dominant meanings and values underscores the degree to which hegemonic ideology remains contested. The repeated focus on cultural resistance within this tradition distinguishes it from past Marxist or neo-Marxist scholarship, which tended to emphasize the mass media's ability to penetrate the consciousness of subordinate groups.

A salient characteristic of critical audience research is its definition of audience members as active participants in their encounters with the media. According to this perspective, media texts do not impose their meanings on passive audiences; rather, meaning is a product of the interaction between these texts and the interpretations of their readers and viewers (see, for example, Allor, 1988; Hall, 1980a; Jensen, 1987; Morley, 1980; Peterson, 1987; Radway, 1984). In a discussion of television and its viewers, Fiske (1988, p. 247) writes that "meaning is produced when the discourses of the viewer meet those of the program in a moment of semiosis." Lewis (1991, p. 47) underscores the "need to understand cultural products (or 'texts') as they are understood by audiences." More broadly, Dahlgren (1988, p. 291) points out that "[r]eception research can be seen as a step towards analytically 'rehabilitating the audience,' placing the active meaning production of viewers in the centre of research focus." By documenting both the complexity of media messages and the varied interpretive strategies employed by audience members in their decoding of these texts, critical audience research has helped to reveal the ways in which a single text will be interpreted in multiple, indeed at times contradictory, ways by its readers or viewers.

Although emphasizing the signification process, hegemony and the active role of audience members in interpreting media messages, studies within this tradition also define media texts as polysemic; that is, these texts are characterized by a multiplicity of meanings. This polysemy encourages diverse interpretations of a single text. Dahlgren (1988, p. 291), for example, describes television news as polysemic because it offers "an array of possible readings." Similarly, Deming (1988) characterizes the meanings within television texts in general as diverse and unstable. Fiske (1987, 1986) repeatedly has stressed the polysemic nature of media texts. He defines television programs as open texts because of their use of certain textual devices, including irony and metaphor, and because of the ideological contradictions they contain. Fiske also argues that these texts include oppositional discourses and that the popularity of television is tied to its polysemy. As we shall see shortly, the degree to which media texts can be defined as open texts remains a subject of debate within critical audience research.

By frequently emphasizing the active role of audience members in constructing meanings, by devoting attention to the ways in which readers and viewers resist dominant ideological meanings and by characterizing media texts as polysemic, researchers within this tradition often explicitly distance their analyses from past Marxist or neo-Marxist media research, including the contributions of the Frankfurt School. This past research is faulted for its exclusively text-based analyses of the media's ideological role and for its explicit or implicit definition of audience members as passive consumers of a univocal dominant ideology distributed by cultural institutions (for examples of this criticism of past research see Allor, 1988; Fiske, 1987; Radway, 1984; Richardson & Corner, 1986). In contrast with earlier text-centered forms of Marxist criticism, Morley (1983, p. 106) provides a representative appraisal of the complexity of cultural analysis: "the meaning produced by the encounter of text and subject cannot be 'read off' straight from textual characteristics. The text cannot be considered in isolation from its historical conditions of production and consumption."

Decoding and Cultural Codes and Discourses

Critical audience research has focused a good deal of its attention on tracing the connections between audience decodings and the contexts in which readers and viewers reside. This research has revealed that social categories, such as class and gender, do not simply determine audience interpretations of media messages. Instead, social categories influence the cultural codes and discourses available to social actors and these codes and discourses help to shape audience interpretations of media texts (see Morley, 1986, 1983; Radway, 1984; Richardson & Corner, 1986, for example). Morley's (1980) research on audience interpretations of *Nationwide,* a British television news magazine program, documents the complex interaction between the structural positions that social actors inhabit, the codes and discourses associated with these positions, and the influence of these codes and discourses on audience interpretations.

Research by Bourdieu (1986) also has underscored the significance of cultural codes and competencies in influencing how people interact with and understand cultural forms. Bourdieu emphasizes the role of the educational system in providing access to discourses and codes that, in turn, shape how people interpret both their world and cultural products. Given structural inequalities in access to material resources and to educational institutions, Bourdieu contends that hierarchies of "cultural competence" are created. In this sense, cultural practices are shaped by educational and class position.

Oppositional Decoding and Cultural Resistance

A significant influence of the encoding/decoding model has been an increased research awareness of and interest in the degree to which readers and viewers resist the hegemonic meanings and values articulated in media texts. Morley (1980) documents oppositional decodings of *Nationwide,* whereas Radway (1984) explores the ways in which women interpreted and used romance novels as a form of real, albeit limited, resistance to patriarchy. Fiske (1987, 1986) stresses the oppositional character of viewers' interpretations of television; indeed, he argues that the pleasure derived from television by subordinate groups is a product of their resistance to the medium's preferred meanings. In a recent contribution, Lewis (1991) explores the ways in which some viewers resist the meanings and values expressed by television news and by *The Cosby Show*. Other researchers have examined oppositional decodings of varied forms of media content, including television situation comedies (Press, 1989), magazine and newspaper content (Steiner, 1988), and a television science fiction program (Jenkins, 1988).

Researchers often have linked these forms of cultural resistance to the codes and discourses employed by marginalized subcultures within contemporary capitalist societies. Varied studies, for example, have examined the interaction between women and media texts, often affirming both the ways in which female readers and viewers challenge patriarchal values embedded in media texts and the tendency of women to seek alternative pleasures from mainstream media texts (see Morley, 1986; Press, 1989; Radway, 1984; Steiner, 1988). In an analysis of newsletters and novels produced by the fans of *Star Trek*, Jenkins (1988, p. 87) argues that these artifacts represent a form of cultural resistance in which "marginalized subcultural groups (women, the young, gays etc.) . . . pry open space for their cultural concerns within dominant representations." Other researchers have examined youth subcultures and their media use; these studies often have focused on the role of rock music and youth culture in articulating oppositional meanings and values (see Grossberg, 1983/ 1984; Hebdige, 1979; Lull, 1987).

Interpretive Communities

Some critical studies on audience interpretations of media texts define particular media audiences as interpretive communities (Jenkins, 1988; Radway, 1984; Steiner, 1988). These communities share certain meanings and interests that shape both their media use and their interpretations of media content. Derived from reader-response criticism (see Fish, 1980), this concept is an effort to explicate similarities and differences in the decoding of media texts. It also highlights the social, not idiosyncratic, nature of reception and, therefore, represents one means by which to place readers or viewers within broader social and cultural contexts.

SOME PROBLEMS CONFRONTING CRITICAL RESEARCH ON AUDIENCE RECEPTION

Although critical perspectives on the interaction between media texts and their audiences have enriched our understanding of the media's ideological role, these studies are plagued by a number of shortcomings. These problems include difficulties associated with the encoding/decoding model and sweeping characterizations of the polysemic character of media texts. In addition, specific studies within this tradition provide problematic definitions of the following concepts: hegemony, oppositional decoding, and interpretive communities.

Pillai (1992), Richardson and Corner (1986), Ang (1985), Streeter (1984), Wren-Lewis (1983), and Morley (1981) have advanced varied critiques of the encoding/decoding model. These critiques have focused on the model's instrumental vision of language, its failure to recognize that both preferred meanings and preferred readings must be *achieved* through complex processes of encoding and decoding, its inattention to the form of media texts, its failure to trace the possible connection between decodings of specific media texts and the general practice of media consumption, and its tendency to define these texts as rather passively reproducing meanings derived from a broader culture. The critical debate focusing on the utility of this model also indicates the need to move beyond a description of decoding positions as dominant, negotiated, and oppositional. Despite attempts to refine this model, too many studies on audience reception continue to employ these generalized characterizations of decoding, ignoring problems associated with the range and nature of audience interpretations within each position. Studies by Steiner (1988) and Jenkins (1988) illustrate the continued use of these problematic generalizations because of their failure to recognize the diversity of discourses in society. As we will discuss shortly, the concept of oppositional decoding in particular needs to be refined.

Sweeping characterizations of the polysemic nature of media texts represent an additional problem in some critical analyses of media audiences. This problem is especially evident in Fiske's work. His description (1987, p. 95) of television texts and their viewers as part of a "semiotic democracy" ignores the degree to which textual meanings and television viewers exist within systems of domination and subordination. By repeatedly emphasizing the openness of television texts, Fiske also neglects the range and depth of research indicating that media texts primarily express hegemonic meanings and values (see Gitlin, 1982, 1980; Hall, 1979; Hallin, 1987; Kellner, 1982; Morley, 1980). Studies affirming the openness of media texts overlook the fact that texts, unlike individual words and images, are constructions and as constructions their polysemy is limited by syntagmatic relations (for a discussion of this issue see Morley, 1981).

In an analysis of critical audience research, Condit (1989) argues that polysemy has become a generalized concept. She contends that a distinction needs to be made between polyvalence, the tendency of readers and viewers to construct varied interpretations of a single text, and polysemy. Condit (p. 107) argues that the "emphasis on the polysemous quality of texts . . . may be overdrawn. The claim perhaps needs to be scaled back to indicate that responses and interpretations are generally polyvalent, and texts themselves are occasionally or partially polysemic. It is not that texts routinely feature unstable denotation but that instability of connotation requires viewers to judge texts from their own value systems." The distinction between polyvalence and polysemy highlights a tension evident in discussions of the latter concept: Is polysemy a product of intertextual relationships? Or is it a product of the constructions or interpretations of audience members?

Given this discussion, critical researchers need to be far more sensitive in their use of this concept. They need to document, not assume, the polysemic character of media texts and they need to define the range of this polysemy. By overemphasizing the polysemic nature of media texts, some researchers have exaggerated the degree to which these texts encourage forms of oppositional decoding. More broadly, the concept of polyvalence offers a useful means to clarify the difficulties associated with the generalized construct of polysemy because it provides an analytical distinction between textual characteristics and the interpretive processes performed by audience members. The degree of ideological openness of media texts remains an empirical question; it can be resolved only through close readings of these texts and through careful analyses of audience interpretations of these messages.

Overstated arguments concerning the openness of television texts and the corresponding tendency to magnify the degree to which these texts produce forms of cultural resistance are a product, in part, of the problematic use of the concept of hegemony. Some researchers conflate hegemony with a unified dominant ideology and, consequently, are surprised by the ideological inconsistencies and variability in media discourse. More sensitive definitions of hegemony stress the mutable and contradictory character of hegemonic meanings and values; these definitions emphasize that the media's hegemonic role evolves in an effort to adapt to changing political circumstances and challenges (see, for example, Hall, 1979; Hallin, 1987; Williams, 1977). O'Shea (1989) points out that Fiske's definition of hegemony, for example, ignores the ways in which this concept draws attention to discursive struggles in a society. O'Shea concludes that

[r]ather than being pleasantly surprised that television displays gaps or spaces in the ideologies of bourgeois individualism or patriarchy [for example], one should expect this; however, "dominant," these are still only two of the discourses in play in modern societies.

Critical researchers also need to devote more attention to their definition of oppositional decoding. This concept, like polysemy, has become far too generalized. Fiske (1987) provides examples of opposition or resistance to television's dominant meanings that range from the trivial to the substantial. Moreover, he provides no empirical support for his sweeping, yet reductionistic, claim that the pleasure derived from television by subordinate groups is linked to their resistance to the medium's dominant ideological meanings. An equally plausible, if still unsupported, contention is that subordinate groups derive pleasure from television precisely because of their identification with hegemonic meanings and values. Fiske's research and other studies of audience reception also fail to specify the degree to which oppositional decodings are representative of wider patterns of interpretations. Similarly, these works frequently fail to acknowledge the limited size of the "critical subcultures" that tend to produce forms of oppositional decoding (for a discussion of this issue see Budd, Entman & Steinman, 1990).

Lewis (1991) points to an additional problem with the definition of oppositional decoding in some studies. By underscoring the fact that some television programs will contain textual emphases antagonistic to dominant ideological meanings or values, Lewis reminds us that a viewer interpreting these meanings in ways consistent with these critical textual emphases is *not* engaged in a form of oppositional decoding. Rather, this type of interpretation "works *with* [emphasis in the original] the message, not in opposition to it" (p. 68). Lewis labels these readings as "resistive" or "popular." He emphasizes that these readings are *not* dependent on the access of audience members to oppositional discourses external to media texts. This analytic distinction is a significant one; it is not made in all critical ethnographies, some of which employ the concept of oppositional decoding in ways consistent with Lewis's definition of resistive or popular readings.

Although Lewis's distinction is a useful one, his terminology is unfortunate. The use of the term "popular" to describe a reading that is congruent with critical or emancipatory moments in television's discourse may serve to exaggerate the tendency of American television to supply these moments. American television remains primarily a means to produce and reproduce dominant meanings. The "popular" tends to be hegemonic, not emancipatory. Similarly, the use of the term "resistive" to describe these readings may serve only to confuse the difference in kind between these interpretations and forms of cultural resistance. To his credit, Lewis recognizes this difficulty (p. 69).

For these reasons, both terms appear problematic. An alternative? These readings may be described as critical but congruent; that is, they are critical of dominant ideological values precisely because they are congruent with the limited number of textual meanings associated with emancipatory moments in the discourse of television.

Research on oppositional decoding also needs to address issues related to the power of media texts to channel and limit forms of resistance.

Modleski (1986) points out that characterizations of audience interpretations as oppositional often neglect the degree to which these "resistances" fall within parameters established by the culture industry. Similarly, O'Shea (1989, p. 377) argues that "[m]any of Fiske's examples of 'subversion' far from connecting to a challenge to the existing social order, can be seen as ways of living out subordination more happily." These views reflect the insights of Adorno and Horkheimer (1979), who underscore the culture industry's ability to incorporate challenges and to set limits on the nature of resistance. This important analytic contribution of the Frankfurt School, a tradition much criticized by researchers working within cultural studies, has been ignored by many critical ethnographies.

The recent emphasis on oppositional decoding and acts of cultural resistance reflects growing tendencies to romanticize media audiences and to overstate their power (for a discussion of these issues see Condit, 1989; Schudson, 1987). Both tendencies are evident in Fiske's (1987, p. 313) argument that in the realm of culture "[m]eanings and pleasure circulate . . . without any real distinction between producers and consumers." This statement overlooks the unequal distribution of power between the constructions and discourses of the media and their audiences. For example, although viewers do negotiate the meanings of the television texts they encounter, their definitions do not match the discursive power of a centralized storytelling institution. The increasingly romanticized vision of audience members may owe less to the empirical reality of mediated encounters than it does to the desire of researchers to "empower" these audiences and to identify constituencies who reject the preferred meanings articulated by media texts.

The preceding discussion is not an effort to deny the reality of cultural resistance. But researchers need to remain aware of the constraints confronting audience members in their interaction with media texts. These constraints include the power of texts to shape audience interpretations, the very availability of specific types of texts at particular historical moments, the historical context that shapes both the production and consumption of texts, and the access of audience members to oppositional codes and discourses. Finally, critical ethnographies need to be more sensitive to the degree of "cultural work" necessary to produce an oppositional reading (for a discussion of this issue see Condit, 1989). Readers and viewers in American society live within a context that actively discourages such cultural work given the recurring emphasis on media exposure as a "simple" form of entertainment and pleasure, devoid of ideological or cultural significance. Within this context, the encounters of audience members with current media texts are shaped, in part, by their previous interactions with and expectations of the media (for a useful discussion of this issue see Biltereyst, 1991). The lack of attention to these constraints in some critical research on audience interpretations of texts leads to an exaggerated sense of the power of readers and viewers to resist media influence (Curran, 1990).

Finally, research on oppositional decoding needs to distinguish between resistances to specific and central hegemonic meanings and values, which represent a challenge to the existing social order, and decodings, which contradict textual emphases divorced from or remote to significant political and social issues. If the concept of opposition or resistance is to have real meaning, both for audience members who engage in this activity and researchers who study this process, it must be reserved for those forms of action that have political consequences. Without distinctions of this kind, the concept of oppositional decoding remains far too generalized. Budd, Entman, and Steinman (1990) stress the need for research to examine the degree to which resistance to hegemonic meanings in media content informs political cognitions and behaviors. Forms of cultural resistance without a connection to broader political knowledge or action would appear to have little or no consequence for the established social order.

A final problematic construct employed in some critical analyses of media audiences is the concept of interpretive communities. This concept remains underdeveloped and poorly defined in studies by Steiner (1988) and Jenkins (1988). Both studies fail to account for the origin of these communities. Steiner and Jenkins also neglect past criticisms of the utility of this concept (see Freund, 1987; Scholes, 1985). In a critique of the use of this concept in reader-response scholarship, Scholes (pp. 149–165) advances multiple concerns, including the lack of a precise definition, the concept's inconsistent application, and the lack of attention to textual properties that construct meanings.

Given the vague manner in which this concept is defined, central questions concerning its character and significance remain unexplored. For example, how are interpretive communities similar to or distinct from social categories such as class or gender? Do social categories influence the formation of interpretive communities? How are interpretive communities similar to or distinct from subcultures and taste publics? If the bonds of interpretive communities are forged primarily by their common uses and interpretations of media texts, is the term community a useful description of these collectivities? (For a more extended discussion of these issues see Carragee, 1990.) At present, this concept needs far more explication and its utility may be limited to those instances where there is direct social interaction between audience members. This condition is fulfilled, in part, in Radway's (1984) study of female readers of romance novels.

CONCLUSION

A discussion of the shortcomings within critical ethnographies of media audiences highlights the need for greater precision in the definition of the following concepts: polysemy, hegemony, and interpretive communities. The problematic definitions of polysemy and hegemony contribute to weaknesses in the development of the concept of oppositional decoding or cultural resistance. While critical research on audience reception has deepened our understanding of the media's ideological role, these conceptual difficulties have weakened the explanatory power of this research.

Future studies should provide detailed analyses of the interaction between specific textual meanings and particular media audiences. These texts and audiences must be located within their proper historical and cultural contexts. A precise definition and application of the concept of hegemony will produce studies that remain sensitive to the systems of domination and subordination that shape the processes of encoding and decoding. Broad characterizations of the openness of media texts and of the power of audience members to construct oppositional readings of these texts are likely to neglect central questions of political, cultural, and economic power.

Additional research should explore the complex relationships between the structural positions social actors inhabit, the codes and discourses associated with these positions, and the influence of these codes and discourses on audience constructions. Morley (1986, p. 43) provides a useful recommendation for future research when he writes of the need to

formulate a position from which we can see the person actively reproducing meanings from the restricted range of cultural resources which his or her structural position has allowed them access to.

Studies also must examine the factors that enhance or inhibit access to oppositional codes and discourses.

More care needs to be devoted to the definition of oppositional decoding. Condit (1989, p. 117) encourages greater specificity in ethnographies exploring forms of cultural resistance: "[i]t is not enough to describe a program or an interpretation as oppositional. It is essential to describe what particular things are resisted and how that resistance occurs." It would be useful, for example, to examine the degree to which the processes of interpretation and resistance vary across media texts that are designed for different purposes; that is, how is cultural resistance realized and what form does it take in interaction with persuasive texts (advertisements), entertainment texts (comedic and dramatic content), and informative texts (news)?

The current generalized definition of cultural resistance inadvertently trivializes that which it seeks to affirm by avoiding distinctions between insubstantial and substantial rejections of textual meanings. The ability of readers and viewers to contradict or reject textual emphases does not necessarily constitute a form of oppositional decoding or cultural resistance. The latter occurs only when audience members resist or substantially modify textual emphases linked to issues of political and cultural power. Finally, oppositional decoding or cultural resistance occurs only when audience members employ discourses external to media texts to critically evaluate dominant meanings and values embedded within media messages.

Cultural resistance that matters informs political knowledge and action. Research examining this concept, then, should focus on central political and social issues and avoid trivializing resistance by equating it with a simple rejection or modification of textual emphases divorced from questions of political power.

Recent research by Gamson (1992) on the relationship between media discourse and political consciousness among working people provides *one* means by which to sharpen the definition of cultural resistance. Drawing on past research examining social movements, Gamson identifies three major dimensions of collective action frames in both media discourse and in the conversations of working people about political issues: an injustice component (an identification of a harm produced by human action), an agency component (a belief that it is possible to change conditions through collective action), and an identity component (the identification of a specific adversary).

Ethnographic investigations of cultural resistance would be well served by examining the degree to which audience interpretations of media texts are related to these collective action frames. In contrast to generalized definitions of the forms of cultural resistance, these frames do have political consequences because of their connection to political knowledge and, in particular, because of their potential connection to collective action. These frames are not, of course, the only potential interpretive pattern with political consequences, but they do suggest one fruitful approach to a more refined exploration of cultural resistance.

Clearly, there will be considerable research debate concerning the degree to which specific textual meanings are linked to issues of political and cultural power; considerable debate also will focus on what rejections of textual emphases constitute meaningful forms of cultural resistance. These debates are unavoidable, indeed essential. The current evasion of these troubling distinctions by some studies inhibits the development of our understanding of how hegemonic meanings and values are both accepted and resisted.

The challenges, then, confronting critical ethnographies of media audiences are many. A proper understanding of the interaction between audience members and media texts demands an analysis of this relationship within specific historical and cultural contexts. A comprehensive understanding of the mass media's ideological role is ill-served by imprecise definitions of cultural resistance and by increasingly romanticized visions of the ability of readers and viewers to resist the centralized discursive power of media institutions.

REFERENCES

Adorno, T. & Horkheimer, M. (1979). The culture industry: Enlightenment as mass deception. In J. Curran, M. Gurevitch & J. Woollocott (Eds.), *Mass Communication and Society* (pp. 349–383). Beverly Hills, CA: Sage.

Allor, M. (1988). Relocating the site of the audience. *Critical Studies in Mass Communication, 5,* 217–233.

Ang, I. (1985). The battle between television and its audiences. In P. Drummond & R. Patterson (Eds.), *Television in Transition* (pp. 250–266). London: British Film Institute.

Biltereyst, D. (1991). Resisting American hegemony: A comparative analysis of the reception of domestic and US fiction. *European Journal of Communication, 6,* 469–497.

Bourdieu, P. (1986). The aristocracy of culture. In R. Collins, J. Curran, N. Garnham, P. Scannell, P. Schlesinger & C. Sparks (Eds.), *Media, Culture & Society* (pp. 164–193). Beverly Hills, CA: Sage.

Budd, M., Entman, R., & Steinman, C. (1990). The affirmative character of U.S. cultural studies. *Critical Studies in Mass Communication, 7,* 169–184.

Carragee, K. (1990). Interpretive media study and interpretive social science. *Critical Studies in Mass Communication, 7,* 81–96.

Carey, J. (1975). A cultural approach to communications. *Communication, 2,* 1–22.

Condit, C. (1989). The rhetorical limits of polysemy. *Critical Studies in Mass Communication, 6,* 103–122.

Curran, J. (1990). The new revisionism in mass communication research. *European Journal of Communication, 5,* 135–164.

Dahlgren, P. (1988). What's the meaning of this? Viewers' plural sense-making of TV news. *Media, Culture and Society, 10,* 285–301.

Dahlgren, P. (1985). The modes of reception: For a hermeneutics of TV news. In P. Drummond & R. Patterson (Eds.), *Television in Transition* (pp. 235–249). London: British Film Institute.

Deming, C. (1988). For television-centered television criticism: Lessons learned from feminism. In J. Anderson (Ed.), *Communication Yearbook 11* (pp. 148–176). Beverly Hills, CA: Sage.

Evans, W. (1990). The interpretive turn in media research. *Critical Studies in Mass Communication, 7,* 147–168.

Fish, S. (1980). *Is There a Text in This Class?* Cambridge, MA: Harvard University Press.

Fiske, J. (1988). Critical response: Meaningful moments. *Critical Studies in Mass Communication, 5,* 246–251.

Fiske, J. (1987). *Television Culture.* London: Methuen.

Fiske, J. (1986). Television: Polysemy and popularity. *Critical Studies in Mass Communication, 3,* 391–408.

Freund, E. (1987). *The Return of the Reader.* London: Methuen.

Gamson, W. (1992). *Talking Politics.* New York: Cambridge University Press.

Gitlin, T. (1982). Prime time ideology: The hegemonic process in television entertainment. In H. Newcomb (Ed.), *Television: The Critical View* (pp. 426–454). New York: Oxford University Press.

Gitlin, T. (1980). *The Whole World is Watching.* Berkeley, CA: University of California Press.

Gramsci, A. (1971). *Prison Notebooks.* New York: International Publishers.

Grossberg, L. (1983/1984). The politics of youth culture: Some observations about rock and roll in American culture. *Social Text, 8,* 104–126.

Hall, S. (1980a). Encoding/Decoding. In S. Hall, D. Hobson, A. Lowe & P. Willis (Eds.), *Culture, Media, Language* (pp. 128–138). London: Hutchinson.

Hall, S. (1980b). Cultural studies and the centre: Some problematic and problems. In S. Hall, D. Hobson, A. Lowe & P. Willis (Eds.), *Culture, Media, Language* (pp. 15–47). London: Hutchinson.

Hall, S. (1979). Culture, media and the "ideological effect." In J. Curran, M. Gurevitch, & J. Woollocott (Eds.), *Mass Communication and Society* (pp. 315–348). Beverly Hills, CA: Sage.

Hallin, D. (1987). Hegemony: The American news media from Vietnam to El Salvador, a study of ideological change and its limits. In D. Paletz (Ed.), *Political Communication Research* (pp. 3–25). Norwood, NJ: Ablex.

Hebdige, D. (1979). Reggae, rastas and rudies. In J. Curran, M. Gurevitch & J. Woollocott (Eds.), *Mass Communication and Society* (pp. 426–439). Beverly Hills, CA: Sage.

Jenkins, H. (1988). Star Trek rerun, reread, rewritten: Fan writing as a form of textual poaching. *Critical Studies in Mass Communication, 5,* 85–107.

Jensen, K. B. (1987). Qualitative audience research: Toward an integrative approach to reception. *Critical Studies in Mass Communication, 4,* 21–36.

Kellner, D. (1982). TV, ideology, and emancipatory popular culture. In H. Newcomb (Ed.), *Television: The Critical View* (pp. 386–422). New York: Oxford University Press.

Lewis, J. (1991). *The Ideological Octopus.* New York: Routledge.

Lull, J. (1987). Thrashing in the pit: An ethnography of San Francisco punk subculture. In T. Lindlof (Ed.), *Natural Audiences* (pp. 225–252). Norwood, NJ: Ablex.

Modleski, T. (1986). Introduction. In T. Modleski (Ed.), *Studies in Entertainment* (pp. xi–xix). Bloomington, IN: Indiana University Press.

Morley, D. (1986). *Family Television.* London: Comedia.

Morley, D. (1983). Cultural transformations: The politics of resistance. In H. Davis & P. Walton (Eds.), *Language, Image, Media* (pp. 104–117). New York: St. Martin's Press.

Morley, D. (1981). The *Nationwide* audience: A critical postscript. *Screen Education, 39,* 3–14.

Morley, D. (1980). *The* Nationwide *Audience.* London: British Film Institute.

Newcomb, H. & Hirsch, P. (1984). Television as a cultural forum. In W. D. Rowland & B. Watkins (Eds.), *Interpreting Television* (pp. 58–73). Beverly Hills, CA: Sage.

O'Shea, A. (1989). Television as culture: More than just texts and readers. *Media, Culture and Society, 11,* 373–379.

Peterson, E. (1987). Media consumption and girls who want to have fun. *Critical Studies in Mass Communication, 4,* 37–50.

Pillai, P. (1992). Rereading Stuart Hall's encoding/decoding model. *Communication Theory, 2 & 3,* 221–233.

Press, A. (1989). Class and gender in the hegemonic process: Class differences in women's perceptions of television realism and identification with television characters. *Media, Culture and Society, 11,* 229–251.

Radway, J. (1984). *Reading the Romance.* Chapel Hill: University of North Carolina Press.

Richardson, K. & Corner, J. (1986). Reading reception: Mediation and the transparency of a TV programme. *Media, Culture and Society, 8,* 485–508.

Scholes, R. (1985). *Textual Power.* New Haven: Yale University Press.

Schudson, M. (1987). The new validation of popular culture: Sense and sentimentality in academia. *Critical Studies in Mass Communication, 4,* 51–68.

Sigman, S. & Fry, D. (1985). Differential ideology and language use: Readers' reconstructions and descriptions of news events. *Critical Studies in Mass Communication, 2,* 307–322.

Steiner, L. (1988). Oppositional decoding as a form of resistance. *Critical Studies in Mass Communication, 5,* 1–15.

Streeter, T. (1984). An alternative approach to television research: Developments in British Cultural Studies at Birmingham. In W. D. Rowland & B. Watkins (Eds.), *Interpreting Television* (pp. 74–97). Beverly Hills, CA: Sage.

Williams, R. (1977). *Marxism and Literature.* Oxford: Oxford University Press.

Wren-Lewis, J. (1983). The encoding/decoding model: Criticisms and redevelopments for research on decoding. *Media, Culture and Society, 5,* 179–197.

Unarmed and Dangerous: The Gibraltar Killings Meet the Press

Andy Ruddock

INTRODUCTION

On March 5, 1988, Mairaid Farrel, Sean Savage, and Daniel McCann were shot dead by the Special Air Service (SAS; the British Army's equivalent of the Green Berets) in the British Colony of Gibraltar. All three had been active members of the Irish Republican Army (IRA). This much can be said for sure. What is less certain is what this event tells us about the war in Northern Ireland. At the time of the killings, British authorities claimed that the three dead had been on a bombing mission aimed at a regularly scheduled military parade. The further announcement that a car bomb had been found close to the site of that parade seemed to close the incident: The SAS's actions had prevented an attack that would have caused an enormous loss of life, both military and civilian (the ceremony in question being a long-standing tourist attraction).

In the days that followed, however, a large body of contradictory evidence emerged, casting doubt in some circles on the official version of events. No bomb had in fact been found, either at the parade ground or anywhere else in the colony, although bomb-making equipment was allegedly discovered in Spain. In addition, none of the dead had been armed. Thus even if Farrel, McCann, and Savage had been planning some sort of attack, they posed no immediate threat to public safety at the time of their deaths. Together with eyewitness accounts that emphasized the premeditated, execution style of the killings, this new information raised a disturbing but familiar question: Does the British Army operate under orders to kill IRA members on sight whenever possible?

Seen from this perspective, the Gibraltar killings represented an ideological crisis for British hegemony in Northern Ireland. Here was a moment in which marginalized definitions of the nature of the conflict between the British government and Republican forces threatened to take center stage, upsetting years of "mainstream" discourse. The process of hegemony involves an ongoing ideological project that protects "commonsense" social meanings from the assault of deviance. This process involves the practice of articulation, whereby the material elements of the social world are connected to a particular meaning or set of coherent meanings from a semiotic universe rich with potential ambiguities (Angus, 1992).

Applied to the Gibraltar killings, the question we need to ask, then, is what are the range of meanings habitually connected to the signifier "IRA" or "IRA member," and how did the actions of the SAS threaten to exploit an inevitable polysemy that is denied by hegemonic ways of seeing?

TERRORISM AND HEGEMONY: WE KNOW IT WHEN WE SEE IT

To begin, we need to understand how dominant views of who the IRA are (with regard to the British context) respond to a very particular set of associations that are a good deal more contestable than is often acknowledged. Generally speaking, the IRA is cast as a terrorist organization. But what does this mean? What is terrorism? Perhaps the best definition of what people normally mean by the term *terrorist* is given by Brian Jenkins, who states simply that terrorism is "what the bad guys do" (cited in Martin, 1985, p. 128). This quote is valuable because it captures both the essence of the term's popular connotation and the absence of any fixed criteria dictating its use. Generally speaking, "terrorism" is used to describe the activities of clandestine military organizations that oppose the recognized political establishment of a nation or group of nations.

However, certain definitions of what represents terrorist activity problematize this view. For example, in Holton's description of terrorism as any act of physical violence aimed at communicating a message rather than achieving a physical objective (the taking of life or ground) (Holton, 1978), we see an expanded meaning that embraces the activities of many state-sponsored agencies. It is clear, for instance, that although the SAS's storming of the Iranian Embassy in London in 1980 was ostensibly aimed at a tangible goal, the rescuing of hostages, it also served a pointed symbolic function in demonstrating a willingness to resort to spectacular forms of violence if provoked.

Indeed the history of the SAS makes it very difficult to think about terrorism as referring to the use of specific strategies of violence. The Regiment has been able to survive the era of postwar spending cuts by demonstrating an ability to adapt to the new demands of the unconventional war theatres that proliferated in the ashes of the Empire. From Kenya to Northern Ireland, the SAS have been the poster boys for strategists such as Brigadier Frank Kitson, who has argued that the only way to fight terrorism is to become the terrorist (1974).

We have, then, units of the British Army operating in much the same way, strategically speaking, as their opponents. If we add this to the argument emerging from Irish Republican positions that the British Army represents, to them, not a benevolent police force but an unwanted army of occupation, then we have a counter-hegemonic problem that threatens to disarticulate conventional connections between signifier (the British Army) and signified (a pro social force operating from a defensive posture). In other words, against a discursive backdrop delegitimizing the Republican cause by connecting it to images of deviance and barbarism, we have an incident, the Gibraltar killings, which offer access to an alternative history. This history, written from a Republican perspective, tells of state-sponsored terrorism aimed principally at the Catholic community, from the Black and Tan search and destroy missions of the 1920s (Burton, 1978) to allegations of Army led drive-by assassinations in the 1970s (Dillon and Lehane, 1973) through to Gibraltar, where eyewitnesses told of watching as the SAS continued to fire at point-blank range into the lifeless bodies of the victims.

As a result, the killings also provide an opportunity to examine the ideological functioning of the news media within the conflict. How was this potential crisis in public meaning negotiated by the media? Did new understandings about the situation in Northern Ireland emerge, or did hegemonic forces make the killings safe by interpreting their meaning within the dominant political schemata of British sovereignty?

METHODOLOGY

I addressed these questions through a qualitative analysis of coverage in *The Daily Telegraph, The Guardian,* and *The Times,* all nationally distributed daily publications that are considered part of the "elite" press. All of these newspapers draw the majority of their audience from the upper and middle classes (Harrop, 1988). They do not, however, share a common political agenda: During the British general election in

1987, *The Times* and *The Daily Telegraph* strongly supported the Conservative party, whereas *The Guardian* sided with Labour (Harrop, 1988). With the Gibraltar incident occurring less than a year after the election, this provides a relatively accurate picture of the general political orientation of the sources at the time. What we are dealing with, then, are two papers standing to the right and one to the left of center on the political spectrum. As this research was conducted in the United States, my access to British newspapers was limited, hence the absence of the tabloid publications.

The analysis draws on David Bordwell's work on scripts and hypothesis testing (1985). Bordwell argues that events or stories become meaningful to us when they are contextualized within the "scripts" we carry, organized sets of beliefs that map out what we already "know" about the world. Perception then becomes an act of "active hypothesis testing" (Bordwell, 1985, p. 31), wherein our beliefs are compared to new information received from our environment. "Top down" or "Bottom up" readings result (p. 31), wherein our scripts are either confirmed or reworked according to the new data. Bordwell's understanding of the dynamics of perception intersects with Carey's view of communication as a process by which reality is "produced, maintained, repaired and transformed" (1989, p. 23). Applied to the Gibraltar killings, the problem to be answered is how did the press coverage position itself in regard to mainstream and more marginalized discursive positions. Were dominant assumptions about the war maintained, or were they threatened by the emergence of conventionally disregarded voices?

Such questions require a thematic analytical approach. Van Dijk (1988) points out that ideological perspectives toward particular situations heavily influence the questions asked of them. To discern the elite press's preferred position on the killings, it is therefore necessary to identify the major thematic structures used, showing how they are related to the discourse surrounding the war. It is also important, however, to recognize the potentially polysemous nature of the news coverage in question. Hence in the analysis that follows, I consider how the stories on the Gibraltar incident positioned themselves in relation to both dominant and oppositional views on the war, locating possible sites at which hegemonic readings break down.

DAY ONE: ARMED AND DANGEROUS

This study begins with a reasonably detailed analysis of the first day's coverage of the shootings. At this stage, when it was believed that a bomb had been found at the parade site and that the SAS's actions had undoubtedly averted a tragedy, news stories carried in *The Guardian, The Times,* and *The Daily Telegraph* allow direct access to dominant political perspectives. Opening coverage in all three sources shares a common thematic core, as the headlines of the lead articles indicate:

- "British police kill 'IRA gang' in Gibraltar" (Walker, Hearst, & Brown, 1988)
- "IRA terrorists shot dead in Gibraltar" (Searle, McEwen, & Wigg, 1988)
- "IRA bomb gang killed by army in Gibraltar" (Brown, Randall, & Bartlett, 1988)

Carried in the *The Guardian, The Times,* and *The Daily Telegraph,* respectively, all mainly focus on piecing together evidence proving that an IRA plot was afoot. All mention that a 500-lb bomb had been found close to the site of a forthcoming military parade to be performed by the Royal Anglian Regiment. The shootings were the culmination of an interactive intelligence operation, conducted by security forces from a number of European countries, which had tracked the Republicans from Belfast to Gibraltar. *The Times* and *The Daily Telegraph* positively identify the dead as Farrel, Savage, and McCann, all known IRA members. All of the reports also describe why it is eminently possible that Gibraltar would have been a target for such an attack: The colony is used for training soldiers in counterinsurgency (Searle et al., 1988) and it is also a stop on an alleged gun running track between Libya and Belfast (Brown et al., 1988; Searle et al., 1988).

As a final point, it is made clear that the detonation of "the bomb" would have caused many civilian causalities due to its proximity to a school and a home for senior citizens. What is more, the subheadline of Brown et al.'s report, "parade carnage foiled as 500lb bomb diffused," establishes a cause and effect relationship between the shootings and the salvation of these civilians.

The most notable thing about the coverage at this stage is the high degree of ideological closure it exhibits; the major themes identified illustrate and confirm dominant readings of the Irish war. The IRA is marginalized in a number of ways. First, the focus on what the IRA *planned to do* rather than on what the SAS *did* performs a pointed political function. The question of who is the aggressor and who the aggressee in the conflict is hotly disputed. The failure to reflect this controversy produces a distinct ideological flavor.

This can be demonstrated by a consideration of *The Times*'s decision to include a particular quote from Tom King, then Home Secretary, without critical comment. King claims that the killings are mainly significant in that they show that "the IRA will not be able to take its bloodshed onto the international stage" (Searle et al., 1988, p. 20). A Father Raymond Murray, who chronicles a savage history of state sponsored terrorism in *The SAS in Ireland* (1990), might well present a different argument. He might argue that the killings prove that the SAS *has* taken its bloodshed onto the international stage. It becomes clear that in portraying the killings as reactive rather than active when, from the perspective of commentators such as Murray, they stand as further proof of state-sponsored aggression (and thus the need for the Catholic community to protect itself), the newspapers create a pro-British ideological framework.

Such questions are largely ignored in favor of the development of other anti-Republican scripts. Importantly, all three sources describe the dead as terrorists, a term holding primarily negative connotations. The BBC, at least in principle, use it to delineate between legitimate and non-legitimate insurrectional military activity. "Terrorist" is used in reference to attacks made on civilian targets, whereas "guerilla" is used in the case of strikes against military targets, which are seen as fair game (Curtis, 1984). In terms of linking this lexical logic to an audience, IRA members interviewed by Burton (1978) feel the word constructs them as criminals rather than the soldiers they see themselves as.

The criminality implied by this label is complemented in early coverage of the Gibraltar killings by other descriptions of the dead, particularly the use of "gang" (Brown et al., 1988) in preference to military terms such as "squad" or "unit." Indeed *The Times* takes an explicit stand against the use of any jargon of credibility by placing the phrase "active service unit," an IRA source's description of the three, in quotation marks. This indicates that the label is that preferred by the Republicans, not the newspaper.

This semantic logic allows us to see the significance of focusing on the civilian rather than the military casualties that would have been caused by the attack. In doing so, the newspapers downplay the argument that the attack would have been aimed at a primarily military target, an argument that hints at a more credible IRA image. Instead readers are presented with the familiar image of the IRA member as murderer rather than soldier. The IRA are exactly who we thought they were, murderers, lunatics. Except this time the forces of sanity caught them before they could do any damage. If you don't believe it, the authorities have the bomb to prove it.

NO BOMB? NO PROBLEM!

But there was no bomb. Three days later it became known that not only had the three been unarmed but also no bomb had been found in the colony. This information creates an interesting testing ground for Bordwell's theory of "top-down" readings. The ideological specificity of the first day's coverage is somewhat obscured by the apparently concrete nature of the evidence favoring the government's case. The presence of the bomb goes a long way toward legitimating the killings by pointing to the immediacy of the threat the IRA members posed. The absence of the bomb therefore casts severe doubts on this conclusion and the credibility of both the government and the newspapers as informational sources.

Moreover the new evidence leads one to believe that the most salient themes to be dealt with on the second day of the coverage relate to oppositional viewpoints. The knowledge that the three IRA members posed no immediate threat to anyone raises doubts about the legitimacy and even the legality of the killings, suggesting that such questions may well have been the most important ones at this stage of the story.

Yet the subsequent coverage of the Gibraltar incident largely ignores this crisis in favor of an elaboration on many of the themes identified by earlier reports. Most notably, despite the fact that the government had, in the kindest reading, been wrong about the bomb, the main developments in the coverage of the killings as a front-page story still focus on what the IRA may have planned to do rather than on what the SAS did:

- "Fourth IRA bomber on the run" (Kennedy & Hearst, 1988)
- "Howe says bombers planned 'dreadful attack' on troops" (Fletcher, 1988)
- "Hunt goes on for IRA car bomb: Dreadful act of terror averted, Howe tells MPs" (Randall, Brown, & Holden, 1988):

Each of these stories mainly hinge on the dissemination of congratulations, gratitude, and warnings.

Indeed the absence of the bomb provides evidence not of problematic aspects of the SAS's actions, but rather the need for continued vigilance; if the bomb was not at the parade site, then it must be somewhere else, so the security forces need to remain alert. If anyone is having doubts about who the "bad guys" are in this story, Geoffrey Howe, then Foreign Secretary, reminds us of the IRA bombing of a Remembrance Day parade in Enniskillen the year before, an attack that actually inflicted the type of civilian casualties predicted in Gibraltar. There is no ideological crisis; only the continued relieved mopping of the brow.

Problematic elements of the government's story are further deflected by the alleged discovery of bomb-making equipment in Spain, which was linked to the IRA:

- "Primed bomb found in IRA missing car" (Kennedy, Hearst, & Brown, 1988)
- "Bomb timing device set to coincide with parade: Explosives in third car found in Spain" (Wigg, Searle, Dawe, Evans, & Ford, 1988)
- "Demands for an inquiry rejected: Police in Spain find IRA's 145lb car bomb. Vindication of Gibraltar shootings, say Tory MPs" (Randall & Jones, 1988)

Each works to put the official version back on the credibility track. This has an important thematic consequence, as the subsequent turning point in the story's front page life continues to revolve around the potential threat to order posed by the IRA.

THE HEARINGS, THE BURIALS

This is even true of moments that explicitly deal with holes in the story. Despite the conclusion drawn by Tory MPs that the discovery of the bomb-making equipment vindicated the shootings, it was decided that an inquiry should be convened. Here, surely, was a theme that would explicitly deal with a critique of army operations. Instead, the decision to conduct an investigation is subsumed into the general topic of the IRA menace.

- "Soldiers to give evidence" (Fairhall, Kennedy, & Hearst, 1988)
- "SAS squad will testify at inquest in Gibraltar" (Wigg, Evans, & Dawe, 1988)
- "SAS names 'must be kept secret' " (Reynolds, 1988)

All position themselves favorably toward the SAS with a dual focus on the regiment's willingness to submit to due process (thus recognizing that as a state sponsored agency it is bound to operate within civil law) and the security problems this decision will cause; in testifying, it is feared that the soldiers in question will expose themselves and their families to IRA retribution. Coverage of the decision to convene an inquiry thus paradoxically enhances the image of the SAS as pro-social.

Stories surrounding the last turning point in the story, the funerals of the dead, also provide examples of how potentially oppositional moments can be used to illustrate hegemonic perspectives. From a Republican standpoint, the funerals were notable for their propensity to physically disprove a key element in the ideological marginalization of the IRA. It is often argued that the IRA can play no part in the negotiation over the North's future because it represents only a minority of the Catholic community. The IRA claims this is untrue, that in fact it represents the majority of working-class Catholics. The funerals gave them an opportunity to prove their point with a show of mass support. Again, this created the potential for a public debate into the mechanics of "commonsense" assumptions about the war. But although *The Guardian* mentioned that security forces feared a Republican propaganda coup, coverage of the funerals generally focused on the threat they posed to public order (Ford, Wigg, Debilius, & Dawe, 1988; Graves, 1988; Kennedy, Hearst, Hetherington, & Carvel, 1988). Thus even in death, Farrel, McCann, and Savage cannot be seen as victims, but as a continued threat.

THE WIDER PICTURE: THE IRA AND INTERNATIONAL TERROR

Generally, then, the Gibraltar incident is met with a thematic focus that assumes that the IRA is the catalyst in the war. But more than this, the elite press' coverage marginalizes pro-IRA sentiments by using a number of the ideological strategies that are habitually mobilized to justify the continued military presence in the North. Armed with the information that the bomb-making equipment found in Spain was of Czech and Soviet origin, and that Farrel, Savage, and McCann had links with Colonel Ghaddafi, the newspapers in question tap into domino logic. Having been linked to the two most potent threats to capitalism in the pre–wall crumbling world (Islam and communism), the IRA is portrayed as part of a conspiracy to overthrow the West. "Ambush on The Rock" (Weaver & Brown, 1988) explains the planned attack not as an attempt to further the goal of national liberation, but to "re-establish . . . [the IRA] as an international terror force" (p. 17). "The network beating the bombers" (Fox, 1988) elaborates on this theme, explaining then recent IRA reversals as the result of the general decrease in public support for terrorist activities all over Europe, with a concurrent increase in cooperation between the security forces of all European Economic Community (EEC) nations. The "war on the West" theme is explicitly invoked here with the conclusion that France's decision to participate in the fight against terrorism is particularly important, as it forms a geographical linchpin in western defenses (sharing borders with Germany, Italy, and Spain, all of whom have active terror groups). This constitutes a most instructive spatial move: The IRA shifts eastward, away from the North of Ireland, away from the issues that give the organization a voice, into the embraces of the crescent and the sickle.

The threat the IRA poses is thus so great that it allows established nation-states to overcome their differences to combat a common enemy. Spanish collaboration with British authorities is particularly important, given that Spain is engaged in its own postcolonial struggle with England concerning possession of Gibraltar. In this sense, it might be argued that the Spanish and the Irish share an agenda. The shelving of these differences tells us that we have to look to the big picture when thinking about the Irish conflict. In fact, we are not really thinking about Ireland, but the world and more particularly the defense of democracy.

OPPOSITIONAL VOICES, HEGEMONIC FISSURES: IDEOLOGICAL SEARCH AND RESCUE

Yet all of this seems too cut and dried. The analysis thus far runs the risk of assuming a homology between the mechanics of colonialism and public discourse on the same. The hegemony thesis avoids such crude determinism by acknowledging struggles in the formation of public meanings; control is not given, but must be won and defended from oppositional onslaught.

And indeed there were questions asked about the morality/legality of the killings. But what were the nature of these questions, and who asked them? The most prominently featured objections came from within the House of Commons, from David Owen (Kennedy, Hearst, & Brown, 1988), a member of the Social Democratic Party, and from a group of Labour MPs who tabled a motion condemning the killings. Yet these objections are constructed from a pro-British rule position. Kenneth McNamara, a member of the Labour party, accuses the government of "creating three martyrs through [the Army's] reckless behavior . . . [hence] damaging British prestige . . . [by jeopardizing] the rule of law and order" (Dudley, 1988, p. 32). Stepping beyond the British Parliamentary framework, former Irish Foreign Minister Peter Barry points to the killings as proof that "the IRA has pulled the SAS down to their level" (Joyce, 1988, p. 1).

This debate perfectly demonstrates hegemonic machinations, absorbing apparently oppositional elements into the state's ideological framework. On closer examination, these objections do not question the morality of British rule in Northern Ireland at all. In fact, the British political establishment is portrayed as victim rather than villain: Rogue elements of the system have threatened to contaminate national morality, making "us" too much like "them." There is no question of reconceptualizing the war by considering the Republican point of view. What is needed is a restoration of British hegemony.

This apparently oppositional dialogue therefore nurtures a profound conservatism at its philosophical core. In the main, debate is only covered insofar as it occurs within the Parliamentary system. Republican voices are either excluded or confined to the later, fine print regions of articles (which may be tantamount to invisibility; cf. Hallin, 1986). The parameters of acceptable public discourse are therefore delimited within the state's institutional structure, marginalizing those outside while valorizing the existing distribution of social power by highlighting its capacity to self-correct.

The national institutional morality is further supported by the rescuing of the army's image. In the face of an incident that threatened to support Murray's thesis, that the army is itself a terrorist organization, readers are presented with a picture of the army as a pro-social entity. The key to understanding the cultural conception of the army lies in coverage that the newspapers devote to the parade which was thought to have been the target of the planned attack.

Against a background of political dilemmas addressing who exactly is on the defensive, and who operates in the best interests of the community they claim to serve, these reports embrace the army as an integral part of law-abiding society while affirming the perceived barbarism of the IRA.

- "Gibralter's old guard take it all in their stride" (Kennedy, 1988)
- "At 11:20 . . ." (1988)
- "Applause and checks for Rock's soldiers" (Randall, 1988)

All provide a series of cues relating to established themes in the main coverage. The reader's image of the targets and likely outcome of the bomb attack is concretized. *The Daily Telegraph* and *The Guardian* provide interviews with several senior citizens gathered to watch the parade. Seated at the front of the crowd, the interviewees would clearly have been killed or wounded in the event of an explosion. The implied barbarism of the IRA is confirmed by a comment from one of the senior citizens, who describes its members as "heathens hiding behind the cloak of religion" (Kennedy, 1988, p. 20). Significantly, he adds that having himself served in the army in Northern Ireland, he knows most of the Irish to be "lovely people" (Kennedy, 1988, p. 20). Here readers are presented with a "wo/man in the street," commonsense marginalization of the IRA, their sincerity and place in the Catholic community dismissed.

These same articles offer a concurrent emphasis on the benevolent nature of the British Army. We are told that the troops involved in the parade regularly set out chairs for the interviewees (Kennedy, 1988). In *The Times* the commanding officer (CO) of the Royal Anglians describes the "enthusiastic" (At 11:20 . . . , 1988, p. 22) welcome the troops receive from the public during the parade. *The Daily Telegraph* describes the ceremony as "part of the way of life" on Gibraltar (Randall, 1988, p. 40). The soldiers, as they march past British style pubs and fish and chip shops (Randall, 1988), are portrayed as a constitutive part of the local community (which again validates British colonialism). Could such people be cold-blooded killers? By implication, the IRA is again cast in a disruptive role. After all, these articles illustrate how the prevention of the bomb plot allowed life on the colony to continue as normal.

As the Royal Anglian regiment marched away, resplendent in the midday Gibraltar sun, so the killings of Farrel, McCann, and Savage were largely put to rest. Although critical positions would subsequently emerge within the mainstream media, particularly in light of an Independent Television (ITV) documentary that alleged that the killings had in fact been summary executions, such questions disappeared at this stage with the funerals of the dead.

PRO-REPUBLICAN SPACES

Yet before concluding this discussion of the elite press' coverage of this incident, it must be pointed out that the ideological functioning of these texts are not as simple or coherent as the preceding discussion may suggest. The work of scholars such as Fiske (1987) and Radway (1984) show that texts can never be seen as univocal; they are polysemous, open to different readings produced by different subjectivities. Accordingly, we must be sensitive to the potential ambiguities in these texts. How might they be read in different ways? Do they really agree on the meaning of the Gibralter incident?

We can begin to examine this question by returning to Bordwell's theory of hypothesis testing. What would happen if a person possessing a pro-Republican script approached the stories in question: Would it be possible to construct a top-down reading that favored the Republican cause? At several points in the coverage, the answer is yes. There are a number of informational fissures and wider thematic constructs that allow such a reading. On a micro level, as the coverage opens one may pay more attention to the military nature of the target than the projections of civilian casualties. One might also pay attention to a range of anti-army cues presented in *The Guardian,* where the shootings are described as having taken place "in cold blood," and are described by Seamus Mullen, an Irish MP, as examples of a "shoot to kill" policy (Kennedy & Hearst, 1988, p. 1). The latter term is an explicit reference to past incidents of violent excess on the behalf of state sponsored agencies. It was used as a popular label for an official investigation in the 1980s into allegations that the Royal Ulster Constabulary operated under orders to kill rather than apprehend IRA members whenever possible (a matter which, incidently, was never satisfactorily resolved).

Similar fissures are apparent in short biographies of Farrel carried in *The Times* and *The Daily Telegraph.* Although these articles can be read as attempts to justify her death by portraying her as an unrepentant terrorist who was determined to continue her IRA activities no matter what the human cost, sympathetic strains are also evident. In "How a schoolgirl chose a career in terror" (Ford, 1988), readers are told that Farrel's grandfather had fought for the Republican cause during the 1920s, and that she had been inspired to join the IRA by the introduction of internment (the imprisonment without trial of suspected terrorists) and Bloody Sunday.

This information stands as an important textual cue supporting the thesis that Republicanism is strongly rooted in Catholic tradition, and the IRA's post-1969 resurgence was not pre-emptive, but was provoked by state-sponsored aggression (Burton, 1978). It also works against the prevailing ideological position of the coverage that seeks to marginalize the

Republicans within their own community. Similarly, although *The Daily Telegraph*'s "I only regret being caught" (La Guardia, 1988) devotes most of its attention to affirming popular perceptions of the IRA by presenting Farrel as heartless, this image is tarnished somewhat by her admission that she had wept for IRA prisoners who died during the Hunger Strikes of 1981. Instead of a vicious automaton, readers are presented with a real human being who genuinely felt her cause was justified.

But perhaps most notably, we should recognize the many places in which *The Guardian* presents the IRA as a legitimate military organization, with rational goals and strategies. First, although the articles "Gibraltar deaths tear huge gap in IRA skills and morale" (Hearst, 1988a) and "IRA loses top gunman" (Hearst, 1988b) can be read as justifications of the killings, at the same time they resist the tendency to portray IRA members as criminals. By pointing to the problems that the organization faces in the wake of the shootings with regard to the "recruiting" and "training" of "volunteers" (1988a, p. 2), and the launching of offensive operations in the absence of "skilled" personnel (p. 2), *The Guardian* connotes a new level of legitimacy through the use of military terms.

But more significantly "Gibraltar deaths . . ." presents an unusual, logical explanation of why the IRA employs the tactics it does. The policy of "Ulsterization" (Hearst, 1988a, p. 2), it is reasoned, removes the problems of the Catholic community from the public gaze by restricting the conflict to the bounds of Northern Ireland. By placing the Royal Ulster Constabulary and the Ulster Defence Regiment (an army reserve unit comprised of local troops) on the frontline of the war, the British authorities have produced a situation wherein "Irishmen kill Irishmen" (p. 2). As relatively few non-Irish soldiers are killed, so the British public become less and less concerned with the North's problems. Bomb attacks on civilian targets are aimed at forcing the conflict to the forefront of the public agenda (Hearst, 1988a). The IRA portrayed in these articles corresponds more to pro-Republican scripts. Its members are not monsters, but genuine political agitators with sincere goals and logical strategies.

CONCLUSION

Despite the presence of these oppositional fragments, we must nevertheless ask about the significance of these moments of resistance. For despite the acknowledgment of textual polysemy, to abandon the notion of the preferred reading is also to abandon the question of power. Although hegemonic theory recognizes the existence of antagonistic discursive formations within a structured social totality, at the same time it is clear that not all of these formations have equal access to or purchase on the public mind. In other words, although coverage of the killings may have contained information that could activate pro-Republican scripts, at the same time we must ask if it is likely that these cues were numerous or prominent enough to significantly change the way a mainstream audience might think about Northern Ireland.

The answer is, probably not. Despite troubling elements in the material evidence available, the vast majority of the stories I looked at steadfastly held on to hegemonic articulations, despite the fact that it was precisely these connections that were at stake. The continued focus on the threat the three dead posed or might have posed, despite the absence of any weapons or explosives, resolutely avoids questions concerning the role of the British Army in the war. This in turn evades attempts to decouple the "Army = benevolence" equation. Indeed, the British establishment as a whole emerges with if anything a somewhat enhanced reputation, demonstrating a willingness to police itself through convening an inquiry into the incident. If Gibraltar gives evidence that something is wrong, then that error resides in deviant elements of the system, rather than the system itself. The most striking thing about the coverage, in this sense, is how an incident that threatened to shake perceptions of national self was molded if anything to confirm hegemonic modes of identity. In the end, the good guys win, even if they get their hands a little dirty in the process.

What this demonstrates, in terms of critical/cultural theory, is how political change cannot depend on the mere existence of material contradiction. The activities of the SAS, in this instance, were not in and of themselves enough to raise questions about the British military presence in Northern Ireland. As Hall suggests in his critique of the British Labour Party's failure to contest Thatcherism on a cultural level (1990), everything is in the presentation; the ideological importance of the event depended on the meanings attached to it by articulatory news practices. Hence, a moment of apparent discursive crisis was able to in fact reaffirm established power relationships and ways of thinking about the war.

BIBLIOGRAPHY

Angus, I. (1992). The politics of common sense: Articulation theory and critical communications studies. In S. Deetz (Ed.), *Communication Yearbook 15* (pp. 536–571). Newbury Park, CA: Sage.

At 11:20 the soldiers returned. Crowds lined the streets. It was the moment the IRA bomb was timed to explode. (1988, March 9). *The Times*, p. 22.

Bordwell, D. (1985). *Narration and Fiction Film.* Madison: University of Wisconsin Press.

Brown, T.; Randall, C.; & Bartlett, G. (1988, March 7). IRA bomb gang killed by army in Gibralter. *The Daily Telegraph*, p. 20.

Burton, F. (1978). *The Politics of Legitimacy.* London: Routledge & Kegan Paul.

Carey, J. W. (1989). *Communication as Culture.* Boston: Unwin Hyman.

Curtis, L. (1984). *Ireland, the Propaganda War.* London: Pluto Press.

Dillon, M., & Lehane, D. (1973). *Political Murder in Northern Ireland.* Harmondsworth: Penguin Books Ltd.

Dudley, N. (1988, March 12). Labour split over "martyrs" in Gibralter. *The Daily Telegraph,* p. 32.

Fairhall, D.; Kennedy, M.; & Hearst, D. (1988 March 11). Soldiers to give evidence. *The Guardian,* p. 1.

Fiske, J. (1987). *Television Culture.* New York: Methuen.

Fletcher, M. (1988, March 8). Howe says bombers planned "dreadful attack" on troops. Hunt for fourth IRA terrorist. *The Times,* p. 1.

Ford, R. (1988, March 8). How a schoolgirl chose a career in terror. *The Times,* p. 3.

Ford, R.; Wigg, R.; Debilius, H.; & Dawe, T. (1988, March 10). Security alert for IRA unit's funerals. *The Times,* p. 9.

Fox, R. (1988, March 9). The network beating the bombers. *The Daily Telegraph,* p. 17.

Graves, D. (1988, March 16). Sinn Fein to turn IRA burials into publicity stunt. *The Daily Telegraph,* p. 2.

Hall, S. (1990). *The Hard Road to Renewal.* London: Verso.

Hallin, D. (1986). We keep America on top of the world. In T. Gitlin (Ed.), *Watching Television* (pp. 9–41). New York: Pantheon Books.

Harrop, M. (1988). Press. In D. Butler & D. Kavanagh (Eds.), *The British General Election of 1987* (pp. 208–221). New York: St. Martin's.

Hearst, D. (1988a, March 8). Gibralter deaths tear huge gap in IRA skills and morale. *The Guardian,* p. 2.

Hearst, D. (1988b, March 8). IRA loses top gunman in Gibralter shooting. *The Guardian,* p. 24.

Holton, G. (1978). Reflections on modern terrorism. *Terror, 1,* (3), 265–276.

Joyce, J. (1988, March 9). Dail uneasy over killings. *The Guardian,* p. 1.

Keegan J. (1988, March 8). Spanish security aid vital to SAS success. *The Daily Telegraph,* pp. 1, 32.

Kennedy, M. (1988, March 9). Gibraltar's old guard take it all in their stride. *The Guardian,* p. 20.

Kennedy, M., & Hearst, D. (1988, March 8). Fourth IRA bomber on the run. *The Guardian,* p. 1.

Kennedy, M.; Hearst, D.; & Brown, P. (1988, March 9). Primed bomb found in IRA missing car. *The Guardian,* p. 1.

Kennedy, M.; Hearst, D.; Hetherington, P.; & Carvel, J. (1988, March 12). Special flight for IRA bodies. *The Guardian,* p. 1.

Kitson, F. (1974). *Low Intensity Operations: Subversion Insurgency and Peace Keeping.* Hamden, CT: Shoe String Press.

La Guardia, A. (1988, March 8). I only regret being caught. *The Daily Telegraph,* p. 17.

Martin, L. J. (1985). The media's role in international terrorism. *Terrorism, 8,* (2), 127–146.

Murray, R. (1990). *The SAS in Ireland.* Dublin: Mercier Press.

Radway, J. (1984). *Reading the Romance: Feminism and the Representation of Women in Popular Culture.* Chapel Hill: University of North Carolina Press.

Randall, C. (1988, March 9). Applause and checks for Rock's soldiers. *The Daily Telegraph,* p. 40.

Randall, C.; Brown, T.; & Holden, W. (1988, March 8). Hunt goes on for IRA car bomb: Dreadful act of terror averted, Howe tells MPs. *The Daily Telegraph,* pp. 1, 32.

Randall, C., & Jones, G. (1988, March 9). Demands for an inquiry rejected: Police in Spain find the IRA 145lb car bomb. Vindication of Gibralter shootings, say Tory MPs. *The Daily Telegraph,* pp. 1, 40.

Reynolds, N. (1988, March 12). SAS names "must be kept secret." *The Daily Telegraph,* p. 1.

Searle, D.; McEwen, A.; & Wigg, R. (1988, March 7). IRA terrorists shot dead in Gibralter. *The Times,* pp. 1, 20.

Van Dijk, T. (1988). *News Analysis.* Hillsdale, NJ: Lawrence Earlbaum Assoc.

Walker, J.; Hearst, D.; & Brown, P. (1988, March 7). British police kill "IRA gang" in Gibralter. *The Guardian,* p. 1.

Weaver, M. & Brown, T. (1988, March 8). Ambush on The Rock. *The Daily Telegraph,* p. 17.

Wigg, R.; Evans, M; & Dawe, T. (1988, March 10). SAS squad will testify at inquest in Gibralter. *The Times,* p. 24.

Wigg, R.; Searle, D.; Dawe, T.; Evans, M.; & Ford, R. (1988, March 9). Bomb timing device set to coincide with military parade: Explosives in third car found in Spain. *The Times,* pp. 1, 22.

Television, Gender, and Sports Hegemony: Prime Time's Portrayal of Female Athletes

Gina Daddario

As many studies reveal, the sports media rarely devote more than 10 percent of their news and photographic coverage to female athletes (Bryant, 1980; Bryson, 1987; Kane, 1988; Reid & Soley, 1979; Rintala & Birrell, 1984). When female sports figures are depicted in sports and general news magazines, in the sports sections of daily newspapers, or on televised sports programming, they tend to be overrepresented in "sex-appropriate" sports—those that emphasize the aesthetic poses and movements of the female body rather than its strength and stamina[1] (Duncan, 1990; Graydon, 1983; Hilliard, 1984; Kane, 1988; Poe, 1976; Rintala & Birrell, 1984). These sports are also characterized as individual rather than team oriented, involving almost no bodily conflict or contact; sports typically associated with female athletes include tennis, golf, gymnastics, ice skating, and swimming. By contrast, male athletes depicted in the mass media are most frequently associated with the sports of baseball, basketball, football, and boxing (Lumpkin & Williams, 1991).

Sports critics accuse the media of not only stereotyping female athletes but of trivializing their achievements and marginalizing their contributions to the institution of sports. Messner (1988) and others (Bryson, 1987; Duncan, 1990; Graydon, 1983; Klein, 1988; Lumpkin & Williams, 1991) argue that the descriptive discourse applied to female athletes deviates dramatically from the discourse applied to male athletes. Female athletes are described frequently in print copy or television commentary according to their physical appearance and desirability to men, whereas male athletes are described according to their physical skills and playing techniques.

Duncan and Hasbrook (1988) argue that television's narrative coverage of women's sports tends to be contradictory and ambivalent. For example, in a telecast of a women's collegiate basketball game, they found that the announcers' play-by-play commentary focused more on the players' aesthetic qualities than on their physical skills. Similarly, in coverage of an international surfing competition, they found that positive commentary of female surfers was juxtaposed with visual images of bikinied body parts, suggesting that television imagery symbolically denies power to female athletes through its inequitable and often denigrating sports coverage.

Inequitable and denigrating television coverage of women is, of course, not limited to the sports arena. Numerous studies conducted in the 1970s on the dramatic and comedic portrayals of women showed that they simply did not exist to the same degree as men on television; rather, their roles were as auxiliaries to men, typically in familial or romantic relationships. Since female characters were confined to sex-dependent roles, such as mothers and housewives, and sex-specific spheres, such as the home and kitchen, they appeared with far more frequency in domestic situation comedies than in dramatic fare (Lemon, 1977; McNeil, 1975; Seggar, 1975).

Some critics argue that, like the institution of sports, television is controlled by, and programming created according to, a patriarchal ideology. Dow (1990) argues that although female characterizations, such as those portrayed on *The Mary Tyler Moore Show, Kate and Allie,* and *Murphy Brown,* may give an appearance of change, none advance a feminist ideology or challenge the status quo. Similarly, a rhetorical analysis of *thirtysomething* reveals that gender roles are constructed according to the "core hegemonic values of a patriarchal society" (Loeb, 1990, p. 258) and that on television, fathers still know best.

My research bridges these two areas of study—feminist analyses of female athletes in the sports media and of female characters on entertainment television—and examines prime-time television's portrayal of females and sport. Feminist media criticism examines the devaluation of women in society, looking specifically at the role of the media in reproducing or challenging the oppression of women. Feminist sports critics often examine how the mass media contribute to the marginalization of women in sport through their scant and stereotyped coverage. Feminist television critics examine women's underrepresentation in comedic and dramatic programming.

Presently, most research on the coverage of women in sport has focused on actual sports reporting, in both print and electronic media. No studies have looked at how the entertainment media take these images and recreate them in a fictional setting, the intention of this study.

Television programs identified for analysis aired between March 1, 1991, and September 1, 1991; the study was limited to prime time programming on the ABC, CBS, Fox, and NBC networks. The six-month sample included first-run and repeat programs from the 1990–1991 television season. Theatrical movie releases and made-for-TV movies were excluded from the sample, as I wanted to look at programs with established characters who were not identified exclusively as athletes to examine how sport is constructed as part of a television character's day-to-day life.

At the time of this study, there were no programs that revolved specifically around a female sports character or a sports theme. Because sport is used infrequently as a plot device or in character development, the use of a random sample of programming would not have yielded substantive data. Instead, I examined *TV Guide* listings for descriptions and synopses of all prime time programming. Programs tape-recorded for analysis included those containing any reference to a female character and sport.

The final sample consisted of eight programs: one drama (*Life Goes On*); one nighttime serial (*Knots Landing*); and six situation comedies (two episodes of *Designing Women* and one episode each of *Full House, Major Dad, Evening Shade,* and *Roseanne*). To be considered in the final sample, a program had to deal at length with females and sport; if sport was incidental to the plot or characterization, a program was eliminated from the final sample. For example, although the initial exposition of an episode of *Growing Pains* took place in a health club when an attractive female trainer complimented forty-something Jason, a husband, father, and psychiatrist, on his physique, the episode ultimately revolved around his wife, Maggie, a television journalist, and her "mid-life crisis," and thus was not included.

This analysis takes a rhetorical perspective in its examination of prime-time television's construction of females and sport. Of primary consideration is the extent to which television's fictionalization of the female athlete is a cultural reproduction of a masculine sports hegemony. As is typically the case in the sports media, is the television athlete restricted to sex-appropriate sports activities, such as tennis or gymnastics? Is she also constructed according to her physical attractiveness or desirability to men? These kinds of questions were addressed through a close examination of characterizations, dialogue, and narrative expositions, conflicts, and resolutions.

TELEVISION SPORTS

The sport most frequently depicted in this sample of fictional programs is baseball, in all cases involving adolescent female and male characters within the context of a little league team. The programs featuring baseball include *Designing Women, Full House, Major Dad,* and *Roseanne.* Like baseball, football is another masculine sport included in the sample and appears in *Evening Shade.*

The remaining sports depicted are considered sex-appropriate and include jogging (*Designing Women*) and gymnastics (*Life Goes On*). Tennis and horse training are both featured in one episode of *Knots Landing* when a wrist injury forces a character pursuing a professional tennis career to change her interests to her real love, horseback riding and horse training.

My analysis suggests that although some differences exist between the sports media's coverage of female athletes and prime-time television's portrayal of them, these are due primarily to the generic conventions of television programming, rather than to ideological considerations. For example, fictionalized representations of female athletes tend to focus on team sports, rather than individual sport. This can probably be explained by the fact that most of the programs in the sample that offer females and sport as a narrative scenario are situation comedies, which, as a genre, rely on situational conflict and character interrelationship. Obviously, a plot revolving around a sports team offers more potential for conflict and interrelationship than a plot revolving around a skater or runner competing against her personal best.

On first viewing almost any of the programs in the sample one might conclude that prime time programming advances women's equality in sport. Unlike the sports media, entertainment television offers many portrayals of adolescent and female athletes engaged in sports that are often perceived as the exclusive privilege of male athletes and spectators. Yet, as Gitlin (1982) might argue, although these portrayals offer the appearance or illusion of change, a closer reading of the texts suggests that they fail to challenge sport as an inherently male-serving domain. This reinforcement is revealed through several hegemonic processes. These processes include: the marginalization of females' participation and achievement in sports; the presentation of female characters' participation in sport from a male protagonist's point of view; the construction of sports competition as gender-specific; and the exclusion of adult females in sport activities. Examples of each are described later.

MARGINALIZATION

Marginalization is a typical media strategy used in portraying female or homosexual athletes (Messner, 1988). When patronizing female athletes is not effective in marginalizing an athlete ideologically, the media cast doubts on her sexuality (p. 205). Similarly, I found several instances where a character's athletic interests and abilities were patronized and where her sexuality was drawn into the ensuing character conflict. Ironically, the patronizing character was usually female and, in some cases, the athletic character's own mother.

One such instance occurred on *Roseanne,* a domestic comedy starring comedienne Roseanne Arnold. The program has been lauded by critics for representing a two-parent working-class family in an honest, rather than buffoonish, manner. Roseanne and Dan Connor are the parents of three children, two girls and a boy. The middle daughter Darlene is depicted as a tomboy and used situationally as a foil or contrast to her more feminine older sister, Becky. With DJ, the family's only son, too young to engage in father-son bonding activities, Darlene is often used as the surrogate son to watch sports with her father. In an episode analyzed for this study, Dan proudly announces, as father and daughter return victoriously from a baseball game, that not only did Darlene pitch an "11 strikeout, no walks" game, but "she made their best hitter cry." Darlene beams with pride and responds: "Yea, I beaned her right in the neck."

However, the plot unravels when Darlene is invited to attend her first school dance, an adolescent rite of passage far more appealing to Roseanne than to Darlene. This becomes apparent in an argument between mother and daughter over a proposed shopping trip.

Roseanne: Come on Darlene, this is something (shopping for dress and accessories) I've always wanted to do with you. It'd be like a girl thing.

Darlene: Mom I have practice on Saturday.

Roseanne: Well, you could just miss it.

Darlene: No, I can't. If I miss practice I might not get to start in the next game!

Roseanne: Well, gee Darlene, this is your first formal dance. It's way more important.

Darlene: Yea, then why don't you go. . . . Why don't you give me this kind of attention when I do *real* stuff like striking out 11 guys without walking anybody.

What is really at conflict is Darlene's internal struggle with her emerging sexuality. A dance invitation, heterosexual romance, and dress shopping with mom can all be considered pubescent manifestations of femininity, or as Roseanne describes them, "girl things." Darlene resists these tugs at her tomboy nature and opts to stay home for an evening of sports and television with her dad. Her date, however, offers a less threatening alternative, one that allows her to keep her androgyny in balance, and invites her out for a pizza instead.

In the last scene Roseanne, who has been forced to recognize that Darlene's athletic achievements are more important to her than a dance invitation or her first prom dress, approaches her daughter with an apology and a gift of baseball shoes. When Darlene opens the package she finds that they are golf shoes instead. When she asks her mother why she bought them, Roseanne replies: "Oh, you mean they're not baseball shoes? I should have listened to the sales guy. But these were way cuter."

This last remark serves to undermine whatever ideological advances have been offered in the program up to this point. Despite her apology and peace offering, Roseanne continues to marginalize Darlene's interest in sports. Her insistence that the golf shoes "were way cuter," although intended as a comedic ploy, reflects an ideology in which appearance take precedence over athletics.

This episode of *Roseanne* is an example of how entertainment television reproduces and reinforces a masculine sports hegemony. Although, on the surface, the values and priorities portrayed on the program encourage young girls to participate and excel in masculine sport, the underlying message is that a girl's interest and participation in sport will not be valued on the same level as her interest and participation in more feminine activities.

A second case where a female character's athletic interests are marginalized by the character's own mother occurs in an episode of *Knot's Landing. Knot's Landing* was a long-running nighttime soap opera spun from *Dallas,* as one of its establishing characters was prodigal Ewing son, Gary, who left the oil ranch in Dallas for a cul-de-sac in Knots Landing, California. Kate, the niece of Greg Sumner, one of the program's major patriarchal characters, sustains a wrist injury that cuts short her career pursuits as a professional tennis player.

As horses are her first love, Kate accepts a summer job as a groom on the Ewing ranch, a decision that ires her mother who had arranged a position for her in Uncle Greg's corporation. Frustrated at her daughter's career choices, Kate's mother dismisses and trivializes her interest in horses: "Greg is offering you a career. This dream you have about making a living working with horses is unrealistic."

In other programs a character's athletic interests are marginalized by family members, colleagues, and even the character herself. A *Designing Women* episode provides some examples. *Designing Women* refers to the four Georgians who work at the Sugarbaker Design Firm, named after sisters, Julia and Suzanne; Mary Jo is one of the partners. Feeling tired and overwhelmed by her responsibilities as a career professional and single mother, Mary Jo convinces Julia to join her in an exercise program of running every morning. She soon tires of the routine and decides to give up running, an action commended by her business partner, Anthony, who dismisses joggers as "real fanatics": "Their eyes are all glazed over and everything. . . . I'm just glad that you and Julia didn't get sucked into that sort of thing."

What her partners have not realized is that the usually sensible Julia *has* gotten sucked into that sort of thing. She runs into the firm donning expensive runner's wear, spouting runner's jargon, and preparing for her first 10K run. She becomes obsessed with running and engages in behavior atypical of her character; she misses important business meetings and hangs out with the "10K crowd," who are portrayed as rich and shallow. Mary Jo laments that they've lost her: "The endorphins have won."

However, the prodigal daughter returns to the firm having traded her jog wear for a business suit and her headbanded ponytail for a coiffed hairstyle. She announces that she has just returned from a physical examination where her doctor reports that she has "shin splints, joint problems, incipient tendonitis, and athlete's foot." A relieved Charlene admits: "Julia, we were starting to get a little worried about you."

This episode was particularly surprising since *Designing Women,* a creation of Susan Bloodworth Thomason, has assumed positions of advocacy on such topical gender issues as pornography, women's self-defense, sex education, and even the Clarence Thomas confirmation hearings. However, the message in this program runs counter to the feminist philosophy usually underlined throughout the show. Fitness and exercise are presented not from an advocacy position, but from an extremist one, where running is portrayed as fanatical and anti-feminist, an unwomanly undertaking.

MALE POINT OF VIEW

One of the criteria for this study was that a program must focus on a female character and that she must be involved situationally or dramatically in a sport activity. Although all of the programs in the sample involve females and sport, not all of the programs are presented from a female's point of view. Obviously, programs starring a female lead or ensemble cast, such as *Roseanne* and *Designing Women,* although effacing a patriachal ideology, are at least presented from a female point of view.

However, when programs feature a male leading character, they depict a female story line from the male protagonist's point of view. *Evening Shade,* the Burt Reynolds comedic vehicle, is an example. Reynolds' character, Wood, is a former professional football player retired to the small Arkansas community of Evening Shade where he coaches the high school's losing football team, a source of much of the humor on the program. In an attempt to recruit new players, Wood opens team tryouts to the entire student body. To his and everyone else's surprise, two sisters, Yvette and Yvonne, show up at football practice.

Yvette and Yvonne are the embodiment of male fantasy[2]; they are sisters, a not uncommon sexual fantasy depicted in male erotic folklore. As sisters, they can be objectified sexually, as they do not require separate characterizations or individual identities. One sister is blonde, the other brunette; their hairstyles are reminiscent of the long, curled tresses of *Charlie's Angels.* They both come to practice attired in jeans and tank tops that reveal their cleavage.

The conflict that ensues is whether Wood will stand by his call for open tryouts and recruit the sisters if they are qualified, or succumb to the townsfolk's taunting and ridicule and ban the sisters from joining the team. Typical of the remarks and advice offered to Wood in the town bar include the doctor, who claims that it is "unnatural" to allow girls to come out for the team: "Men play football. Women don't. It's a hallmark of civilization. It's part of what separates us from those third world countries."

A female townsfolk approaches Wood about designing uniforms for the female players. She shows him her sketches pointing out the "padded upper torso panel" and the "little Peter Pan collar." Meanwhile, another bar patron shouts out: "Are you going to change the school colors to lavender and mauve?"

Wood reveals to his wife that he is personally opposed to the sisters joining the team, not because it challenges tradition but because it puts the girls at risk for injury. His wife responds that "boys can get hurt too, right?" Wood agrees, but sees getting hurt as an integral part of the socialization process for boys: "Boys grow up understanding about football. Part of the game is getting hurt."

In front of the press and his players, Wood announces that Yvonne and Yvette have made the all-male team. Although we have seen them only in workout (tank tops as well as sweats) attire, rather than actually working out, we are to assume that they are competent qualified players. After some half-hearted grumblings of protest, Wood responds:

I know, I didn't like it anymore than you do. I thought we were being the laughing stock of the state, but we already are the laughing stock of the state. We might as well do it for a good cause. This is not about women and men. This is about change, about people getting the chance to do what they do best. These two deserve a chance like that. We may not win any games this fall, but this spring we're going to do the right thing.

Coach Wood's decision is constructed dramatically as an act of individual courage, a point that is conveyed through narration at the end of the program. As the image dissolves from the locker room to a long shot of the high school, a male narrator is heard: "Wood Newton had many opportunities to show his courage on a football field, but he thought they ended with his playing days. It just goes to show that the more things change, the more they stay the same."

This particular tag line reveals as much about the cultural reproduction of sports and gender on entertainment television as it does about Wood's public displays of courage; the more things change for the advancement of females in sport, the more they stay the same. On the one hand, the program challenges traditional notions about high school and football by portraying female athletes as competent, competitive, and capable of trying out and making an all-male team. On the other hand, the portrayal of the sisters is consistent with stereotypes of female athletes offered throughout the sports media, which tend to emphasize physical appearance, attractiveness, and desirability to men.

In a study on the photographic depiction of male and female Olympians, Duncan (1990) argues that physical attractiveness, or "cosmetic perfection," helps determine whether a female athlete receives press coverage since athletes who "embody the feminine ideal" (p. 26) are more likely to be photographed than athletes who do not. She found that photographs of sprinter Florence Griffith Joyner and skater Katarina Witt, athletes most reporters and spectators would consider attractive and glamorous, appeared in the sports and general news media during the 1984 and 1988 Olympic periods far more frequently than photographs of their less attractive, yet comparably victorious, peers.

Duncan's study may help explain the entertainment media's preference for female football players who embody, rather than challenge, the feminine ideal. The sports media, which are comprised primarily of males, favor attractive female athletes and non-athletes, such as spectators and fans, in their coverage. A similar study on the photographic depiction of females in *Sports Illustrated* found that the magazine devotes more pictorial coverage to non-athletes than athletes; a large percentage of these non-athletes are models posed in its annual swimsuit issue (Daddario, 1992).

Major Dad is another program that presents a female character's story from a male's point of view. As its title implies, *Major Dad* is a domestic comedy set on a military base. When the title character, Mac, marries a single mother who also enjoys a career as a professional journalist, he becomes the stepfather of her three daughters. In the episode under analysis, middle daughter Robin is wrongly identified in the marine base newspaper as the "goat" who, through a bad play, forfeits her school's baseball game. The major, greeted by his commanding officer at work with "maaaaaaa," urges Robin, a young adolescent, to submit a retraction to the newspaper; she is reluctant to comply, preferring instead to put the humiliating experience behind her. Mac is awakened in the middle of the night by the realization that he wants the retraction more for himself than he does for Robin. After much introspection and self-analysis, Mac decides to honor Robin's wishes and drop the issue as well. Meanwhile, the Major's secretary, a female sergeant, writes a letter to the newspaper pointing out the sports reporting error, a gesture that satisfies and reunites the familial characters. Both Robin and the Major are vidicated, she without drawing further attention to herself, and he without compromising his relationship with her.

As in *Evening Shade,* this is the male protagonist's, not the female athlete's story. Robin is depicted as depressed and sullen during most of the program. Initially, Mac is depicted as insensitive and self-serving. However, like Wood, after much introspection and analysis, Mac undergoes a self-transformation and ultimately does the "right thing." Yet, neither of these programs do the right thing for the adolescent athletes.

Because the sports media construct competition as an almost exclusively masculine experience, it seems fitting that male characters should dominate the sporting experience in the situation comedy as well. The programs' creators allow both Mac and Wood to take the female characters' athletic successes (and failures) and reconstruct them as their own.

GENDER AND COMPETITION

Critics argue that sport, perhaps more than any other American institution, has shaped our cultural definition of masculinity (Kane, 1988; Trujillo, 1991). According to Bryson (1987), "sport privileges males and inferiorizes women" (p. 350), as sport is almost the exclusive territory of men.

Almost all feminist sports scholarship cite the classic work of Methany (1965) who observed that sport is inherently masculine unless it has been gender differentiated or socially sanctioned specifically for female participation. The relationship between women and sports is essentially one of exclusion or "otherness." For example, women are discouraged from engaging in sports requiring bodily contact, conflict, or face-to-face opposition, or in sports requiring great exertions of strength and stamina.

Klein (1988) argues that, because of biological differences between males and females relating to body size, strength, and weight, sports participation and achievement can be seen as a type of "natural" sex differentiation. This natural sex differentiation acts as an ideological agent in legitimizing sport-specific forms of masculinity and femininity. A masculine sport requires great physical strength, speed, and control (Trujillo, 1991, p. 291). Conversely, a feminine sport requires glamour and grace, and poses little risk of visible bruising or severe injury (Duncan & Hasbrook, 1988). Therefore, as Klein's argument goes, female athletes, by "nature," participate in individualized sports, such as gymnastics, swimming, and skating, whereas male athletes participate in team sports, such as football, baseball, and wrestling.

Birrell (cited in Duncan & Hasbrook, 1988) characterizes individual sports as events in which an athlete competes against herself or against a standard of excellence, such as a world record or personal best. Team sports, on the other hand, are those in which athletes compete directly against each other in a challenge for power and control. Men, by nature, are assumed to be more competitive than women, a trait that is socially sanctioned and culturally reproduced by the sports media.

A third hegemonic process at work in several of the programs involves women's struggle against "nature" and coming to terms with competition. Mary Jo, one of the interior design partners, experiences this struggle in an episode of *Designing Women* when she is the coach of the firm's little league team. Her son, Quint, is on the team as is Julia's young ward, Randa; Quint is portrayed as the timid player, whereas Randa is the aggressive one.

The first scene takes place at the Sugarbaker firm where Mary Jo is depressed at losing the last six baseball games and seeks advice on coaching from her colleagues. Suzanne, one of Mary Jo's partners and beauty pageant veteran, observes: "I know what your problem is Mary Jo, you just don't know how to kick little butts." Julia agrees with Suzanne's sentiment and encourages Mary Jo to coach her players more competitively.

The next scene takes place at the ballfield where Quint is pitching unsuccessfully for the Sugarbaker team. When the umpire calls a ball, Mary Jo approaches the large, physically imposing male with the following reproach: "That last pitch, well, I thought it looked sort of like a strike." Speaking more as a mother than as a coach she urges the umpire to reconsider his call: "I just think it would be so great for his [Quint's] self-esteem if he could strike one person out." The umpire sarcastically replies: "Lady, you must be confusing me with Phil Donahue."

Julia steps in and insults the umpire and chastises Mary Jo for failing to pull Quint out of the game and for failing to approach the game more competitively. Suzanne, a former Miss Georgia, chimes in: "There's a word for you people that worry that competition is a bad thing—losers." Mary Jo responds defeatedly: "I don't have a competitive bone in my body. When we were growing up, little girls were taught it wasn't nice to compete. So now almost all women feel just a little uncomfortable about straight-out competition."

The denouement is reached when Mary Jo challenges Julia to an arm-wrestling match and wins. In anticipation of the next game she declares:

"I'm going to be tougher and you're [Julia] going to be more diplomatic." Mary Jo becomes not only more tough but more "male" as well. At the next game she chews gum like a ballplayer chews tobacco, and takes on the umpire in an insult match.

These mannerisms suggest that in order for a female to approach a sport in a less passive, more aggressive manner, she has to assume a less feminine, more masculine posture. Due to the social sanctions and participatory restrictions relating to competitive sports and gender, there are few, if any, female role models by which Mary Jo can pattern her behavior so she resorts to stereotyped, even caricatured, male behavior.[3]

Like Mary Jo in *Designing Women,* Kate in *Knots Landing* finds that she is not competitive by nature either. When her tennis career is cut short by a wrist injury, she expresses relief at not having to play tennis anymore: "My uncle's right, I don't have the killer instinct. I really like playing tennis but I hate the competition." She finds sanctuary grooming horses, a solitary activity.

An episode of *Full House* deals with a similar theme, an adolescent's internal struggle with her feminine and competitive natures. *Full House,* a situation comedy that could easily be subtitled, "Three Men and Three Babies," takes place in the Tanner household. Danny Tanner, a widower and father of three daughters, invites his brother-in-law and best friend to move into his home following the death of his wife; all males assume parenting roles and responsibilities.

In the episode under analysis, ten-year old Stephanie is infatuated with a young classmate, Bret, and is advised by her older sister, DJ, to adopt Bret's favorite hobbies and activities to win his eye and establish common ground. As one of Bret's interests is baseball, Stephanie joins a competing team and becomes an overnight legend for her no-hit pitch, the "Tanner Twist."

Bret approaches Stephanie on the eve of their teams' playoff and, not wanting to risk humiliation in front of his family, requests that she ease up and allow him to get a hit in the game. The following day Stephanie has second thoughts when the score is tied and she finds herself on the pitcher's mound facing a bat-clutching Bret at home plate. With the outcome of the game resting on this one play, Stephanie calls a quick time out and summons her sister to the mound. In response to DJ's advice, "What's more important, self-respect or true love?" Stephanie is observed striking Bret out of the game.

Stephanie is not smiling when her team members lift her victoriously on their shoulders; she does not join in the chorus of "we're number one." She is despondent and assumes that Bret has dumped her until he shows up at her house the following day and congratulates her for winning the game; she apologizes for striking him out. He, in turn, apologizes for asking his girlfriend to cheat for him.

Although Stephanie's actions may be motivated by self-respect, nowhere is she portrayed as respecting herself. Rather, when contemplating the choice of self-respect or true love, it is true love rather than self-respect she desires. Ironically, her sister presents these choices as mutually exclusive; a young girl can have one only at the expense of the other. However, once she trades her uniform for adolescent wear and her baseball cap for a hair ribbon, her boyfriend comes around to accepting her actions.

A final incident occurs in *Life Goes On,* an hour-long family drama which deals with significant human issues, such as AIDS and Down's syndrome, among others. Becca, a high school student, sees her female gymnastics coach's temporary leave of absence as a convenient time to quit the gymnastics team because of her involvement in other after-school activities. The coach's replacement, a young attractive male, talks Becca into staying with the sport by using such seductive prose as: "To me, gymnastics is God's ultimate expression of art"; and "Gymnastics adds to your self-confidence, your toughness, your joy."

Becca develops a romantic crush on the coach. Her new sense of athletic drive is motivated by him. For example, Becca is fearful of the vault and does not want to participate in the vaulting event. Her coach then shames her into facing her failings: "I know girls like you, you're not real good at something, you don't want to do it." Becca begins practice on the vault.

The denouement is reached late one afternoon at practice when Becca kisses her coach as he helps her up from a fall; he does not kiss her back. Humiliated, she skips practice and intends to drop out of the upcoming gymnastics meet. The coach, sensitive to her embarrassment, visits her home and convinces her to come back. The final scene takes place at the meet where Becca completes a successful vault. From the "winning" smile on her face and the congratulatory hugs from her teammates, it becomes clear that Becca has survived both her romantic rejection and competitive fears. As her coach predicted, gymnastics has added to her self-confidence, toughness, and joy.

As these examples illustrate, females' participation in sport is motivated, not by a competitive spirit, but by other reasons. Mary Jo's maternal instincts prompted her participation in coaching. Stephanie's initial interest in baseball was motivated by true love. Finally, Becca's decision to train in gymnastics was precipitated by her infatuation with a male.

SPORT AND SOCIALIZATION

Bryson (1987) observes that the primary participants in sport are men and children; up to the age of fifteen years, boys and girls are equally likely to exercise or engage in athletic activity. Generally, sports do not become gender or sex differentiated until children reach puberty. Until that time, girls and boys' body size, strength, and weight are comparable physiologically. After puberty, not only do sports assume sex-specific forms of femininity and masculinity, but women drop out of sport activities in far greater numbers than do men.

All of the programs in this sample involve adolescent or teenaged females, rather than adult females, participating in sports. Further, except for Becca's participation in gymnastics in *Life Goes On,* all of the females are involved in competitive team sports, primarily, baseball, and in the case of *Evening Shade,* football.

The only programs that involve adult females in sport are *Designing Women,* where Julia is portrayed as a jogger, and *Knots Landing,* where Kate is portrayed as an aspiring professional tennis player. Both characters are also portrayed as abandoning their athletic interests. Julia abandons what is depicted as the fanatical world of recreational jogging, whereas Kate abandons what is characterized as the competitive world of professional tennis. Both characters' withdrawal from sport is motivated by physical injury—Julia by shin splints and Kate by a wrist injury.

As illustrated in the preceding examples, prime-time television's world of females and sport is reserved for adolescent and teenage participation. Given that reservation, however, opportunities abound; females can participate in competitive team sports such as baseball and football. They can strike out boys, make batters cry, and join traditional all-male teams.

However, this recreational freedom is short-lived. On entertainment television, there are few sport opportunities for the adult female athlete. Rather, she is frightened by competition and disuaded by injury. This dilemma might prompt one to think that Wood in *Evening Shade* was right, that boys, unlike girls, grow up understanding about sports; getting hurt is part of the game.

CONCLUSION

Feminist sports critics have long argued that female athletes depicted in the mass media do not enjoy the same coverage or privilege as male athletes. Similarly, feminist television critics argue that female characters, even seemingly liberated ones, are constructed according to a patriarchal ideology. An examination of television's fictional portrayal of women and sport suggests that the prime-time athlete is also a cultural reproduction of a masculine sports hegemony.

Unlike the sports media, which underrepresent female athletes in what are considered masculine sports, entertainment television offers many portrayals of adolescent and teen athletes engaged and succeeding in team sports. Two sisters break tradition in the small prime time town of Evening Shade by training and qualifying for an all-male football team.

However, a feminist reading of the texts suggests that most programs reinforce rather than challenge a masculine sports hegemony. For example, hegemonic processes are at work in *Roseanne* through the title character's insistence that shopping is more important than sport. They are also at work in prime time's presentation of female athletes' sporting experience from male protagonists' point-of-view.

Hegemonic processes are at work in *Full House,* which offers sport and heterosexual romance as separate spheres, or "self-respect" and "true love" as conflicting agendas. They are also at work through the presentation of sport as an adolescent or teen activity. In the few instances where adult females are associated with athletics, the characters are depicted as either fanatical about sport or fearful of competition. This is reflective of a larger masculine hegemony that excludes female participation from most team and competitive sport.

Despite prime-time television's advancement of the female athlete in traditionally masculine sports, such as those depicted in this analysis, what still matters most to the athlete's family, her peers, and even to herself, is her physical appearance, as driven home by Roseanne; her romantic status, as concerned by Stephanie and Becca; and her perceived desirability to men, as emphasized in *Evening Shade.*

Bryson (1987) is among the critics who argue that sport is so thoroughly masculinized that it seems "unlikely that it can be reclaimed to serve women's interests" (p. 350). However, through critical examination of the sports and entertainment media's contributions to the reproduction and reinforcement of hegemonic masculinity, perhaps women can begin laying claim to their roles and achievements in sports.

NOTES

1. Although sex-appropriate sports pertain to feminine activities such as tennis and golf, sex-inappropriate sports are those that challenge traditional beliefs about "ladylike" behavior (Kane, 1988). Additionally, Rintala and Birrell (1984) consider whether a sport is high risk, such as car, horse, and speedboat racing, or team-oriented when creating sex-inappropriate sport categories.

2. In February 1989, *Sports Illustrated* (*SI*) released a twenty-fifth Anniversary Swimsuit Issue that included a retrospective of all *SI*'s cover page swimsuit models. Ironically, the 1976 swimsuit issue depicted identical twins, Yvette and Yvonne Sylvander, on its cover. Yvette is clad in a one-piece bathing suit and Yvonne in a bikini.

3. In a study on media coverage and sports role models, Marovelli and Crawford (1987) found that female high school athletes are more likely to identify with male athletes than female athletes, suggesting that the media's underrepresentation of women in sports leaves young women with few same-sex role models (p. 236).

REFERENCES

Bryant, J. (1980). A Two-Year Selective Investigation of the Female in Sport as Reported in the Paper Media. *Arena Review, 4,* 32–44.

Bryson, L. (1983). Sport and the Oppression of Women. *The Australian and New Zealand Journal of Sociology, 19*(3), 413–426.

Bryson, L. (1987). Sport and the Maintenance of Masculine Hegemony. *Women's Studies International Forum, 10,* 349–360.

Daddario, G. (1992). Swimming Against the Tide: Sports Illustrated's Imagery of Female Athletes in a Swimsuit World. *Women's Studies in Communication, 15,* 49–64.

Dow, B. J. (1990). Hegemony, Feminist Criticism and *The Mary Tyler Moore Show. Critical Studies in Mass Communication, 7*(3), 261–274.

Duncan, M. C. (1990). Sports Photographs and Sexual Difference: Images of Women and Men in the 1984 and 1988 Olympic Games. *Sociology of Sport Journal, 7,* 22–40.

Duncan, M. C. & Hasbrook, C. A. (1988). Denial of Power in Televised Women's Sport. *Sociology of Sport Journal, 5,* 1–21.

Gitlin, T. (1982). Prime Time Ideology: The Hegemonic Process in Television Entertainment. In H. Newcomb (ed.), *Television: The Critical View* (3rd ed., pp. 426–454). New York: Oxford University Press.

Graydon, J. (1983). "But it's more than a game. It's an institution." Femininist Perspectives on Sport. *Feminist Review, 13,* 5–16.

Hilliard, D. C. (1984). Media Images of Male and Female Professional Athletes: An Interpretive Analysis of Magazine Articles. *Sociology of Sport Journal, 1,* 251–262.

Kane, M. J. (1987). The "New" Female Athlete: Socially Sanctioned Image or Modern Role for Women? *Medicine and Sport Science, 24,* 101–111.

Kane, M. J. (1988). Media Coverage of the Female Athlete Before, During, and After Title IX: *Sports Illustrated* Revisited. *Journal of Sport Management, 2,* 87–99.

Klein, M. (1988). Women in the Discourse of Sport Reports. *International Review for Sociology of Sport, 23,* 137–151.

Lemon, J. (1977). Women and Blacks on Prime-Time Television. *Journal of Communication, 27,* 70–79.

Loeb, J. C. (1990). Rhetorical and Ideological Conservatism in *thirtysomething. Critical Studies in Mass Communication, 7*(3), 249–260.

Lumpkin, A. & Williams, L. (1991). An Analysis of *Sports Illustrated* Feature Articles, 1954–1987. *Sociology of Sport Journal, 8,* 16–32.

Marovelli, E. & Crawford, S. (1987). Mass Media Influence on Female High School Athletes' Identification with Professional Athletes. *International Journal of Sport Psychology, 18,* 231–236.

McNeil, J. C. (1975). Feminism, Femininity, and the Television Series: A Content Analysis. *Journal of Broadcasting, 19,* 259–271.

Messner, M. A. (1988). Sports and Male Domination: The Female Athlete as Contested Ideological Terrain. *Sociology of Sport Journal, 5,* 197–211.

Methany, E. (1965). *Connotations of Movement in Sport and Dance*. Dubuque, IA: Wm. C. Brown.

Newman, B. (1989, February). Birds of a Feather. *Sports Illustrated*, pp. 141–142.

Poe, A. (1976). Active Women in Ads. *Journal of Communication, 26*, 185–192.

Reid, L. N. & Soley, L. (1979). *Sports Illustrated*'s Coverage of Women in Sports. *Journalism Quarterly, 56*, 861–862.

Rintala, J. & Birrell, S. (1984). Fair Treatment for the Active Female: A Content Analysis of *Young Athlete* Magazine. *Sociology of Sport Journal, 1*, 231–250.

Seggar, J. F. (1975). Imagery of Women in Television Drama: 1974. *Journal of Broadcasting, 19*, 273–282.

Snyder, E. E. & Kane, M. J. (1990). Photo Elicitation: A Methodological Technique for Studying Sport. *Journal of Sport Management, 4*, 21–30.

Sports Illustrated. (1989, August 28). Front page.

Trujillo, N. (1991). Hegemonic Masculinity on the Mound: Media Representations of Nolan Ryan and American Sports Culture. *Critical Studies in Mass Communication, 8*(3), 290–308.

TV Guide. (1991, August 3). Listings, p. 62.

Green but Unseen: Marginalizing the Environment on Television

James Shanahan

> We believe that we live in the "age of information," that there has
> been an information "explosion," an information "revolution." While
> in a certain narrow sense this is the case, in many important ways
> just the opposite is true. We also live at a moment of deep ignorance,
> when vital knowledge that humans have always possessed about who
> we are and where we live seems beyond our reach. An Unenlighten-
> ment. An age of missing information.
>
> McKibben, 1992, p. 9

Recent cultural wars have been and are being fought over the environmental question. But what information is missing? How much do we
really know about our natural environment? How can something as
"ubiquitous" as the environment be marginalized in our consciousness?
Is there really a diminution in awareness about the environment, or is it
simply a matter of the quality of that awareness? In the past thirty or so
years there has been a vigorous if circumscribed debate over this question, as various camps (academic, commercial, and activist) have sought
to define what makes someone aware of his or her environment, and
what makes that meaningful to the society at large. This chapter assumes
that it *is* indeed possible to marginalize the environment, and also that

it is possible to marginalize the environment even at a time when apparently unprecedented "attention" is being paid to it.

Unquestionably, there is much public attention to the *attitude* known as "environmental concern" or "environmental awareness." One's attention is often directed to the environment in the marketplace, in business, at school, and in the mass media. For instance, in the marketplace, products are now using "green" labeling and packaging as a means to encourage purchase of the product, basically as a marketing ploy. In business, managers and decision makers are becoming more environmentally conscious as means both to placate policy makers and to better public perception of their operations. In schools, the environmental ideology is being propounded at all levels, culminating in the proliferation of environmental studies programs in many colleges and universities. And then, in the mass media, there are news stories about the environment and entertainment programs which sometimes have environmental themes embedded in them.

From this, one would suspect that the average person must be acquiring environmental awareness, and that the environment would benefit from this. Or perhaps the picture is not so rosy, especially if we make a distinction between attention and awareness. "Attention" implies that one's view may be directed toward an object or concept. Unquestionably, at this moment, significant attention is being given to the environment. This even extends to "concern" among certain social groups. "Concern" is the state where one's normal mental ease is troubled by something, in this case the natural environment. But what about awareness? Webster's defines "awareness" as the state of having or showing realization, perception, or knowledge, and the term implies something beyond the act of paying attention or even being concerned. Being aware of something means having it always be in your consciousness at some level, and having a fundamental understanding of how it works and how it can be changed.

The term "environment" itself is subject to many possible confusions, and thus terms like "environmental awareness" are loaded with interpretational possibilities. Besides confusing "awareness" with "concern" or "attention," we can confuse the natural environment with the informational or "symbolic" environment. Any society, via social processes, chooses its mainstream and delineates what is at the margin. More fundamentally, all societies "choose" an environment. They don't choose their natural environment, of course, but they create symbolic environments, which have extremely real and important consequences for the natural one. The socially constructed environment "contains" both the mainstream and the margin; it is a "ground" against which the "figures" of mainstream and margin are defined. This symbolic environment is a message space in which the "important" messages of our everyday life obtain meaning. In the symbolic world, the environment is whichever information is best seen as background information, privileging whatever informational "figure" interests us. The symbolic environment is that information, by definition, which *least* "occupies" our conscious but collective social mind. But the fact that it occupies our mind least also leads to the conclusion that the environment is that which we most intuitively understand. The symbolic environment is what we take for granted and know best.

Thus, the environment we take for granted today is neither air nor water. It is, rather, information (broadly defined). Because we make a living by manipulating information, it is the information background that we see as nurturing. Instead of hunting, we do research. Instead of farming we cultivate databases, libraries, and archives. Instead of wearing natural items as personal totems we identify with information totems such as product logos and designer clothes. And, instead of creating our own stories of the natural world, of the gods who rule our fates, and of the rules we must follow, we have TV.

It is the thesis of this chapter that modern society is not well-equipped to provide environmental awareness, although it is well-enough suited to generate concern and even a sensationalistic sense of impending doom. We may recycle ourselves into oblivion, with little impact on the true problem. In particular, this chapter focuses on the role of the mass media in developing environmental awareness, both from a normative and a practical perspective. This chapter includes an analysis of data that are, as far as I am aware, the only extant content analysis of environmental information in entertainment programming in this country.

Although U.S. television is an enormously complex industry, serving many functions, it is clear that its prime function is to sell advertising. It does this through the time-honored technique of storytelling. Although the technological aspects of the television medium may be relatively new, the social role that television has assumed has always been with us. Storytellers and their stories allow us to make sense of the world in which we live, and allow us to perceive our role in the social structures that protect us from danger and give meaning to our lives.

This storytelling function means that television has a quasi-mythological role to play. In this sense, a myth is simply a story about social reality that most members of the culture believe to be important or true. Obviously, because television tells so many stories it may also create many myths, but one can suspect that there are also higher-order characteristics of different stories which begin to "hang together," because the overall social structure of stories cannot afford to be too contradictory.

Given this, it's not surprising that television could assume the role of myth-maker in the area of the natural environment. All cultures have a vision of their environment, although they may differ radically. Nature may be seen as devilish wilderness, benign Providence, or simply as abstract beauty. Still, for all of us, a mythical conception of nature seems fundamental. In 20th-century America, if we wish to understand how we think about our environment, we should also understand the stories we tell about it. Although many scholars have analyzed the works of nature-thinkers such as Thoreau or Muir, surprisingly few have addressed what is a patently more important question: What are the important mythologies about the environment for the everyday person? To answer that question we must look at television.

MEDIA AND ENVIRONMENT: HOW IT COULD BE

Let's say that Bill Cosby (or Roseanne, or Seinfeld, or any other TV character) in a series of programs, mentions issues like whaling, ozone depletion, and acid rain. Tens of millions of people hear these issues mentioned. One would be tempted to assume that the audience becomes more environmentally aware. Perhaps even more pointedly, let's say that a program like *Northern Exposure,* also viewed by tens of millions of people, not only consistently talks about environmental issues but includes native characters and deals with traditional environmental ideologies. Again, one assumes that the effect of this on environmentalism would be necessarily beneficial.

Based on examples like these, many people would argue that television is perfectly placed to play a role in the generation of environmental awareness. It has become fairly routine for the media to examine environmental problems, Hollywood stars have made the issue a pet, and the environment has become more of a focus in news coverage over the past few years. Concurrently, public opinion polls have registered increasing levels of public "concern" about the environment (Gillroy & Shapiro, 1986), although people always tend to "say" they are environmentally aware. Seeing that more light has been shed on environmental topics, and also that more people are saying they are concerned, it is tempting to conclude that increased media coverage results in increased public awareness.

Indeed, as we consider the issue, it makes some sense that media would be well-positioned to extend our awareness, making it possible for us to be more informed about the environmental consequences of various things that we do. This is a fairly simple notion: technology made it possible for us to affect much more than just our local environment, so why should not media technology make it possible for us to be aware of the consequences, even if they can only be measured at farther and farther distances?

The idea is that media are information resources and they also are part of an information environment, and ideally speaking, they should feed back information to us that lets us know when we are polluting, and also tells when we are taking positive actions. As Meadows argues,

A paradigm is upheld by the constant repetition of ideas that fit within it. It is affirmed by every information exchange, in families, churches, literature, music, workplaces, shopping places, daily chats on the street. The key to paradigm stability and coherence is repetition. Therefore when people learned how to repeat information on a mass basis—to make printing presses and send messages over electronic waves—they not only created tools with the potential to improve vastly the information flows in systems, they also inadvertently invented potent techniques for paradigm affirmation and, theoretically, for paradigm change. (Meadows, 1991, p. 74)

If our media system were actually structured in a way that promoted paradigmatic change, what would it look like? Media would position themselves to *measure* or *discover* pollution, and environmental destruction, and report back on this to the public regularly. They would produce programs to make sure that people *understand* that environmental harms are something that have economic and personal consequences. They would adopt a *consistent* position on environmental issues (reconciling the usually oppositional attitudes of growth/consumerism and environmentalism). They would also proactively seek to inform people, rather than depending solely on marketplace mechanisms to achieve higher levels of environmental awareness. Most importantly, media would actually have to deemphasize their own social importance, so that people could actually return to the environment to experience its own logic and order.

Now, this is idealism at best, utopianism at worst. Nevertheless, such a system would require a *decentralized* media structure. Information should flow easily from sender to receiver but should also flow as easily back. The mass media network architecture would have to be, rather than the hub and spoke architecture that is most common around the world, more of a star-shaped or even neural architecture, with less emphasis on centralized points of distribution. It may be that new technologies will begin to develop the possibility of such an architecture (granting that, historically, such advances have always been dominated by commercial interests). Such a pattern would prevent breakdown in the function of the system if one of the key points in the system were to fail in the creation of environmental awareness. It would also tend to return more environmental information back into the system and to its users.

Program producers would have to become schooled in the meaning of the environment in today's times, so that they can effectively *propagan-*

dize the point that environmental costs, although not measured in dollars, are still real economic costs. This is currently happening with some media producers, but only at a very slow rate.

Although the technology of media become decentralized, there should also be a greater *conceptual* centralization in the planning of program schedules by individual programming entities. Programs with environmentally aware messages should not have to be overwhelmed by programs whose messages are either environment-apathetic or even explicitly anti-environment. If there are more environmental messages this partially solves the problem, but all programs need to be produced with an eye toward the lessons they teach us about the environment. This conceptual centralization, when matched with architectural decentralization would provide a more efficacious environmental awareness machine. The problem here, of course, is that this contradicts the sanctity of information in our culture, which equates corporate commercial control with freedom and democracy.

Finally, there must be a conscious decision by media owners and managers to become environmental *activists*. This is a highly controversial position (see LaMay and Dennis, 1991), but some journalists have begun to debate the worthiness of this idea. Coming from an objectivity-obsessed institution such as American journalism, that is an important development. However, such media environmental activism would best encompass the entire range of media institutions, from news to editorials to entertainment and other forms of message sending and storytelling. Obviously, we are some distance from such a system.

Some environmentalists think that media are, by essence, anti-environmental because they represent technology and technology is what damages the environment. Tokar, for instance, a Green, says about computer use that "[t]he real impact of early computer use on many children is a reduction of experience to what can be represented on the screen and an invitation to view the world as an object for manipulation and control" (1987, p. 95). This suggests that there is no content that would make computers hospitable to the environment. He makes the same argument about television, taking something of a technological determinist position about communication media in general. Ellul (1964) argues that technology itself is what distances us from natural reality. My position is that technology will always accompany civilization; thus, there must be some acceptance of a humanizing and pro-environmental role for the media as technology, or we are doomed. However, it is the way in which our society appropriates technological developments that contributes to the appearance that high technologies such as communication media are environmentally damaging. This "social construction" of the media is the focus of the next section.

MEDIA AND ENVIRONMENT: THE WAY IT IS

Clearly, the media are not organized in the ways just described. Most members of media institutions would argue that the policies discussed are impossibly naive, or even malevolently socialistic. That is because, to them, the symbolic environment that privileges freedom of information and freedom of exchange is more valuable and inviolable than the symbolic environment that privileges life.

Although the media are "free"—in the sense that content is not directly dictated by the government—they are owned by businesses. Also, they themselves are businesses. This creates a tension between the need to produce attractive programs that the public will consume and the need to advance the agenda of corporate institutions. In the past, the corporate agenda was anti-environmental; nowadays the corporations deny this. Thus, in the past, media could ease the tension by avoiding environmentalism as an issue within most programming, while still serving the needs of advertisers. But now, the public, whose mainstream ideology incorporates aspects of environmentalism, must be appeased at some level, and it demands some amount of environmentalism from its corporate mentors (even if only for the sake of appearances). But the nature of the environmentalism presented is of course very inoffensive and minor when compared to the fundamental ideology espoused of consumption and individualism. The result is that the media are slowly adopting a lite-green form of environmentalism to gratify public demand without subverting the corporate agenda. The media, although devoting attention to the environment, are not structured to provide "awareness." Thus, Cosby's hypothetical attention to the issue would be admirable but does little to change the underlying ethic. Even *Northern Exposure,* while reflecting a romanticized notion of environmentalism that is very popular, has little ability on its own to contradict the massive messages of consumption and individualism that pervade corporate culture.

Several things are happening in the environmental debate that should be of concern to any genuine environmentalist. First, environmentalism is being co-opted by business and media, so that the meaning of the term becomes "rational consumption of consumer products" rather than "realization, perception, or knowledge" of environmental issues. Of course, it is difficult to prove that business is trying to co-opt environmentalism for its own purposes. But the recent flurry of activity in this area is instructive. Peggy Filis, an expert on "green marketing," writing in the media trade journal *Electronic Media* (January 6, 1992) notes that "[n]ew products, new packaging, repositioning, seal-of-approval certifications and green advertising are all elements of the marketing quest for what is expected to be a $10 billion pot of gold within a very few years" (p. 36).

However, it is likely that business attention to green issues will fade as public attention turns elsewhere.

Second, environmentalism is being channeled into non-threatening directions and is being associated with admittedly important strategies such as recycling and bottle-return, as opposed to radical restructuring of the national philosophy toward damaging the environment. This is not to denigrate various efforts at environmental clean up, which are necessary components of an environmental strategy. But this form of concern is being exploited to prevent more far-reaching forms of concern. Small-scale consumer-based strategies alone will not address the root problems, although one gets this impression from the media.

Third, the media themselves do not "create" environmentalism, they ride the bandwagon, which has gained momentum after thirty years of media's ignoring the situation. Once they have made the problem seem important, the media use the issue to retain credibility and also to create new ways to pursue their main goal, which is to sell products. Thus we obtain the ultimate absurdity of promoting environmentalism through the sale of more products, when what we patently need is less consumption and an economy on a more rationalized or sustainable scale. There seems to me no way to dispute the assertion that media do not, in the main, set social trends, they adapt them and make them evident to the masses. Media are most effective at presenting a sanitized version of the mainstream, and reprocessing individual expression to make it risk-free. In this instance, environmentalism can only be represented to the masses after the masses have conferred mainstream status on it. Then the media will repackage the issue, de-authenticating it in the process.

Fourth, when measured objectively rather than subjectively, media seem to depress environmentalism rather than encourage it. Although hardly any data exist on this topic, what evidence there is shows that exposure to television is negatively related to environmental awareness (Shanahan & Morgan, 1990; Shanahan, 1993). That is, heavy viewers of television are less likely to express environmental awareness than light viewers. Although the causal link between television and environmentalism is not clear, it seems logical that this occurs because the mainstream of television's messages has to do with entertainment, and entertainment, self-gratification, and consumption are undoubtedly components of the cycle fueling our environmental problem. It is true that the statistical evidence regarding the negative cultivation of environmental concern is meager; there are very few studies in this area. One of the major pieces of evidence lacking is a systematic content analysis of the presentation of the environment in television entertainment. Such analyses are fairly common for TV news, but naturally, most people are watching entertainment when they watch television, and entertainment is clearly one of the more effective ways to reinforce the anti-environmental ideology that all

Americans implicitly accept (or are almost forced to accept). The absence of data on this point prompts the analyses that form the rest of this chapter.

Finally, perhaps the most important issue is the way in which environmentalism is presented as an individual attribute, so we believe that the solutions for environmental problems must come from individuals rather than social change. These factors, taken together, show how it is possible for the environment to enter the mainstream discourse at the same time that it is being marginalized. In a way, this very entry guarantees its marginalization, because the mainstream discourse is not configured to handle a topic like the environment properly. This is how media, and especially television, can detract from environmental awareness even as they become noticeably "green."

This research builds on the "cultural indicators" (CI) framework, a well-known form of communication research designed to measure what the culture is teaching its pupils at the broadest possible levels. Mostly this is done through an analysis of the issues presented in television programming. In "cultural indicators" analysis (Gerbner, 1973), it is customary to perform content analyses to determine the central ideological thrust of television programming, to formulate hypotheses about the expected impact of viewing television. These analyses also serve as the ongoing cultural "indices" from which CI theory takes its name. Mostly, CI's analyses have focused on topics such as violence, sexism, and political issues. Apart from brief items in the standard CI coding instrument, none of these analyses have focused on environmental issues. Thus, this analysis presents the first systematic examination of environmental messages in prime-time television.

The underlying assumption was that prime-television is really not as environmentally concerned as we might expect. Because no previous analyses exist to serve as benchmarks, there is no way to comparatively evaluate the strength of this hypothesis: this was the first such time the phenomenon has been measured. However, the content analysis was somewhat disingenuously implemented knowing ahead of time that there really is precious little environmentalism in prime-time entertainment. I firmly expected from the start that there would be little reference to the environment in programs that have traditionally avoided mention of most important issues, let alone the environment. Because of this, the analysis was designed to accomplish more than simply to measure the frequency of environmental "mentions" in the mass media. An additional focus was the analysis of environmental themes in comparison to others, so that the hypothesized dearth of environmental issues could be more easily seen in comparison to television's prevalent coverage of issues such as interpersonal relations, crime, money, and other things. Also, the analysis was oriented toward providing complete detailed textual descriptions of all environmental images encountered, so that there would a base from which to argue about the quality of environmentalism on television in the absence of high quantity. To this end, I report not only statistical information on the incidence of environmental information in the mass media, but I concentrate on some of the interesting cases that were encountered.

HOW THE RESEARCH WAS CONDUCTED

In two week-long time periods (starting November 11, 1991, and January 25, 1993) all programs appearing on the three Boston network affiliates were recorded from the prime-time slot (7–11 P.M.). All programs were analyzed, even if they were not network programs. The sample included network news programs, local feature/magazine programming, local news programming, syndicated first-run programming, and regular network entertainment (including some "off-network" syndication). Four hours of programming were coded on three networks on seven evenings in two weeks, yielding 168 hours of sample content, or 216 programs.

Each program was examined using a four-part coding scheme. The first part was based on the coding scheme long used in cultural indicators research to record basic information about the themes appearing in programs. The various themes (there were a total of sixteen) included things like "relationships between the sexes," "media/entertainment," "law enforcement/crime," "health," "science," and so forth. A theme for "nature," also used in the CI coding scheme, was included. (Although "nature" and "environment" are not quite the same, this preserves continuity with other cultural indicators research. In any case, the rest of the instrument is designed to give a very detailed picture of environmental images on TV.) The coding scheme employed allowed for themes to be coded as absent, representing a minor focus, representing a secondary focus, or representing a prime focus.

Dealing with environment more specifically, I coded how many environmental "events" occurred in each program. An environmental event was defined as any episode involving spoken words or physical action in which environmental issues were specifically implicated or denoted. Environmental images were more difficult to code, since almost any image could be given an environmental interpretation. Events were coded as either environmentally "concerned," "neutral," or "unconcerned." "Concerned" statements were those that expressed approval of the importance of environmental issues or implicitly supported environmental positions. For instance, if a character in a sitcom mentioned recycling and either explicitly or implicitly supported the technique, that would be a "concerned" event. "Neutral" events took no position but mentioned the environment. "Unconcerned" events were those where specific opposition was taken to environmental issues or where such opposition was implicated. In some cases, for instance, environmental issues became the focus of a joke or putdown. Criticizing someone as a "tree-hugger" would be an example of an unconcerned environmental event.

The next part of the instrument coded details about the fictional environmental event. Demographic information about who performed the event was coded, as was interpretational information about the event, such as its political focus, the object to which it was directed, and so on. Information about whether the act was dramatic or serious was also obtained. Finally, information about what specific environmental themes were included was coded. This analysis compiled an extensive list of environmental problems and issues to see what specific kinds of problems TV was best and worst at covering. Each environmental event was coded separately.

Data were coded by the author and two assistants. Coding pretests were done to enhance intercoder reliability prior to recording the data in each of the two separate years. However, content analysis of television programming is extremely expensive and subjective, and extensive reliability testing and double-checks of data were not possible.

RESULTS

In the sample, sitcoms dominated the programming (about 30 percent), with feature programs, game shows, news, and other kinds of dramatic series making up most of the rest of the lineup (about 10–15 percent each). Table 1 shows the distribution and importance of the various themes that were encountered in these programs, using the CI coding scheme.

The major foci of programs in the sample were home/family, law enforcement, finance/success, relationships, health, and media/entertainment issues. Nature was absent from about three quarters of all programs, was a significant issue in about 10 percent of programs, but was almost never the outstanding issue.

It was also rare to find environmental "events" in programming. Among 165 fictional programs coded, fourteen had an instance of an environmentally concerned event, seventeen programs contained environmentally neutral actions, and three programs contained an environmentally unconcerned event. As Table 2 shows, however, 1993 saw relatively more environmental events, reflecting the increase in nominal environmental concern, as already discussed. This was particularly noticeable for "concerned" actions or events. Environmentally concerned actions generally took place in the context of sitcoms. Neutral events were spread more widely among a variety of genres such as sitcoms,

Table 1
Themes Coded, Their Frequency and Importance

Theme	Not Present	Present, but minor	Significant Issue	Outstanding Issue
Home/family	33.0	23.9	25.7	17.4
Relationships	47.3	12.7	23.6	16.4
Law enforcement	52.3	5.5	18.2	23.9
Health	52.3	17.4	21.1	9.2
Finance/success	59.6	19.3	8.3	12.8
Media/entertainment	62.4	12.8	11.0	13.8
Politics	72.5	9.2	11.9	6.4
Nature	72.7	12.7	12.7	1.8
Science	74.3	20.2	4.6	0.9
Minorities	74.3	17.4	8.3	0.0
Business	77.1	12.8	10.1	0.0
Education	79.8	11.9	6.4	1.8
Military	81.7	8.3	8.3	1.8
Supernatural	84.4	5.5	6.4	3.7
Consumer issues	89.0	5.5	3.7	1.8
Religion	89.9	9.2	0.9	0.0

movies, and comedy-variety. The unconcerned actions also took place in a sitcom, usually as a joke.

Most programs (42.1 percent) took place in an urban location, whereas only about 13 percent took place in a small town or rural location. The remainder of the programs were set in mixed locales. Many of these mixed locale programs were news programs with stories from various locations; these programs concentrated on urban environments as well. More than half of the programs were entirely or primarily shot in the studio, whereas only 26.5 percent were shot mostly outdoors. Again, however, there was an increase in the number of "outdoor" shows between 1991 and 1993. Environmentally concerned events were not more likely to occur in programs that had been primarily shot outside, and neither were unconcerned events more likely to take place in primarily studio shows. In fact, since most environmentally concerned actions were in sitcoms, they were more likely to have been shot in a studio.

The simple statistical picture that emerges is one where environmental and natural images appear infrequently in fictional programming. Programs are mostly shot indoors and in urban locations, focusing more on relationships, sex, crime, and family issues. Thus, "attention" is certainly being paid to the environment but it is not something that one really sees throughout prime-time. The result may be that one's *awareness* is

Table 2
Number of Environmental Events Encountered

	Percentage of Shows with Environmental Events		
Year	Concerned	Neutral	Unconcerned
1991	4.7	7.0	2.3
1993	12.7	13.9	1.3

directed toward things besides the environment. Indeed, the major focus on relationships, family, crime, and so on is quite a-environmental, if not explicitly anti-environmental. The fact that the natural environment is seen less often than indoor environments probably emphasizes our leanings toward being an indoor culture. The emphasis on urban settings also does this. In any case, the dichotomy between news and entertainment programming about environmental issues is striking. Whereas news may bring consciousness of environmental issues, the lifestyle impacts of these issues are apparently not addressed in fictional programs.

As we have seen, there were few environmental events in our programs (compared to violent events, for instance, which occur six to eight times per hour). So it makes little sense to analyze them statistically. It is more useful to examine the environmental events themselves to get a sense of how they fit in programs, whether they are important or not, whether they are treated humorously or seriously, and so on.

First let's look at the 1991 sample. One "environmentally concerned" event was encountered in the ABC program *Step-by-Step,* in which an adolescent male character commented on the natural beauty of a location in which the family was camping. Specific mention was made of the lack of cars and how "this is the life." This particular event is typical of the few events that we did encounter: they were mostly apolitical and praised the beauty of the natural environment in comparison to the drudgery of city life. This kind of concern is typical in the marginalization of environmentalism: it supports the basic idea of beauty, wilderness, and nature, but in no way deals with the political subtext. By making it a "background" issue, it in fact lends support to the idea that the environment is already healthy, and remains so.

In the NBC program *Sisters,* there was a dispute between neighbors about a tree on the border of their property. One neighbor demands that the tree be chopped down, and specifically complains about having so many trees around. The protagonist neighbor says that "trees are beautiful" and defends the right of the tree to exist. Thus, we have two environmental events, one concerned and one unconcerned, although again the level of politicization on the issue is minimal. In fact, the tree dispute is a dramatic device used to introduce a later resolution in which we find out that the mean-old-tree-hater is really lonely because of the recent death of his wife. He eventually saves the tree-lover's son who falls out of the same tree and there is a happy ending as the neighbors get together for a friendly dinner. In the end, the tree stays.

One movie, *Deadly Medicine* on NBC, had two environmental events, both judged to be "neutral." The setting of this movie alternated between small town and city, but occasionally moved to a rural location where the protagonist's husband was building a house. This movie was about a doctor who was unfairly charged with killing her patients. The lead (played by Veronica Hamel) twice states her reasons for moving to the "hill country" as environmental beauty. The two events were of such minor importance that they could only be judged as neutral. This is also an example of how one has to "stretch" to consider an episode an "environmental event." I was very liberal in defining such events, which is important because if one is not liberal in one's definitions one encounters even fewer.

An episode of *Designing Women* contained a section where a character expressed anti-hunting views. This was coded as a "concerned" event, although many hunters consider themselves environmentalists. Another character responded to her in a separately coded event that hunting was necessary to keep the deer population down. In any case, the general thrust of the interchange was comedic rather than informational, since the point was to portray one of the characters as a macho rural rube, in opposition to the enlightened urban stance of the protagonist.

In an event typical of the way sitcoms deal with the environment, *The Royal Family* went camping, bringing bio-degradable and ozone-friendly products along with them. In this episode, the environment (that is, the camping milieu) was the enemy of urban comfort, with the green products an obvious sop to Hollywood's environmentally correct ideology.

An episode of *Cosby* was addressing the stereotypes of young black males. Cosby was speaking to a class of students on this issue as a concerned member of the community. Two of the youths were joking about how they get blamed for everything bad that happens in society. They commented to humorous effect how they might be blamed for the "greenhouse effect" and one character said "If whales are missing, we stole it!" This event was coded as neutral, but was the only explicit mention of endangered species or global warming in the week's programming.

As mentioned, the 1993 sample had more events to look at. On *Knot's Landing*, recycling was part of a public service punishment meted out to a character. Similarly, recycling appeared on *Major Dad*, when the major indicated that he planned to spend a particular day recycling (as part of a joke). Both actions were very quick in the scheme of the show, but they do indicate how Hollywood scriptwriters have been persuaded to include mentions of environmental themes in their shows.

Jeopardy, as American's schoolteacher, occasionally touched on environmental themes. One "answer" had to do with Chernobyl and the fact that some sheep had been poisoned. On another occasion, "conservation" was an entire category of answers. One of the answers had to do with a spill from a Coors beer plant, which killed many fish.

"Environmental correctness" sometimes became the focus of jokes in sitcoms. For instance, on *Golden Palace,* a spin-off of the popular *Golden Girls,* one character put down another by saying "you are a spotted owl in the forest of life." Or, on the popular *Wings,* the following exchange occurred:

"Hey, if you're finished with that soda can, can I have it? I'm recycling."

"Sure, I'm all for helping the environment."

"Oh, I'm just doing it for the money to pay you back."

Sometimes environmental concerns of the past come back in old movies. For instance, in *Cannonball Run II* the characters got out of a speeding ticket by telling the officer they were carrying radioactive material from a meltdown.

On *The Commish,* a character commented "I am the social equivalent of toxic waste." On *Funniest Home Videos* a video trick depicted a horse with six legs. The affable host offers this: "this is why you should never build a dude ranch next to a nuclear reactor."

On *Coach,* the coach visits a rainforest group to convince them that his daughter's donation is written on a bad check. He jokes: "The rainforests? Now isn't that a stupid cause, they're not even going to be around in ten years!" The rainforests were again a focus on *Family Matters,* when a character was said to use a "rainforest tape" for relaxation, including sounds of bulldozers, chainsaws, and animals shrieking.

Finally, in a Hitchcockian twist, one of the dinosaurs on ABC's eponymously entitled show was reading a newspaper with the headline: "Environmentalists Name Top Corporate Polluters."

So, environmental information in entertainment is usually incidental. This is obviously one technique of marginalization. Even though most Hollywood writers and producers probably consider themselves environmentalists, they minimize the environment by treating it as an ancillary issue or as a device for jokes, plot twists, or character development. At a deeper level, the very absence of environment, and the inattention to it, work to create a mind that knows very little about the natural world. Of course, there have been programs where environment is the main focus, but they are few in number.

There certainly were news stories that covered environmental themes. The focus of this chapter is entertainment, however, for a specific reason. Entertainment dominates prime-time television, and entertainment is the reason most people tune in to TV in prime-time. They are there to escape or relax or be diverted. During this time, they are particularly open to portrayals of the world and how it is structured. Because the focus is on the plot or characters, background issues come to be seen as "common sense."

Let us return to the idea of "myth." Roland Barthes considered this process in his well known essay "Mythologies" (1957), where he argued that one function of signs is to convert social History into inevitable Nature. For Barthes, this was a kind of depoliticization of speech. If things could be made to seem "natural," then the issue of human political bias could be avoided. As Evernden (1992) points out in his discussion of Barthes, even the natural itself can be de-historicized, becoming Nature in the process. Because conceptions of nature have always been social, they have varied over time. But we paradoxically tend to see Nature as that which is beyond such a social construction. This may be arguably true of physical nature, but certainly not of social Nature.

As far as prime-time television is concerned then, it seems that even Nature is subject to "naturalization." In this process, the stories of television take place in a new environment, one constructed by television itself. Cosby's mention of the whales, say, implies a natural order that would be salvageable if indeed the whales could be saved. That's not a conspiracy of the producers of *Cosby,* it's just a feature of the story system to which they belong. The new environment of television is very hospitable to drama, comedy, news, and other genres, of course; after all, that is its function. It is a message or story environment. But this environment does not really exist, and it marginalizes both the real physical environment and movements struggling to develop sane and survivable environmental policies.

DISCUSSION

It could be argued that it is not the role of entertainment to deal with political and social issues. Nevertheless, entertainment does deal with such issues all the time, and therefore places itself in a position where the stances it takes can be legitimately criticized. Although the environment is somewhat present in news, it is relatively absent in entertainment. News can certainly bring attention to issues, but it is legitimate to ask how attention can become translated to awareness and eventually behavior.

Television performs an important and ancient function: it tells stories. Stories have always given us lessons about our environment; they play an extremely important role in defining what is natural and what is unnatural. That is, the story is a powerful socializing agent. Moreover, the story, through its narratives and styles, focuses our attention on issues and especially ways of perceiving issues. Because of this, it is important to note not only what issues stories tell us about but how they do it. Simply depicting environmental catastrophes does not ensure that citizens will become more environmentally concerned, aware, or active, any more than the endless depiction of violence rouses citizens to take anti-violence measures. The depiction in TV stories of environmental issues treats them as extremely minor side issues, peripheral to the important concerns of relationships, materialism, consumption, law enforcement, and so on.

If television wishes to be an environmental force it will have to adopt a more socially concerned perspective throughout its programming schedule. How much would be enough? No specific amount is needed, rather, some consistency is necessary. The vast majority of programming promotes old-paradigm thinking: the car commercial that says "It's about style, it's about power, it's about control," is an example of the sort of thinking on man-nature relationships that are emphasized by consumer mass culture.

In the long run, television will lose its superficial interest in environmental issues as it has done in the past. Only if the environment absolutely forces us to take notice can we expect continued coverage from our mass media, and that is a frightening prospect.

NOTE

I would like to thank Anniken Naess and Katherine McComas, who assisted in the collection of these data.

REFERENCES

Barthes, R. (1957). *Mythologies.* New York: Hill and Wang.
Ellul, J. (1964). *The Technological Society.* New York: Vintage.
Evernden, N. (1992). *The Social Creation of Nature.* Baltimore: Johns Hopkins University Press.
Gerbner, G. (1973). Cultural indicators: The third voice. In G. Gerbner, L. Gross & W. Melody (eds.), *Communications Technology and Social Policy.* New York: John Wiley and Sons, pp. 555–573.
Gilroy, J. & R. Shapiro. (1986). The polls: Environmental protection. *Public Opinion Quarterly, 50:* 270–279.
LaMay, C. & E. Dennis (eds.). (1991). *Media and the Environment.* Washington, DC: Island Press.
Meadows, D. (1991). Changing the world through the informationsphere. In C. LaMay & E. Dennis (eds.), *Media and the Environment.* Washington, DC: Island Press, pp. 67–79.
McKibben, B. (1992). *The Age of Missing Information.* New York: Random House.
Shanahan, J. & Morgan, M. (1990). Television and environment. Paper presented to the American Psychological Association, Boston, MA.

Shanahan, J. (1993). Television and the cultivation of environmental concern: 1988–1992. In A. Hansen (ed.), *Mass Media and Environmental Issues.* Leicester: University of Leicester Press.

Tokar, B. (1987). *The Green Alternative.* San Pedro: R. and E. Miles.

Initial Lessons in Popular Orientalism from *National Geographic* Magazine

Linda Steet

This chapter focuses on Orientalism in *National Geographic* magazine from the end of the 19th century through the 1920s. This age was the height of European empires and when Ottoman rule of the Arab world was challenged and displaced by Western colonialism. European scientific and technological advances were such that certain Western European countries became dominant military powers in the world, against which the Ottomans were no match. In this period, European expansion in search of resources, markets, and colonies culminated in the French and the English having developed the two greatest colonial systems in the world. Arabs witnessed and experienced this changing international balance of power, firsthand.

In the 19th century, France completed (1830–1847) the first major European conquest of an Arabic-speaking country, Algeria. In 1839, Britain occupied Aden and, in due course, Egypt, Sudan, Tunisia, Morocco, and Libya fell under European domination. By the end of World War I, the Ottoman Empire was completely destroyed and, except for parts of the Arabian peninsula, the whole of the Arabic-speaking world (including Syria, Lebanon, Palestine, Iraq, and Transjordan) was divided up among European powers, primarily England and France. The political structure under which most Arabs had lived for four centuries, the Ottoman

Empire, came to an end and European colonial systems were entrenched in all areas of life. Arab commerce, finance, raw materials, agricultural production, schooling, government, import and export markets, and the like were in the hands of Europeans.

National Geographic's most current portrayal of this historical period will usher us into an examination of Orientalism in the magazine's first thirty years. In January 1987, as it entered its one-hundredth year and, again in January 1988, for its anniversary issue, *National Geographic* shared with readers reflections on the magazine's history and a description of the late 19th century, the era during which it was founded. Looking back a century, *National Geographic* saw a time "of action, and the relevant word was conquer—be it wilderness, disease, paganism, or ignorance."[1] This framing of colonialism as something of a gigantic good works project is one we shall encounter repeatedly, and see how its various components are identified, employed, and "conquered." The heroes of the late 19th century were said to have been "daring explorers" who matched the industrial tycoons of the day "in initiative, and in go-getter spirit."[2] The magazine says of that historical period:

The formation of societies like the National Geographic Society was just one expression of the demand for progress through organization and efficiency spawned by the experience of handling large numbers of men and machines during the Civil War. Indeed, the individual explorers became heroes, because they stood out as individuals—exotic examples of a new "can do" mentality that overtook Americans in the decades after the Civil War. As symbols, they represented those Darwinian, survival-of-the-fittest emerging "captains of industry."[3]

This period of "heroic exploration," or colonialism, was portrayed in the 1980s by *National Geographic* as a generally high-spirited, positive time. Against this interpretation we go back in time and examine "heroes," "the demand for progress," and social Darwinism at work.

Before we enter that era, another quotation from *National Geographic* in the 1980s further sets the historical scene for us:

The youthful United States was coming of age—going through a sort of national puberty and maturing as a world force. . . . Missionaries and businessmen were scattering into Asia and Latin America. Our explorers were competing with Europeans to reach far recesses of the world. . . . With equal vigor inventors and entrepreneurs were grabbing for shares in the industrial revolution. . . . Hand in glove with this ferment was the growth of national research and exploration societies.[4]

The characterization of becoming a world force during the era of colonialism as going through puberty explains that particular historical system of appropriation and exploitation as both natural and boy to man growth (this gendering operation is a favorite we encounter often in the magazine). Here national puberty is marked along a masculinist growth chart and the activities of American and European missionaries, explorers, and businessmen "in the far recesses of the world" are framed as manly competition. Made completely invisible in all of this, because of particular interests being supported, are the peoples of those "far recesses," which allows *National Geographic* to offer readers a rather clean, nostalgic look back at the heroic era of colonialism.

THE GEOGRAPHIC LINES OF DIFFERENCE

National Geographic's 1894 annual address by the president was given by Gardiner G. Hubbard and titled "Geographic Progress of Civilization." The address begins:

If parallels of latitude were drawn around the earth about fifteen degrees north and fifteen degrees south of Washington, the land within these parallels would include all the countries of the world that have been highly civilized and distinguished for art and science. No great people, except the Scandinavians and Scotch, who, from their climate, belong to the same region, ever existed outside these limits; no great men have ever lived, no great poems have ever been written, no literary or scientific work ever produced, in other parts of the globe. . . . The nearer man lives to the polar regions the greater his inferiority in intellect, the greater his barbarism.[5]

Hierarchical difference was geographically charted with only a minor break necessary in the parallel of latitude to include Scandinavia and Scotland. Continuing the geography lesson, readers learned that changing the starting point and drawing two parallels fifteen degrees north and fifteen degrees south of the equator, would delineate the region of the world with the richest lands and greatest varieties of vegetation and animal life. In these countries were found "both animal and vegetal life carried to the highest perfection, save only in the case of man, for whose development a different zone has been required."[6]

But Hubbard was optimistic that advanced man (read white man) and the world's richest environmental zone (read non-European countries) could successfully be united. This optimism was based on the power of Western industrial advances:

In the progress of civilization man with his inventions and discoveries, by the applied power of steam and electricity, has practically annihilated time and space. In the early history of man he was controlled by and subject to his environment, which shaped his life and formed his character; now he in turn controls his environment.[7]

Thus, so it would seem, the lands *outside* of Hubbard's parallels of difference were assumed the property of those people's *inside* the parallels of latitude. In fact, this period, with its relevant word being "conquer" and its "go getter spirit," as characterized by *National Geographic* in the quotations from the 1980s, found the Western world taking over the non-Western world.

These two worlds were clearly distinguished as such by the magazine from its earliest days, and this difference was not without assigned value. Hubbard's address set up man/nature as a binary opposite in which the former dominates the latter; along with industrial/non-industrial and civilized/primitive. Subtitles in the text of the address signaled these hierarchies for the readers: "The Changeless People of the Nile," "Slow Progress of the Dark Continent," "The Decadence of the Savage," and "Where Whites Fall before Blacks."

Interestingly, the Arab world fell within the geographic zones of both civilization and barbarism. Unlike European exceptions to latitudinal lines of difference, even those Arab countries in northern Africa and the Arab Gulf cut in two by the line fifteen degrees south of Washington were not given exceptional status. Actually, within the geography lesson's logic, having the Arab world straddle the zones could help explain both the area's great past civilizations and achievements and its later "backwardness" and need of colonization. The science that drew these lines of difference along parallels of latitude was what Said would refer to as "imaginative geography."[8] What is presented as natural fact, including geographic information, is so often human invention. Hubbard's geographic zones of difference were so imaginary and arbitrary that he had to allow for great latitude in exceptions to the rule. To make the lines confirm the realities of Western expansionist drives and the accompanying construction of race, breaks in the parallels of latitude, to include or exclude a given country, were acceptable.

"PRESTIGE OF THE WHITE RACE"

A good, bare-bones definition of racism is offered by Memmi who says it is: "the generalized and final assigning of values to real or imaginary differences, to the accuser's benefit and at his victim's expense, in order to justify the former's own privileges or aggression."[9] How this plays itself out may be seen in reports about a visit to Sudan, one of the Arab countries that falls outside of the civilized region produced by drawing parallels fifteen degrees north and fifteen degrees south of Washington. In a 1929 *National Geographic* article, it was reported that since British rule "amazing change" had taken place in Sudan. It was previously a land of "war, famine, disease, and more war. Life was cheap." As the article's author listened to the stories of the British Assistant District Commis-

sioner, a Scottish captain of the native Camel Corps, and a Scottish doctor, he wondered how it was that the millions of "wild men" who
inhabited "savage Sudan" were ruled by so few such Englishmen who
managed to live unprotected and, yet, be "absolute masters and gover-
nors of all?"[10] His explanation to the readers was:

> Courage, unshaken belief in their race and their caste, and rigid, absolute, un-
> swerving, impeccable justice have given to these administrators this mastery over
> the warlike and still fanatically religious tribes of the Sudan. It is because of this
> prestige of the white race that the British administrators have established . . .
> [their authority].[11]

Arrogance and racism driving this account of Sudan are among attitudes
and assumptions basic to the colonizing project and its racist underpinnings.

"WOOING WHITE MEN"

National Geographic established difference through an intricate racial
grid that created and assigned value to physical and mental markers. And
so it was, we read, that while traveling through Egypt and Sudan one
found: "In color these Arabs range from coalhole black to taffy yellow.
From Luxor to Khartum the Arab and the Negro have become a blend."[12]
In Morocco, the Berbers "looked and dressed alike. Their skin was swar-
thy, features rather flat, eyes small and brown."[13] In the Arab world one
found "unwashed children, with the limpid eyes of Arabs."[14] And, Arabs
are "often far lighter in color than a sunburned European. Their eyes,
which are very beautiful, belie their jealous and deceitful natures."[15]
     A visit to Sudan found old black women "as gentle as the 'mammies'
of our own Southland" and "discover[ed] the American Negro's love for
watermelon is a hereditary influence. All these black people were excessively fond of melons."[16] Traveling past Khartoum it was reported that:
"the characteristics of the natives changed. So far, we had seen only Arabs
and mixed breeds. Here we met Negroes and Negro-and-Arab half castes.
The Negroes were genuine savages; they wore feathers in their hair and
rings in their noses."[17]
     How one was able to distinguish between these breeds was explained:

> One finds it easy to recognize the Negroes with a mixture of Arab blood. The eyes
> betray them. The Arabs have eyes of a peculiar and distinctive luster, moist and
> luminous, and shaded by long eyelashes. The dirtiest little Arab girl can perform
>   cks with her eyes that are astonishing. It was amusing to see those half-caste
> girls attempt to woo the white men with their eyes.[18]

But not only eyes help sort out breeds, castes and half-castes: "For all his sins, the Arab is one of the strongest and brainiest individuals the world ever produced. Show me a black boy . . . with one percent Arab blood in his veins and I will show you one who is smarter than his fellows."[19] This seeming compliment to Arab intelligence plays out much like beautiful eyes which belie deceitful natures. Paralleling what Said calls a " 'bad' sexuality" ascribed to Arabs, we shall also find that Arab intelligence was a "bad" intelligence of cunning and plotting.[20]

Still at the work of establishing race, we read in *National Geographic* that the Nubas were "one of the wildest tribes of the Sudan . . . dirty, savage, and suspicious." And their "woolly hair, thick lips, and dusky hues show how their race, though mixed in origin, remains essentially Negro."[21] Nile blacks are said to be "shiftless, vain, noisy, and warlike." And, "no one yet has devised a plan for making the native Africans work. They seem to wish for nothing that is not free and under their hands. . . . Meanwhile, the land and civilization languish."[22] All of these examples work within Memmi's definition of race. It is by assigning and then continually pointing to the essentially negative physical and mental characteristics of others, that race becomes a natural fact accounting for all manner of traits.

"TO BECOME GOOD MOORS"

Clearly, establishing race was (is) a very complicated matter. One had to see difference everywhere and keep seeing it or risk it falling apart. Throughout this early period, *National Geographic*'s search for difference was relentless. In Morocco, reported French practices of not interfering with Moslem customs or architecture, and building French towns outside native villages were explained as understanding that: "The Moors are not an inferior, but a different, race from the French. We want them to become good Moors, not poor Frenchmen."[23] This is a good example of how different but equal worked—the French were to colonize Morocco, enforce segregation, and train Moroccans how to be good Moors. There can be no doubt that such difference was riddled with value judgments allowing one side to dominate the other. This is the very same racism—no milder—as preceding statements on Sudan. As we shall now see, helping Moroccans become good and doing something about the aforementioned "languishing of land and civilization" were mere drops in colonialism's bucket of good works.

"ON THE FRINGE"

Stam says that "Colonialist historians, speaking for the 'winners' of history, exalted the colonial enterprise, at bottom little more than a gigantic act of pillage . . . as a philanthropic 'civilizing mission' motivated by a desire to push back the frontiers of ignorance, disease and tyranny."[24] It is from this same perspective that *National Geographic* speaks of colonialism. And the open, self-righteous way it does so reveals the depth of the West to non-West hierarchy.

In Algeria, a key region necessary to control the Sahara's important north-to-south caravan routes was described as "difficult to manage" because "fanatical nomads of the interior long prevented fuller knowledge of the peoples and places of the center of the great desert."[25] To end this situation, the French put together a trans-Sahara automobile expedition that included specially constructed Citroens mounted with rapid-fire guns. This expedition was said to have added an important page to France's record of exploration in Africa, and to have helped it develop a political and commercial link between its northern and western African colonies. And with it, "civilization approached a bit nearer to the heart of Africa's most mysterious domain."[26]

An amazing turn of logic blames people of an area for being in the way of acquiring knowledge about them and their area. A blaming-the-victim strategy works here because it was already understood that only the West can know. Moreover, without the slightest degree of self-consciousness the article reported that machine guns were mounted on vehicles to clear the way of any Arabs resisting (thereby read as fanatics) the French quest for knowledge and, incidentally, caravan routes. In the end, learning that "civilization approached nearer" enabled readers to make sense of the expedition; nothing more need be said. It was, after all, as *National Geographic* reported: "the age of swelling empires and shifting frontiers" that saw "Greater-France-in-Africa . . . 20 times larger than France-in-Europe" and "Great Britain, with a territory 30 times larger than the British Isles."[27] This European swelling from the right to know and own was colonialism in its heyday.

EDUCATING MEN AND TRAINING WOMEN

National Geographic readers learned that because of Morocco's simple sameness it was necessary for the French to work hard and spend great sums of money. "All Moroccan mosques, medersas, homes, shops, and cemeteries look more or less alike, forming an incomparable setting for a people whose dress, regardless of station, is alike in form and coloring." In all this Moroccan sameness the French "had to build extensively"—administrative buildings, barracks, warehouses, railway stations, post offices, hotels, shops, and homes. They reforested the hills, tamed the rivers, and built irrigation ditches; archeologists unearthed Roman ruins; and France "spent a small fortune on the port of Casablanca . . . home of most of the European residents."[28]

However, not all Moroccans were grateful for French good works. There were still some "rebellious" tribes in, as of yet, "regions unsubdued." But, "profiting by their mistakes in Algeria and Tunisia, the French have made a steady advance in pacification, unification, and progress." Moroccan "aristocrats are being educated" for future military and municipal positions, and "women of the leading families are being trained." The fate of "warriors who have been thorns in the side" of European colonialism in Morocco is sealed; they are surrounded by a "pacified zone," which spells their "ultimate subjugation, the fate that has overtaken equally brave aboriginal tribes blocking Civilization's path throughout the world."[29]

For those resisting civilization there were pacification and unification programs—to which the barracks previously mentioned would no doubt have had some relation. For others, there were French programs to educate aristocratic Moroccan men and train women of leading families, that is, produce good Moors of the upper class. Training Arab women was a colonizing strategy not particular to Morocco. For example, in a 1914 article we read about "modern education" in Tunis in the form of an Arab girls' school headed by a French woman who, "thoroughly understands Mohammedan ways":

No effort is made to proselytize or influence them in any way, the desire is simply to make these young girls intelligent and useful members of the community, so that when they marry they may have attractive homes and be intelligent companions to their husbands. They are taught plain, common-sense sewing, hygiene, common-sense cooking, how to set a table properly, to read and write; also arithmetic and bookkeeping.[30]

It was with complete self-confidence in their ability to know others and prescribe what they needed, that this French woman and *National Geographic* could so matter-of-factly report colonial efforts to uplift Arab women. One never gets a hint of self-doubt in descriptions of such unilaterally developed projects for the natives' betterment. It went without saying, it would seem, that Westerners could identify problems and set solutions for the colonized population.

Arab women were also in need of serious training in motherhood. During a 1914 visit to Palestine, an author reported that, "Mortality among the babies is great and is not to be wondered at, for in view of the rough treatment they receive, it becomes a question of the survival of the fittest."[31] The evidence given of this bad treatment was: while working in the fields mothers erected small hammocks from sticks and cloth to hold the babies, babies were carried tied onto the backs of mothers, and in some districts babies in crude wooden cradles were carried on mothers' heads.

The women, rather than any economic and health conditions, were held responsible for the mortality rate of infants. And, given the evidence offered, this was due to their non-Western mothering practices. The logic at work here was that by training Arab women to use Western baby carriages the infant mortality rate would drop. The Western model of motherhood, in all its detail, was that to be adopted. Arab mothers were identified as the cause of the high mortality rate among children and, thus, there was clearly the need for their training by colonial teachers of domesticity and motherhood.

The objectives of colonial programs to train Arab women were, in essence, the same as those discussed by Hunt in her analysis of the Belgian *foyer* system in Africa. Citing Ester Boserup's work, Hunt points out that "colonial notions of development for women meant 'training for the home.' " She argues that the *foyer* project points to "important connections between Western family ideology, the colonial construction of womanhood and domesticity, and the emergence of a colonized African urban elite."[32]

The Belgian system, like the French, intended to achieve support for the colonial state from upper-class natives who could, through education and training, learn to cooperate with the colonizer. These education programs were an important part of colonial efforts to strengthen class structure and inscribe within it "colonial standards of prestige and status." And they "worked to establish, maintain, and enhance hierarchies" of gender, class, and race.[33]

Training Arab women in basic, commonsense activities of running the nuclear family household held up Western womanhood and Western patriarchy as models to imitate. This carried with it the denigration of Arab women's culture and the Arab family unit, both of which became signs of backwardness in colonial training programs. It is also important to note that domesticating Arab women during this era did not speak to any economic role for them. They were being trained to keep house and be suitable companions for men, for Arab men, that is. The colonizer/colonized hierarchy was never lost in education and/or training programs that, as Hunt puts it, as part of the racist context of colonialism, do not aim at assimilation or Westernization, but at "colonial mimicry."[34]

"BORN OF THE DESERT"

Among the descriptions of Arabs often used was: "born of the desert." Arabs were routinely identified in *National Geographic* as sons or daughters of the desert, an essentializing move that accomplished quite a bit. "Of the desert" denied one being part of a human community or nation as, for example, a son of France would be. Being a daughter of the desert placed one too close to nature, and produced a primitive woman who, since nature was understood as something to be conquered and controlled, needed to be pacified, trained, subjugated, and so forth. Further, since this particular piece of nature was a desert, and deserts in *National Geographic*'s Western gaze were empty wastes, except when economic or military significance could be spotted, the daughter of the desert, with sexual significance already located in her as primitive woman was, like the land, there for the taking with nothing in the way.

The whole Arab world seems to have been little more than an empty desert until the good works of colonialism. In Egypt, an author of a *National Geographic* article stopped at a railway station "set in the waste" where "voluble Arabs made the usual din, apparently about nothing." He noticed that "the desert Arabs live in desperate squalor, on the fringe. On what they subsist is . . . a mystery. The hot sun burns up their filth; otherwise they must of necessity all die." And, predictably, Arabs were found "covered with contented flies."[35]

Flies, usually contented, were a regular part of constructing the primitive. Flies performed several functions; most obviously they meant a lack of personal and public hygiene; they signaled that Arabs were too lazy to even shoo flies away; they pointed to the animality of Arabs who, unbothered, were at one with the contented flies; and lastly, flies on Arabs created an image of the Arab world as a decaying corpse. This was an important image to hold against that of Western expansion; it could explain so much.

In *National Geographic,* Sudan was described as "a country of calamities" where medical missionary work had doctors "literally giving their lives to save the black man from savagery and ignorance and disease." We read that only the lucky ones came out alive, nevertheless, "when one dies, another comes in."[36] This was not the only example of British sacrifice in the Sudan; passing Kitchener's camp, readers were reminded that "the great British soldier spent something like three years equipping an army with machine guns and artillery to go into the Sudan to subdue a religious zealot and his fanatical followers."[37] All this sacrifice was not for nothing, the author speculated that some day Sudan would be a great cotton producer supplying Britain with all that it then bought from the United States.

Readers learned from *National Geographic* that Italian fascists also had a colonization program full of good works. Tripoli, Libya, was said to be a "promising modern Italian colony" where "Italy is turning to good account the martial instincts of the restless sons of the desert."[38] The difference between the Arab world and Western civilization (including fascism) was made clear throughout a 1925 article:

Arabs and Negroes, wrapped in the universal dingy white woolen shroud . . . shuffle by groups of smart Italian officers in khaki and silver and Fascisti in black shirts and caps. Arab and Negro women, with only one eye peering from beneath an all-enveloping cloak, use that eye to stare at the short skirts and silk stockings of European ladies. Thus East and West meet.[39]

Once leaving this main street, "one plunges into the Arabian Nights," where the market sights include sellers who "recline silently at their ease, waiting, like true Easterners, for customers to come to them" and one shop owner "dozes among baskets of carrots and cabbages."

Creating the other as lazy and violent, and using Western women's dress as a sign of freedom was all routine within colonialist discourse. What makes the preceding example striking is that in it even European fascists were represented as more civilized, more advanced than Arabs. It was the martial instincts of the sons of the desert, not those of fascists, that needed to be controlled. In the zone where the Italians had established control there was "peace, justice, order, freedom, and coming prosperity. Outside it lie the stony desert . . . where lawlessness still exists." And while "Italian soldiers have pacified" most of the western province, for extra protection they built a wall around their area against "raids by bands of desert warriors."[40]

In another *National Geographic* article, readers learned that sons of the desert were not only violent, Syrian Bedouins were said to be "robbers by nature and tradition." At the same time, when shown an American tractor and plow, they "were as enthusiastic as children with a new toy."[41] Contradictions were the stuff of primitivist discourse.

TIME

One of these contradictions is that although the primitive was constructed as existing outside of time, there was (is) nothing so timeless as primitivist discourse itself. Traveling from Syria to Baghdad, the author found it "the dust heap of the world," where "*Arabian Nights'* splendor has departed." His disappointment in Baghdad was due to it having "existed in the minds of most people only as a mythical city, for in childhood they had read the fascinating *Arabian Nights' Entertainments.*" However, the British presence in Baghdad brought about "miraculous change" said to have made the city almost unrecognizable from ten years earlier. Roads, bridges, motor vehicles, a taxi-cab service of luxurious cars, an efficient police force, a new town for Europeans, electric fans, ice factories, and heat resisting architecture were listed as examples of "civilization's conveniences" brought by the British to Iraq. In addition, there was a club with polo, tennis, and golf facilities, and a race track—because "wherever the Briton has penetrated, he has taken his sport with him."

Alongside this world of Western progress was another world: "Baghdad is still the real East"; once you entered the bazaar gates you found that "civilization has halted."[42] The familiar time warp also held in Morocco, where *National Geographic* readers learned that: "shadowy figures . . . hooded, shrouded in ghostly white . . . seemed to belong to an age long past. . . . Little changed since prehistoric days." But with the entry of France, Morocco was brought "face to face with civilization in its most advanced stage—the railroad, the automobile, the airplane."[43] Within Orientalism centuries may be run together and Arabs easily thrown back into prehistory all because of a white shroud.

In a 1914 article, readers learned that "Palestine, often called the Holy Land, is in a general way familiar to all of us from our study of the Bible [notice the assumed audience]. Few, however, realize that the manners and customs which prevailed there in Biblical days are still unchanged, even after an interval of 3,000 years."[44] This is quite a time warp, but Biblical times was one of *National Geographic*'s favorites to conjure up while in the Arab world.

Another favorite time period within which to locate the Arab world was in the 8th and 9th centuries—the time of the *Arabian Nights*. In fact, there was even an "An *Arabian Nights* Type" still to be seen in 1925, as the caption to a picture of a Moroccan woman informed readers. The woman in this photo was wearing a turban heavy with gold jewelry, large gold earrings and necklace, and gold belt. The excess jewelry was part of the general excess imagined to exist behind doors in the Arab world. This "*Arabian Nights* Type" of woman was positioned to the side of an open door standing in a very unguarded, submissive pose with hands behind her back—she seems to invite you into the harem, that is, the common Western representation of harem as brothel.

One need not even actually be on the ground in the Arab world to work up an *Arabian Nights* fantasy. In 1928, while flying over Baghdad, an author reported that if not for keeping to his schedule he would have liked to land "where storytellers in turbans drone the racy, unexpurgated tales of *Arabian Nights;* or to sample that seductive arrack drink and hear the East's oldest flute tune played while a lithe-limbed girl dances."[45] In another article, this whole sense of Arabs out of step with time was put most succinctly—on seeing some "old Arabs in doorways" the author remarked: "Here, as elsewhere, the Arab is an anachronism."[46]

ARABIAN DAYS

Through text and photographs *National Geographic* created not only Western fantasies of *Arabian Nights* and entering harems but, just as deliberately, the mundane. "Forced realism," when signs are deliberately put into a picture to suggest it is a natural or truthful scene, was one of the ways through which this is done.[47] For example, a photo titled "A Daughter of the Libyan Desert" used a rock wall as background; cotton clothing, as opposed to silks and brocades; a pose meant to suggest the woman was acting naturally by fixing her head covering, although the actual effect is a very rigid and awkward pose; and lastly, the caption informed readers that: "Her elaborate jewelry includes a commonplace key, a safety pin and a piece of a comb." Noting these everyday items hanging off the necklace helped produce the desired realism.

The items pointed out in the caption were commonplace Western objects that could create a sense of the mundane—commonplace Arab objects could not perform the same function for a Westerner. Additionally, that the Arab woman was making inappropriate use of a key, safety pin, and comb is an example of what Torgovnick calls "culture contact" photographs—"indigenous peoples incorporat[ing] Western materials into their dress, rituals, and art."[48] In *National Geographic* this image was regular fare used more to designate culture clash than contact as such. Arabs' inappropriate use or misinterpretation of Western culture was always the point being made; it never seemed to occur the other way around.

In addition to the arrangement of details for forced realism, a desired photo may also have been produced by staging events to photograph. During a visit to Sudan, a *National Geographic* author tried to set up a sham battle between two tribes thinking it "might make an interesting picture to stage." The chiefs of the tribes had their enthusiasm for the idea "aroused by a promise . . . of much sugar and cloth." However, the followers were not equally enthusiastic fearing the possible danger from even a mock battle between two tribes that have been "deadly enemies for generations." The author assured them, "no one will be hurt. This will not be real, only a game. You . . . will only play together." The requested performance did not take place, but later in his travels the author did get a tribe to perform a battle with no opposing side.[49]

The author could not convince the tribes' members that the battle would not be real, only a game, nor would the magazine's readers easily be convinced of this. That is to say, even after reading that photographs representing the Sudanese as violent and warring were staged by *National Geographic*, it would still be a struggle not to see such photos as Sudanese reality. With so much about the natural link between Arabs and violence already in place in the West, the magazine's credibility as an educational journal would be safe despite the admitted artificiality of the photographs. The stereotype of the angry, violent Arab man was already known, therefore, pictures corresponding to that image became real enough.

According to Schick, throughout the late 19th and early 20th centuries "photographers scoured the Middle East and North Africa in a relentless quest to classify and catalog their ruins, markets, monuments, holy places, and especially their many 'exotic' peoples." Of the taxonomies they created, Schick asserts: "Any taxonomy fundamentally relies on the classifier's perspective; type, after all, lies in the eye of the beholder."[50] And *National Geographic* was also a beholding eye.

National Geographic produced and taught about its types through visual images and text. For example, readers learned about types of Arab women: the difference between Berber and Moor women was that the former were "taller and leaner than their harem-bred sisters . . . in the cities where Moorish beauty runs to avoirdupois."[51] A picture of a Libyan woman identified her as "A Town-Bred Arab Woman." Since identifying women as city- and town-bred meant a connection to the harem according to *National Geographic*'s categories, the Libyan woman was dressed in silks and excessive jewelry, and posed against rich curtains while leaning on a balcony railing with one hand on her hip.

Similar, but not the same, was the dancer type often appearing in the magazine. A 1917 picture of an Algerian woman (wearing the familiar ten pounds of jewelry) was staged as though the camera caught her daydreaming. The lengthy caption read:

A Desert Flower

"Somewhere in the Sahara" lived this child of the Desert until she came to Biskra, the "Garden of Allah," to earn her dowry as a dancer. One would imagine that she is dreaming of some turbaned knight left behind and counting the days until she may return to her natal tent.[52]

The reader/viewer had to participate in creating this woman as a dancer by accepting that this was a candid shot, not a studio portrait, and agreeing to imagine, along with *National Geographic,* that she was dreaming about a man. Leaps of imagination were often required in popular Orientalism.

Another example was an outrageous explanation of veiling that introduced some additional categories of Arab women. Readers were informed that: "In Cairo all Mohammedan women cover their faces—the ugly ones with black knitted veils and the pretty ones with sheer white chiffon, which reveals the face clearly and endows it with a glorified complexion."[53] Assuming this information was correct, which I would not suggest one do, readers were left to imagine how, when, and by whom these "Mohammedan women" were declared ugly or pretty and assigned their appropriate veil colors.

THE MOHAMMEDAN MIND

In the preceding quotation from *National Geographic* the term "Mohammedan" was used; what does it mean? The word "Mohammedan" is not used in Arabic; how did it come to be employed in the West in place of or synonymously with the word Muslim? Discussing how Christian thinkers interpreted Islam, Said says that: "since Christ is the basis of Christian faith, it was assumed—quite incorrectly—that Mohammed was to Islam as Christ was to Christianity."[54] With this assumption at work, Mohammed was, therefore, understood by Christians as an impostor because only Christ was/is the son of God. How Muslims themselves understood Mohammed, the prophet, and his role was neither here nor there. Christians who employed the term Mohammedan did so from an analysis of Islam that ignored Muslims' interpretations of their own religion. This arrogant way of knowing others set Christians up with the one true God leaving Mohammedans with Allah—not God. And, thus, the Arabic word "Allah" did not get translated into English (God) in *National Geographic*—it could not translate within the context of a Christianity/ Islam hierarchy.

Together, the Christian ability to know Mohammedans and the knowledge produced could make sense out of reading that dismantlement of a Muslim religious shrine helped establish colonial control because: "holy places are very dear to the Mohammedan mind" and one could eventually "develop into a disturbance center."[55] This same knowledge secured meaning in another *National Geographic* article where it was learned that one should gauge conversation with Muslims because "all Mohammedans hate the Christians and . . . they dislike being seen talking to them."[56] This could make immediate sense given what was already known about Mohammed as an impostor and Islam as a competitor religion to Christianity.

In a 1909 article, the author shared with readers three anti-Christian incidents he encountered while traveling through the Arabian peninsula. One happened during a stop at an oasis in northern Arabia (present day Saudi Arabia) and was his "first real experience of Arabian superstition and hatred of the Christian." The author said that he was not allowed to occupy a guest-room but was, rather, told to sleep with the cattle in the stables. He did so but was then ordered to move away from the animals because his presence might cause their deaths. He was then given a place alone in the palm grove but, once again, was forced to move because it was thought close contact with the palms might harm their fruit bearing. Finally, he was "confined in a tent to keep company with one afflicted with a disease not unlike leprosy."[57] Creating a Christian/Muslim opposition could not but frame the colonizer/colonized opposition also in religious terms, which, in turn, allowed religion to be used to legitimate colonial activity.

As Kabbani notes, a Christian sense of religious superiority was founded on seeing Christianity as "the only system of belief that was correct and could enlighten . . . those less fortunate."[58] The less fortunate as non-Christian was clearly established in *National Geographic*. For example, in a 1909 article tracing the route of Moses out of the desert, the author's religious journey came to an end at the town of Aqaba, Jordan, where he found: "wretchedness and filth personified. . . . The people are despicably poor in their persons and characteristics, having lived like leeches on the Egyptian caravans to Mecca for centuries."[59] This description packed quite a bit: it represented Muslims as so morally poor they *even* rob Muslim pilgrims, it left *National Geographic* readers to wonder what a Muslim would do to Christian pilgrims, and the image of leeches robbing reproduced familiar stereotypes of the Arab thief and the unproductive Arab.

It is this same representation of Arabs found in a 1914 anecdote from a French officer in Tunis. The anecdote that "illustrates the Arab character" told of an Arab who had sown his fields with wheat but at harvest time a swarm of locusts devoured it all. During the destruction of the crop, the Arab just looked on impressed with Allah having created such a small but powerful insect and "improvised a poem, without trying to drive them away."[60] This contrasted to the Western, Christian character, which, through its energy and industriousness would, of course, have saved the crop.

Another example of the magazine's Christian bias was in a 1924 report of the British District Commissioner of a Muslim province in Sudan. He explained to readers that when called upon to settle an argument over responsibility for the death of a bull, he carried his Bible into court having found a "suitable judgment" in the twenty-first chapter of Exodus, thirty-fifth verse.[61] The colonial commissioner's open use of the Christian Bible as authority over colonized Muslims speaks to both the link between colonialism and Christianity, and the Christian/Muslim hierarchy in place and being reproduced in the magazine.

The Christian colonial disrespect for Islamic beliefs and practices revealed in *National Geographic* was indicative of the level of religious superiority so taken for granted that attempts to cover it were unnecessary. Another example of this lack of Christian restraint can be found in a description of Muslims dancing in religious celebration during the holy month of Ramadan:

Off across the square, tom-toms beat perpetually and white figures of dervishes danced to the wild music. . . . Three musicians shuffled backward in a perpetual circle. . . . From time to time figures broke away from the tightly packed mob . . . and danced furiously. . . . Around and around they went, barefooted fanatics, leaping and gyrating in their long white robes and odd white turbans. One minute they struck a self-appreciative pose and held it; the next, they were in a frenzy again. They resembled nothing so much as chickens with their heads cut off, fluttering in the purposeless dance of death.[62]

Muslims were made hideous and out of control in this description of their religious celebration. Everything in the account served to distance readers from weird and wild Muslims. *National Geographic* established a strange, incomprehensible non-Christian religion with these reports and, here, it portrayed Islamic holidays as meaningless.

DANCING GIRLS

The preceding description of what sounded like nothing short of Muslim insanity was framed as a Christian watching Muslims dance. However, there was another dance spectacle more integral to *National Geographic's* Orientalist representations of the Arab world—Western men watching Arab women dance. Brown says that the "Middle Eastern 'dancing girl' is an indispensable part of the Orientalist repertoire of images . . . used to suggest lasciviousness and sensuality, exciting both enjoyment and disapproval in Western viewers."[63] Brown also points out that the Western association between public dancing and prostitution runs through images of the "dancing girl."

This enjoyment and disapproval tension produced reports on the dance in *National Geographic* that created an erotic moment suddenly punctured with denial. Listen to two different, yet same, accounts of Arab women dancing:

We could see five graceful young girls facing one man. The girls were alternately advancing and retreating as they danced—at first slowly, rhythmically, and then, still keeping the rhythm, with an ever-increasing speed. Suddenly, before Schoedsack and I realized what was happening, the women, still unsmiling, not changing their rhythm at all, turned and danced right up to us, . . . the five of them stopped as one, shook their braided curls in our faces, and then hastily retreated—as we did.[64]

And:

Her dancing! She moves on her toes, but barely raises them from the platform. In her hands she holds a silk handkerchief behind her head or waves it occasionally in the air. But feet and hands, legs and arms, do not enter much into the dance; she performs chiefly with the muscles of her neck, breast, abdomen, and hips. . . . The eyes of the interested spectators sparkle as they gloat on the dancer's charms and movements. To them she is the poetry of motion, but to a European she is almost repugnant.[65]

This sudden coming to one's Victorian senses after such an intense gaze corresponds with Kabbani's assertion: "The Orient of the western imagination provided respite from Victorian sexual repressiveness. It was used to express for the age the erotic longings that would have otherwise remained suppressed.''[66] The focused and lengthy descriptions given to women dancing were not likewise offered about women weaving, caring for children, working in fields, etc. Only women dancing received such concentrated treatment in *National Geographic.*

Although it was Orientalism that focused attention on dancing girls— the "blame" was put on Arab women. This operation brings to mind Berger's discussion of the painting, *Vanity,* by Memling. He calls the moralizing in it hypocritical: "You painted a naked woman because you enjoyed looking at her, you put a mirror in her hand and you called the painting Vanity, thus morally condemning the woman whose nakedness you had depicted for your own pleasure."[67] This same sort of hypocritical treatment went on in *National Geographic.*

A 1917 picture of a dancing girl carried the following caption: "An Arab Shod with Fire: She is a dancer of Algeria and the slow, throbbing music of the Orient is just as necessary . . . as the jewels and coins with which she adorns herself."[68] The erotic, sexual desires of the Western man were put on the Arab woman he portrayed as an essentially throbbing, burning dancing girl. His needs were hidden through the invention of hers—his sexual motives were displaced onto her.

In this representation, familiar signifiers were employed—the rock wall as background, excessive jewelry, the sexy pose, and a cigarette. The cigarette prop not only signified the loose woman, but also functioned as a pun. In the picture of a dancing girl holding a cigarette and "shod with fire," the cheap word and visual puns carried the message that the woman was even cheaper than the pun. The fire and the throbbing music and gold said to be necessary to her turned the Arab woman into a whore and a prostitute. *National Geographic,* in search of the Orient, created the hot dancing girl through costumes, props, and poses; and *then* proceeded to "find," categorize, explain, and display her for lessons in popular Orientalism.

Although each fragment of this picture (and others) may on its own have been "authentic," in total design they became the Westerner's image of an Arab woman, letting go any link to "authenticity." No doubt the rock wall behind the dancer shod with fire was truly rock, no doubt the jewelry was from the Arab world, no doubt the outfit was made by Arab hands, and no doubt that was a cigarette she was holding. But when one tries to take in the excess, make sense of the pose, and think about why, from all possible backgrounds, a rock wall was chosen, the picture's authentic pieces collect into a lie. Alloula speaks to this very issue saying: "Truthfulness in details may very well not constitute the truthfulness of the whole, however. The elements of dress and the jewels, viewed separately, are factual, but their arrangement on the model fails to produce an impression of veracity."[69] No matter how painstakingly constructed, this "realism" fails, it does not manage to "rise above trivial reductive-ness."[70]

In looking at photographs of Arab women in *National Geographic,* something is learned about the relationship between those on either side of the camera. Denzin calls the anthropologist's and tourist's camera an "instrument of power."[71] And Berger argues that "men act and women appear. Men look at women."[72] In the activity of constructing the Arab dancing girl we can see both of these claims come to life. More insidi-ously, such pictures take on a life of their own in that the more often they appear, the more real the image. The power of the West to represent the non-West, and the power of men to represent women came together on the body of the Arab woman with such force that she became the fake, and representations of her the truth. Sontag summarizes this process saying: "Photographs do not simply render reality—realistically. It is re-ality which is scrutinized, and evaluated, for its fidelity to photographs."[73] Arab women could not remove Orientalist images of the Arab woman off of them.

But there was more than gender going on here. Berger's argument that men act and women appear, men look at women, becomes more com-plicated when the relationship is also one of West to non-West. Working from Berger's words, we can characterize what went on in *National Ge-ographic* as: Western men act and non-Westerners appear or, for the specific concern of this study: Western men act and Arabs appear. Arab men, as well as Arab women, were made into objects to look at. In ad-dition, another hypocritical operation took place when, not only did Western men look at the women, but they used Arab men as an excuse to do so. This fits within what Said calls a " 'bad' sexuality" given to Arabs. Thus, when *National Geographic* wanted to peek inside the harem or watch dancing girls, it was framed as examining what Arab men do to Arab women.

BREASTS

When I take up the subject of *National Geographic* looking at women, it is from a perspective that agrees with Suleiman's on the female body:

The cultural significance of the female body is not only (not even first and fore-most) that of a flesh-and-blood entity, but that of a symbolic construct. Everything we know about the body . . . exists for us in some form of discourse; and dis-course, whether verbal or visual, fictive or historical or speculative, is never un-mediated, never free of interpretation, never innocent.[74]

From here, a fundamental question needs to be addressed: How did *Na-tional Geographic* get away with producing pictures of bare-breasted women that even in the 1990s are not to be seen in other popular magazines, except for pornographic publications?

Berger defines mystification as "the process of explaining away what otherwise might be evident."[75] It is through mystification that bare-breasted women were displayed in *National Geographic.* Discussing French postcards of Algerian women, Alloula says that in the quest for the harem, the obsession has produced an exhibition of breasts that amounts to "an anthology of breasts."[76] As well, the breast might serve as a logo for *National Geographic.* So how do we explain away pictures of bare-breasted females?—what McElroy identifies as the "stock-in-trade for ethnographic photographers" and "titillating in their photographic objectification of non-European women."[77]

Miles' discussion of nudity in religious painting points out that images of nudity "must be carefully balanced with other visual content so that an erotic response does not dominate, causing the viewers engagement with the painting to collapse into 'mere' sensuality." *National Geographic*'s photographs of nudity have a balance between the erotic and the educational. In educational photographs, as in religious paintings, "nudity must be depicted naturalistically enough to evoke the viewers' erotic interest: on the other hand, it must not be dominant enough to render this erotic attraction primary."[78]

For example, a 1924 *National Geographic* photograph of four women positioned something akin to a police line-up and with breasts fully exposed was merely captioned: "From left to right, mother, daughter, grandmother, and great-grandmother in Darfur."[79] Thus the breasts were "ignored" and the magazine's readers looked at different generations of women as they naturally appeared. They could track the four generations through physical variations and not "just" or even necessarily be looking at women's breasts. Additionally, this particular photograph concentrated within one frame an "anthology of breasts."

Mosse's examination of nudism within the German life-reform movement that gained momentum in the late 19th century explains how their nudes were presented as different from pornography. Among the primary means employed were calling up the Greek tradition of idealized beauty and framing nudity in a natural setting, such as the sea or meadows. In addition, to further secure a distinction from the nudes of pornography, the movement "advised the use of glossy paper, which would heighten the artistic merit of the female nude without arousing lust."[80] All three of these conventions were also used in *National Geographic.* Clearly, there were established ways of getting away with producing images of nudity.

These, by the way, also applied to displaying the male body. Analyzing some nude photographs taken in the 1920s–1930s of the African-American actor, Paul Robeson, Dyer asserts that he was put into "a position of 'feminine' subordination within the dynamics of looking that are built into any portrait-image of a human being in this culture."[81] Dyer explains that while one would assume nude photos to be heavily coded as erotic, those of Robeson were able to produce a "double articulation" through poses similar to statues of classical antiquity. By referring to classical nudes, an erotic image can carry with it its own denial of eroticism and insist it celebrates the human form on a higher level.

This double articulation was identically produced in photos of women in *National Geographic* that obviously appealed to classical nude images. In one such picture a woman was displayed wearing a toga style robe that exposed her right breast. She stood against a rock wall to inject naturalness and, at the same time, was distanced from "real" nudity by looking off to the heavens in a statuesque pose. For additional security, the photograph was captioned solely by a few lines of poetry from Byron:

A Daughter of Araby

"Full many a flower is born to blush unseen,
And waste its sweetness on the desert air."[82]

It is noteworthy that, as Kabbani points out, Byron, who traveled to the Arab world in the first half of the 1800s, was an avid consumer of Orientalist travel accounts.[83]

With a rock wall, toga, statuesque pose, and poetry, *National Geographic* could cover its erotic photograph with appeals to naturalness, classical images of the body, and high literature. (It also managed to slip in the idea that women were wasted on Arab men.) This corresponds to what Gimblett found in her study of the exhibition of humans beginning in the first half of the 19th century in Europe and America. She says, "reframing of performance in terms of nature, science and education rendered it respectable."[84]

The "Daughter of Araby" picture also brings up an issue mentioned by Kappeler concerning women viewers of such photographs. She says that "what women find objectionable in pornography, they have learnt to accept in products of 'high' art and literature."[85] And so it was that the systematic objectification of women for men's interests by *National Geographic* could pass by women viewers with appeals to high culture and, of course, education. It was also within this framing that the magazine was to be understood as useful for children.

All these different readings exist because, as Miles, echoing Barthes, reminds us: "All images are polysemous, they imply, underlying their signifiers, a floating chain of signifieds" and the viewer can "choose some and ignore others."[86] It is this looseness that enables *National Geographic* to supply, "voyeuristic eroticism . . . under the guise of scientific curiosity and self-improvement."[87] Different readers/viewers take what they need and walk by other meanings simultaneously available. The magazine was always innocent because one could not "prove" an erotic reading was meant. The erotic photograph, distinct from the pornographic, as Barthes understands it, does not have to show sexual organs (let alone, as with the pornographic, have them at the center) but "takes the spectator outside its frame," letting the viewer complete the picture.[88] Eroticism can be there and not be there when *National Geographic,* an educational magazine, represented women.

In another picture of a toga-clad Arab woman with a breast exposed, the woman was positioned near, actually in, vines to signify naturalness and was carrying a water jug. This added prop served as a visual and verbal pun—jug meaning breast, a slang term in use since the early 1900s.[89] This device, as Torgovnick points out, "exploit[s] the visual image's power to say things by juxtaposition that would be unacceptable to put into words."[90] The caption to the photograph further enhanced sexual meaning—while simultaneously offering a high culture connection—once again, poetry from Byron:

A Bedouin Beauty

"Around her shone
The nameless charms unmarked by her alone,
The light of love, the purity of grace."[91]

Jugs would seem so cheap a pun as to clash with the injection of high culture, but the correlation made by the viewer between objects in a picture not directly linked by narrative is a connection, as Williamson argues, "not on a rational basis but by a leap made on the basis of appearance, juxtaposition and connotation."[92] This transference of significance carried out by the viewer could seemingly leave *National Geographic* out of the meaning-making process and this was how it got away with it—the reader/viewer had to make, or not make, possible connections.

If the peep show is, as understood by Kappeler, essentially a place where men observe women but do not encounter them, then *National Geographic,* which identified itself as a "window on the world," may, in terms of this study, more precisely have been a peep show on the Arab world.[93] This characterization of the magazine's early period is based on its production of representations (both textual and visual) of Arabs firmly lodged within Orientalism, which was also a very gendered discourse. Clearly, as a popular educational journal, *National Geographic* shared responsibility for bringing initial lessons in Orientalism to the U.S. public.

NOTES

Based on material in *Imaginative Geography: Teaching Orientalism in U.S. Popular Education through* National Geographic by Linda Steet. State University of New York Press, forthcoming.

1. *National Geographic,* ed., "One Hundred Years of Increasing and Diffusing Geographic Knowledge," *National Geographic* 173, no. 1 (January 1988): 1.

2. William H. Goetzmann, "Tell Me if Your Civilization Is Interesting," *National Geographic* 173, no. 1 (January 1988): 17.

3. Ibid.

4. *National Geographic,* ed., "Editorial," *National Geographic,* 171, no. 1 (January 1987): editorial page.

5. Gardiner G. Hubbard, "Geographic Progress of Civilization: Annual Address by the President," *National Geographic* 6 (January 1894): 1.

6. Ibid., 1–2.

7. Ibid., 22.

8. Edward W. Said, "Orientalism Reconsidered," *Cultural Critique* 1 (Fall 1985): 90.

9. Albert Memmi, *Dominated Man: Notes Towards a Portrait* (Boston: Beacon Press, 1969): 185.

10. Merian C. Cooper, "Two Fighting Tribes of the Sudan," *National Geographic* 56, no. 4 (October 1929): 465–486.

11. Ibid., 465–466.

12. Felix Shay, "Cairo to Cape Town, Overland: An Adventurous Journey of 135 Days, Made by an American Man and His Wife, Through the Length of the African Continent," *National Geographic* 47, no. 2 (February 1925): 127. This entire issue is devoted to the Shay's "adventurous journey."

13. Harriet Chalmers Adams, "Across French and Spanish Morocco," *National Geographic* 47, no. 3 (March 1925): 332.

14. Shay, 125.

15. Captain Cecil D. Priest, "Timbuktu, in the Sands of the Sahara," *National Geographic* 45, no. 1 (January 1924): 77, 79.

16. Shay, 137.

17. Ibid., 139.

18. Ibid., 140.

19. Ibid., 235.

20. Edward W. Said, *Orientalism* (New York: Vintage Books, 1979): 315.

21. Cooper, 467–468.

22. Shay, 141–142.

23. Adams, 342.

24. Robert Stam and Louise Spence, "Colonialism, Racism and Representation—An Introduction," *Screen* 24, no. 2 (March–April 1983): 5.

25. *National Geographic,* ed., "The Conquest of the Sahara by the Automobile," *National Geographic* 45, no. 1 (January 1924): 87, 88.

26. Ibid., 92.

27. Adams, 327.

28. Adams, 345, 347, 351.

29. Ibid., 345, 347, 351.

30. Frank Edward Johnson, "Here and There in Northern Africa," *National Geographic* 25, no. 1 (January 1914): 62.

31. John D. Whiting, "Village Life in the Holy Land," *National Geographic* 25, no. 3 (March 1914): 261.

32. Nancy Rose Hunt, "Domesticity and Colonialism in Belgian Africa: Usumbura's Foyer Social, 1946–1960," *Signs* 15, no. 3 (Spring 1990): 448–449.

33. Ibid., 474.

34. Ibid., 469.

35. Shay, 131.

36. Ibid., 133–134.

37. Ibid.

38. Colonel Gordon Casserly, "Tripolitania, Where Rome Resumes Sway: The Ancient Trans-Mediterranean Empire, on the Fringe of the Libyan Desert, Becomes a Promising Modern Italian Colony," *National Geographic* 48, no. 2 (August 1925): 137.

39. Ibid., 131.

40. Ibid., 132, 133, 135, 149, 156.

41. Major F. A. C. Forbes-Leith, "From England to India by Automobile," *National Geographic* 48, no. 2 (August 1925): 211, 214–215.

42. Ibid., 215–219.

43. Adams, 331–332.

44. Whiting, 249.

45. Commander Francesco De Pinedo, "By Seaplane to Six Continents," *National Geographic* 54, no. 3 (September 1928): 253.

46. Shay, 235.

47. Malek Alloula, *The Colonial Harem,* Translated by Myrna Godzich and Wlad Godzich (Minneapolis: University of Minnesota Press, 1986), 40.

48. Marianna Torgovnick, *Gone Primitive: Savage Intellects, Modern Lives* (Chicago: The University of Chicago Press, 1990), 79.

49. Cooper, 481.

50. Irvin Cemil Schick, "Representing Middle Eastern Women: Feminism and Colonial Discourse," *Feminist Studies* 16, no. 2 (Summer 1990): 350.

51. Adams, 341.

52. *National Geographic,* ed., "Photo Essay," *National Geographic* 31, no. 3 (March 1917): 261.

53. Shay, 131.

54. Said, *Orientalism,* 60.

55. Shay, 137.

56. Priest, 75.

57. Archibald Forder, "Arabia, the Desert of the Sea," *National Geographic* 20, no. 12 (December 1909): 1045.

58. Rana Kabbani, *Europe's Myths of Orient* (Bloomington: Indiana University Press, 1986): 105.

59. Franklin E. Hoskins, "The Route over which Moses Led the Children of Israel out of Egypt," *National Geographic* 20, no. 12 (December 1909): 1038.

60. Johnson, 93.

61. Major Edward Keith-Roach, "Adventures among the 'Lost Tribes of Islam' in Eastern Darfur: A Personal Narrative of Exploring, Mapping, and Setting Up a Government in the Anglo-Egyptian Sudan Borderland," *National Geographic* 45, no. 1 (January 1924): 71.

62. Shay, 137.

63. Sarah Graham Brown, *Images of Women: The Portrayal of Women in Photography of the Middle East 1860–1950* (New York: Columbia University Press, 1988): 170.

64. Cooper, 480.

65. Casserly, 230.

66. Kabbani, 36.

67. John Berger, *Ways of Seeing* (New York: Penguin Books, 1977): 51.

68. *National Geographic* (March 1917): 267.

69. Alloula, 54.

70. Ibid., 89.

71. Norman K. Denzin, "Reflections on the Ethnographer's Camera," *Current Perspectives in Social Theory* 7 (1986): 106.

72. Berger, 47.

73. Susan Sontag, *On Photography* (New York: Farrar, Straus and Giroux, 1977): 87.

74. Susan Rubin Suleiman, ed., *The Female Body in Western Culture: Contemporary Perspectives* (Cambridge: Harvard University Press, 1986): 2.

75. Berger, 15–16.

76. Alloula, 105.

77. Keith McElroy, "Popular Education and Photographs of the Non-Industrialized World, 1885–1915," *Exposure* 28, no. 3 (Winter 1991–1992): 41.

78. Margaret R. Miles, "The Virgin's One Bare Breast: Female Nudity and Religious Meaning in Tuscan Early Renaissance Culture." In Suleiman, 203.

79. Keith-Roach, 49.

80. George L. Mosse, *Nationalism and Sexuality: Middle-Class Morality and Sexual Norms in Modern Europe* (Madison: University of Wisconsin Press, 1985), 51.

81. Richard Dyer, *Heavenly Bodies: Film Stars and Society* (New York: St. Martin's Press, 1986): 120.

82. *National Geographic* (March 1917): 263.

83. Kabbani, 33.

84. Barbara Kirshenblatt Gimblett, "Objects of Ethnography." In Karp and Lavine, 397.

85. Susanne Kappeler, *The Pornography of Representation* (Minneapolis: University of Minnesota Press, 1986): 103.

86. Miles, 196.

87. McElroy, 50.

88. Roland Barthes, *Camera Lucida: Reflections on Photography,* Translated by Richard Howard (New York: Farrar, Straus and Giroux, Inc., 1981): 59.

89. Robert L. Chapman, ed., *The New Dictionary of American Slang* (New York: Harper and Row, 1986).

90. Torgovnick, 79.

91. *National Geographic* (March 1917): 271.

92. Judith Williamson, *Decoding Advertisements: Ideology and Meaning in Advertising* (New York: Marion Boyars, 1984): 19.

93. Kappeler, 76.

REFERENCES

Adams, Harriet Chalmers. "Across French and Spanish Morocco." *National Geographic* 47, no. 3 (March 1925).

Alloula, Malek. *The Colonial Harem.* Translated by Myrna Godzich and Wlad Godzich (Minneapolis: University of Minnesota Press, 1986).

Barthes, Roland. *Camera Lucida: Reflections on Photography.* Translated by Richard Howard (New York: Farrar, Straus and Giroux, Inc., 1981).

Berger, John. *Ways of Seeing* (New York: Penguin Books, 1977).

Brown, Sarah Graham. *Images of Women: The Portrayal of Women in Photography of the Middle East 1860–1950* (New York: Columbia University Press, 1988).

Casserly, Lieut. Colonel Gordon. "The White City of Algiers." *National Geographic* 53, no. 2 (February 1928).

Casserly, Lieut. Colonel Gordon. "Tripolitania, Where Rome Resumes Sway: The Ancient Trans-Mediterranean Empire, on the Fringe of the Libyan Desert, Becomes a Promising Modern Italian Colony." *National Geographic* 48, no. 2 (August 1925).

Chapman, Robert L., ed. *The New Dictionary of American Slang* (New York: Harper and Row, 1986).

Cooper, Merian C. "Two Fighting Tribes of the Sudan." *National Geographic* 56, no. 4 (October 1929).

De Pinedo, Commander Francesco. "By Seaplane to Six Continents." *National Geographic* 54, no. 3 (September 1928).

Denzin, Norman K. "Reflections on the Ethnographer's Camera." *Current Perspectives in Social Theory* 7 (1986).

Dyer, Richard. *Heavenly Bodies: Film Stars and Society* (New York: St. Martin's Press, 1986).

Forbes-Leith, Major F. A. C. "From England to India by Automobile." *National Geographic* 48, no. 2 (August 1925).

Forder, Archibald. "Arabia, the Desert of the Sea." *National Geographic* 20, no. 12 (December 1909).

Gimblett, Barbara Kirshenblatt. "Objects of Ethnography." In *Exhibiting Cultures: The Poetics and Politics of Museum Display,* edited by Ivan Karp and Stephen D. Lavine (Washington: Smithsonian Institution Press, 1991).

Goetzmann, William H. "Tell Me if Your Civilization Is Interesting." *National Geographic* 173, no. 1 (January 1988).

Hoskins, Franklin E. "The Route Over Which Moses Led the Children of Israel out of Egypt." *National Geographic* 20, no. 12 (December 1909).

Hubbard, Gardiner G. "Geographic Progress of Civilization: Annual Address by the President." *National Geographic* 6 (January 1894).

Hunt, Nancy Rose. "Domesticity and Colonialism in Belgian Africa: Usumbura's Foyer Social, 1946–1960." *Signs* 15, no. 3 (Spring 1990).

Johnson, Frank Edward. "Here and There in Northern Africa." *National Geographic* 25, no. 1 (January 1914).

Kabbani, Rana. *Europe's Myths of Orient* (Bloomington: Indiana University Press, 1986).

Kappeler, Susanne. *The Pornography of Representation* (Minneapolis: University of Minnesota Press, 1986).

Keith-Roach, Major Edward. "Adventures among the 'Lost Tribes of Islam' in Eastern Darfur: A Personal Narrative of Exploring, Mapping, and Setting Up a Government in the Anglo-Egyptian Sudan Borderland." *National Geographic* 45, no. 1 (January 1924).

McElroy, Keith. "Popular Education and Photographs of the Non-Industrialized World, 1885–1915." *Exposure* 28, no. 3 (Winter 1991–1992).

Memmi, Albert. *Dominated Man: Notes Towards a Portrait* (Boston: Beacon Press, 1969).

Miles, Margaret R. "The Virgin's One Bare Breast: Female Nudity and Religious Meaning in Tuscan Early Renaissance Culture." In *The Female Body in Western Culture: Contemporary Perspectives* by Susan Rubin Suleiman (Cambridge: Harvard University Press, 1986).

Mosse, George L. *Nationalism and Sexuality: Middle-Class Morality and Sexual Norms in Modern Europe* (Madison: University of Wisconsin Press, 1985).

National Geographic, ed. "Editorial." *National Geographic* 171, no. 1 (January 1987).

National Geographic, ed. "One Hundred Years of Increasing and Diffusing Geographic Knowledge." *National Geographic* 173, no. 1 (January 1988).

National Geographic, ed. "Photo Essay." *National Geographic* 31, no. 3 (March 1917).

National Geographic, ed. "The Conquest of the Sahara by the Automobile." *National Geographic* 45, no. 1 (January 1924).

Priest, Captain Cecil D. "Timbuktu, in the Sands of the Sahara." *National Geographic* 45, no. 1 (January 1924).

Said, Edward W. *Orientalism* (New York: Vintage Books, 1979).

———. "Orientalism Reconsidered." *Cultural Critique* 1 (Fall 1985).

Schick, Irvin Cemil. "Representing Middle Eastern Women: Feminism and Colonial Discourse." *Feminist Studies* 16, no. 2 (Summer 1990).

Shay, Felix. "Cairo to Cape Town, Overland: An Adventurous Journey of 135 Days, Made by an American Man and His Wife, Through the Length of the African Continent." *National Geographic* 47, no. 2 (February 1925).

Sontag, Susan. *On Photography* (New York: Farrar, Straus and Giroux, 1977).

Stam, Robert and Louise Spence. "Colonialism, Racism and Representation—An Introduction." *Screen* 24, no. 2 (March–April 1983).

Suleiman, Susan Rubin, ed. *The Female Body in Western Culture: Contemporary Perspectives* (Cambridge: Harvard University Press, 1986).

Torgovnick, Marianna. *Gone Primitive: Savage Intellects, Modern Lives* (Chicago: The University of Chicago Press, 1990).

Whiting, John D. "Village Life in the Holy Land." *National Geographic* 25, no. 3 (March 1914).

Williamson, Judith. *Decoding Advertisements: Ideology and Meaning in Advertising* (New York: Marion Boyars, 1984).

Refugees and Representation: Politics, Critical Discourse, and Ethnography Along the New Guinea Border

Stuart Kirsch

One problem all refugees face, regardless of the circumstances of their migration and resettlement, is the numerous limitations on their ability to speak for themselves. Among these constraints are the trauma of past experience, the enormity of their daily struggle for survival, the fear of reprisals against family members left behind, the prejudices and resentment of host communities, and the difficulties in communicating across barriers of language and culture. The refugee experience is reduced to a vast silence that is easily ignored. Refugees are treated like nameless figures jumping the turnstiles of national borders, and they are unable to raise their voices to challenge this characterization.

This is not to suggest that there is no discourse about refugees, rather that refugees themselves are afforded few opportunities to contribute to it. Their point of view is frequently neglected or ignored. In this chapter, I describe some of the consequences of this general failure to take refugee perspectives into account in discussions about their fate. Most discourse about refugees falls into three general categories, which I call the "political," the "critical," and the "pragmatic."

In political discourse, refugees are primarily of concern in regard to the problems that they pose for relations between nation-states. Refugees typically cross international borders, raising questions about the integrity of the nation-states involved and potentially jeopardizing their relations. Political discourse seeks to minimize complications resulting from refugee action, including perceived threats to national security. Relatively little attention is given to efforts to understand the origins or cause of the refugee movement. Politicians, political scientists, and some journalists commonly engage in this kind of discourse. Political discourse is distinguished by its emphasis on the political ramifications of refugee action, rather than with the fate of the refugees themselves.

Refugees become the subject of critical discourse largely because their actions highlight political processes that the advocates of this discourse wish to critique. Whether from a Marxist perspective, from an indigenous rights platform, or in opposition to oppression and hegemony in all their guises, critical discourse focuses on refugees to advance a particular theoretical agenda or political cause. Scholars from a variety of disciplines, including geography, anthropology, and sociology, contribute to critical discourse on refugees. Journalists and other media specialists in television and film also frequently participate in critical discourse as defined here. Although such discourse is intended to increase awareness of the problems faced by refugees, broader political and theoretical issues remain the primary focus of critical discourse about refugees.

The third form of discourse about refugees is characterized by its pragmatic orientation. The work of refugee service personnel and relief organizations generally falls into this category. Their interests are largely applied, and range from concrete problems such as the provision of medical care to planning for complex processes like integration into the host society. A common feature of such discourse is its urgency, which may preclude effective refugee participation in the planning process (Baker, 1992), even though such participation is generally regarded as essential to success in all development projects (Cernea, 1985). A variety of external considerations, such as time constraints on spending, media attention, and regional political pressures affect the delivery of aid to refugees in ways that may have little to do with their needs or long-term goals (Cuny, 1983). Although some of the criticisms levied against political and critical discourse apply here as well, in this chapter I do not consider pragmatic discourse at length.

This chapter is therefore primarily concerned with political and critical discourse about refugees. More generally, the topic that I address is the politics of representation. I argue that political and critical discourse often marginalize and dehumanize the refugees in the process of enhancing their own rhetorical power. Rather than focusing on refugee experience and addressing refugee concerns, advocates of these forms of discourse seek to advance their own political and theoretical agendas. Their work may even have detrimental consequences for the refugees about whom they write.

As an alternative to these forms of discourse, I argue that greater attention should be given to person-centered ethnographic accounts of refugee experience. Despite the current crisis of representation in anthropology (Marcus and Fischer, 1986; Clifford and Marcus, 1986), ethnography compares favorably with competing critical and political discourse with regard to the ability to describe and analyze the circumstances faced by refugee populations. In my conclusions, I discuss the value of ethnography as a form of political representation.

REFUGEES ALONG THE NEW GUINEA BORDER

This chapter is based on two years of research among the Yonggom, a group of about 15,000–20,000 people living in the interior lowlands of southern New Guinea, on both sides of the border between Irian Jaya, Indonesia, and Papua New Guinea (see Kirsch, 1991; Schoorl, 1993).[1,2] The area occupied by the Yonggom is bounded to the north by foothills leading to the island's central cordillera, and to the east and west by the Fly and Digul rivers. The Yonggom exploit a variety of resources in their rain forest environment. Their staple food is sago, a starch harvested from the pith of the *Metroxylon* palm. They also practice slash and burn horticulture, raise pigs, and supplement their diet with hunting and gathering. The Yonggom are involved in the regional cash economy as well. In addition to wage labor, particularly in the service sector, they sell forest and garden products in local markets and produce small quantities of rubber for export.

Despite the so-called "bamboo curtain" that surrounds the militarized Indonesian province of Irian Jaya, there are numerous reports of political and military terror regularly inflicted on its inhabitants (e.g., Suter, 1982; Osbourne, 1985; Whittaker, 1990). Even though transmigration programs moving thousands of peasant farmers and their families to Irian Jaya from Indonesia's inner islands have slowed in recent years (Arndt, 1986), large areas of land have already been alienated from local ownership and use. Mines and timber companies operate in the province with little regard for either traditional land rights or ecological impact. Melanesians living in Irian Jaya face pervasive racism as well as political and economic inequality.

In 1984, more than 10,000 people from Irian Jaya fled eastward into Papua New Guinea (PNG) as refugees, settling in camps along the border. The exodus followed an aborted attempt to raise the flag of independence in Jayapura, the capital city of Irian Jaya, and subsequent military reprisals by the Indonesian government, the details of which are not well known (Smith and Hewison, 1986). Both the protest in Jayapura and the refugee movement were coordinated by members of the "Organisasi

Papua Merdeka" (OPM) or "Free Papua" political movement, which has pursued sovereignty in Irian Jaya for more than twenty years.

Nearly half of the 10,000 refugees who left Iran Jaya for Papua New Guinea are Yonggom.[3] What do they say about their experiences in Irian Jaya and their reasons for coming to Papua New Guinea? To answer this question, it is important to note that the Yonggom refugees themselves do not speak in terms of racism, cultural imperialism, and ethnocide, the favored vocabulary of many outside commentators. And unlike the educated leaders of the OPM, one of whom wrote to me that "God the creator will[ed] that each nation be free from colonialism" (anonymous, p.c.), the Yonggom refugees themselves do not speak about the domination of Third World nations over Fourth World tribal peoples.

Instead the refugees refer to the Indonesian refusal to establish reciprocal relations with them. This is particularly significant given that for the Yonggom, the denial of reciprocity is regarded as an affront to their humanity (Kirsch, 1991). This idea is illustrated in their myths in which *unrequited reciprocity* results in persons becoming animals. One example from this genre of myths is the story of the children who turned into flying foxes after their father's sister, who had adopted them when their parents died, decided that she would no longer take care of them:

Once there was a woman who was called upon to raise her brother's orphaned children. The woman had to work hard to make enough sago flour to feed them all. She grew weary of the labor involved and one morning, in a fit of anger, called out to her nephews and nieces, telling them to look after themselves, for she would no longer feed them. Then she stalked off into the rain forest.

The children were shocked; they did not know what to do. Finally, the eldest picked up some pieces of wood and some branches with leaves and made himself a pair of wings. He ran around the yard, jumping and flapping his arms up and down. He leaped high into the air and flew into a tree beside the house. He called down to his brothers and sisters and told them to make their own wings and fly up to join him.

That afternoon when the aunt returned, she felt contrite. She was puzzled at the fact that the house was silent and she called out to the children, telling them to come eat the food she brought from her gardens.

When she heard noises in the trees overhead, she turned to look up: her nieces and nephews had become flying foxes. They called down to her: "Oh, aunt, you did not feed us, so now we are going away," and off they flew, every last one of them.

In Yonggom myth, when exchange relations are abrogated and people are denied reciprocity, they cease being human and take on animal form. In this case, the children were refused food by the adult responsible for them, and they became flying foxes as a result. Unrequited reciprocity is thus regarded as a threat to one's humanity.

Hence Yonggom assertions about the Indonesian refusal to treat them as equals or to establish reciprocal relations with them represent serious grievances to the Yonggom. This is also the language in which the refugees usually spoke to me about their departure from Irian Jaya and their determination to stay in Papua New Guinea until they achieve their goal of political sovereignty. From their perspective, to do otherwise would be to accept the Indonesian evaluation of them as less than human.

The Yonggom refugees also make reference to unrequited reciprocity in their attempts to imagine political solutions to their problems. Elsewhere (Kirsch, n.d.) I have described how the Yonggom seek to extend their myths into the present to make history. In one example of this process, the refugees have elaborated on a series of myths involving a man named Kamberap. In the first of these myths, which are central to Yonggom male cult ritual, Kamberap manages to symbolically overcome the problems caused by unrequited reciprocity. In subsequent episodes of the myth, he mediates Yonggom interaction with colonial authorities. In a new episode of the myth told by the refugees, Kamberap has a son living abroad who will one day return to help them in their quest for independence from Indonesia. The advent of the son is expected to lead to political change. In one version of the myth, Kamberap's son is identified as Jesus Christ, and his return likened to the second coming of Jesus Christ. The myth seeks to universalize concern for the refugees by linking their fate to broader notions of human salvation. The refugees express their political aspirations by elaborating on a body of myths that, through the actions of Kamberap, hold the key to overcoming the problem of unrequited reciprocity.

A significant dimension of the Yonggom experience as refugees is their emotional response to social disruption. Great sadness and pathos is associated with being alone, a condition they call *iwari*. During a speech concerning a dispute between villagers and refugees about competition over scarce food resources, an elderly refugee man stood and addressed those assembled:

I am an old man. I came here by myself and I have no family with me. I am alone *(iwari)*. Just look at my body; I am no longer strong. I am short of breath, so I don't leave my house. I just sit inside all day long. I have no sons or daughters, no brothers or sisters. In the morning I wake up and make a fire . . . and wait to see whether anyone will bring me food. I will stay here and die; they will bury me here.

His speech was intended to remind those listening, particularly angry villagers, of the great hardships that the refugees face by living in Papua New Guinea.

The separation of the refugees from their land also presents them with emotional and psychological difficulties. Among the Yonggom, in the course of a lifetime, one's activities inscribe personal history onto the landscape. For example, the Yonggom maintain individual networks of trails, camping places, and catchments for drinking water. They plant trees and clear areas for gardens. They fell trees to make canoes and build houses. Gradually the landscape is transformed so that it comes to reflect, or is inscribed with, a person's biography (see Battaglia, 1992). The rain forest thus acquires the force of memory.

This inscribed history extends beyond an individual's lifetime. For example, a person mourning a friend or relative may refuse to leave the village for several weeks or even months to avoid confronting memories of the deceased that echo throughout the landscape. Thus, for the refugees, being away from their land involves more than a simple physical separation; it also entails the displacement of memory.

PERSON-CENTERED ETHNOGRAPHY

The anecdotes just discussed represent fragments of a person-centered ethnographic account of Yonggom refugee experience. Person-centered ethnography has undergone something of a renaissance in anthropology over the last decade (Rosaldo, 1984, p. 138). Langness and Frank (1981, p. 1) describe person-centered ethnography as the attempt to "convey directly the reality that people . . . experience." In presenting this material, my intention is to describe refugee experience from the Yonggom point of view.

Such an undertaking necessarily relies predominantly on "experience-near" constructs, which reflect how someone "might himself naturally and effortlessly . . . define what he or his fellows see, feel, think, imagine, or so on, and which he would readily understand when similarly applied by others" (Geertz, 1984, p. 124). Such constructs stand in contrast to the more analytic "experience-distant" language more commonly employed in the social sciences. Yonggom *iwari* or loneliness is experience-near, while the assignment of refugee status, which is primarily a political and legal category, is experience-distant. Person-centered ethnography may also draw on intersubjective constructs that are neither experience-distant nor experience-near. These concepts are formulated by the ethnographer to translate particular cultural idioms, and as such, are not directly employed or necessarily recognizable by members of the culture. The concept of "unrequited reciprocity" is an example of an intersubjective construct used to represent cultural differences in experience.

Person-centered ethnographic inquiry into refugee experience should be able to address questions such as: How do the refugees describe their experiences? What are their primary concerns? How do they articulate their responses to political developments, and how do they challenge or resist actions and events that they regard as unfavorable? Although this is not the forum for detailed discussion of the answers to these questions, I can suggest preliminary responses. The refugees interpret political relations in Irian Jaya in terms of the experience of unrequited reciprocity, and any resolution to the contemporary political struggle in Irian Jaya is dependent on reversing the underlying conditions of inequality. This is much more than a matter of instrumental desire for resources; rather, it reflects an existential position about equality and what it means to be human. Feelings of loneliness and separation from family, place, and history are central factors in Yonggom experience as refugees.

Given the limited participation of refugees in political, critical, and pragmatic discourse about their affairs, ethnographic accounts of refugee experience should be incorporated into these discussions. This is equally appropriate for discussion about practical matters, such as resettlement programs, and for more general debates about regional cooperation. In fact, the field of refugee studies is growing in significance within anthropology (see DeVoe, 1992; Hopkins and Donnelly, 1993). Although direct refugee participation is the ideal, political representation through person-centered ethnographic accounts is clearly preferable to the current pattern in which refugee perspectives are largely ignored. I now turn my attention to the representation of refugees in critical and political discourse.

CRITICAL DISCOURSE

Critical discourse about refugees from Irian Jaya is characterized by its recourse to conspiracy theories and its advocacy of millenarian solutions, positions that are generally advanced without regard for refugee perspectives or for the impact that such discourse may have on the refugees themselves.

Let me begin with an example that illustrates these claims. In 1987, an article by David Hyndman in the *Cultural Survival Quarterly* was partially reprinted in a national newspaper in Papua New Guinea. The essay discussed the recent infestation of pigs in the highlands of Irian Jaya with the tapeworm *Taenia solium,* a parasite that can cause cysticercosis in humans, leading to convulsions and death. Hyndman, an anthropologist, argued that the tapeworms had been deliberately introduced into Irian Jaya as a form of biological warfare against indigenous Melanesian populations. He made these assertions despite the research of a parasitologist sponsored by the World Health Organization (Desowitz, 1987), who concluded that the parasites had been inadvertently introduced into Irian Jaya when a number of pigs were brought as gifts from Bali, where the parasite is endemic. Hyndman further suggested that the domesticated pigs raised by the refugees were hosts to the parasite, even though there is no medical evidence to support this position (Fritzsche, 1988; George Nurse, p.c.). The original article, cleverly titled: "How the West (Papua) Was Won," made quite a splash. Had its speculative claims of Indonesian genocidal conspiracy through biological warfare been true, endangering the refugees as well as their neighbors in Papua New Guinea, the situation would certainly have provoked international intervention.

Given that Hyndman's argument has not been substantiated, however, what was its impact on the Yonggom refugees? Several weeks after the essay was reprinted locally, there was an outbreak of influenza in the refugee camps along the border in which a number of refugees lost their lives. The Yonggom usually attribute such deaths to sorcery, and may hold divination ceremonies they call *awon monbe* to identify the responsible party.

In these divinations, several arrows are left overnight on the grave of the deceased, whose spirit is called on to identify the sorcerer. The following day, the members of the village or refugee camp stand in a broad circle with an adult pig in the middle. The arrows are shot at the pig, which runs away from the center of the circle, shrieking in its death throes and seeking to escape from the crowd. Like bullfighters braving a charge in the ring, everyone must stand their ground as the pig runs toward them. Only at the last second might the pig veer away and run in another direction. If the pig should collide with someone, marking him or her with blood, it implicates them, or a member of their clan, in the death. After the pig collapses, several knowledgeable men test a series of hypotheses about the identity of the sorcerer by seeing how the pig responds to the statements. If the pig blinks, kicks its legs, or otherwise reacts strongly to one of the statements, it is regarded as confirmation that the statement is true. Typically these assertions refer to tensions in social relations, particularly violations of exchange obligations, such as the failure to pay bridewealth.

At one such *awon monbe* divination in the refugee camp, held in response to the deaths from the influenza epidemic, I heard a surprising line of questioning. Standing alongside the group of men huddled around the pig, one man asked, "Did the Indonesians poison our pigs?" "Was that the cause of the deaths?" "If it's true," he said to the pig, "then blink an eye, kick your leg, or give us a sign." Thus Hyndman's unsupported claims about biological warfare were directly transformed into refugee fears about being poisoned by the Indonesian government.

In other examples of critical discourse about the refugees from Irian Jaya, the attempt to present the strongest possible case against Indonesia sometimes leads to false or exaggerated claims. Such assertions may have the unintended consequence of striking fear into the hearts of the very people that proponents of the argument claim to support. Sensationalist reports about helicopter gunships and armed river trucks patrolling the

Fly River (Nietschmann and Eley, 1987) or phantom OPM operations blockading the shipment of copper and gold from the Ok Tedi Mine along the Fly River (Matthews, 1992) do little to calm the refugees.

More than simply inciting terror, however, such discourse also encourages the refugees to seek a military solution to their predicament, a strategy that must be regarded as millenarian. Yonggom members of the OPM sometimes boast of magical techniques that enable them to transform themselves into crocodiles at river crossings to evade capture, or rites that permit them to withstand a volley of Indonesian gunfire without harm. Encouraged by outsiders, the OPM train in the rain forest along the border with their bows and arrows, machetes, and vintage weaponry.

Not only is the hope for a military solution to the problems in Irian Jaya unrealistic, but this perspective also discourages the refugees and the OPM from pursuing alternative political strategies. Political moderates among the refugees even risk denunciation as traitors. Thus the conspiracy theories and millenarian solutions of critical discourse are promoted at the expense of any possible rapprochement between the refugees and the Indonesian government. Proponents of critical discourse often overlook refugee interpretations of events and ignore the impact of their discourse on the refugees themselves.

POLITICAL DISCOURSE

When politicians discuss the problems in Irian Jaya or the refugee situation in Papua New Guinea, they typically focus on their implications for international relations. The governments of the region have been reluctant to criticize Indonesia for its treatment of the indigenous population of Irian Jaya, or to question the neocolonial status of the province. For example, several years prior to the current refugee crisis, an Australian politician rejected the claim that Australia should provide the people of Irian Jaya with assistance in their struggle for independence from Indonesia, arguing that:

Australians today are still in the lead in raising false hopes and fears in Papua New Guinea on the subject of west New Guinea [Irian Jaya]. It must therefore be emphasized that to this day, no state will officially condone a process for severing some part of another state. Such a principle would lead to the breakup of such large entities as the USSR. (Whitlam, 1980)

In retrospect, this was not the best choice of analogy. The problem, as exemplified by the post–Cold War realignment in Europe, is that questions about the legitimacy of borders and states can spread to destabilize an entire region. Hence politicians in the Pacific have failed to challenge Indonesia's presence in Irian Jaya.

The initial response of the governments in the region to the refugee crisis of 1984 was to downplay the seriousness of the situation. The Papua New Guinea government dismissed the refugees as "traditional border crossers" under the provisions of a border agreement between Indonesia and Papua New Guinea (Kirsch, 1989; Dorney, 1990). It was only after missionaries visited the refugee camps and discovered a number of newly dug graves and scores of children suffering from malnutrition that international organizations such as Save the Children and later the United Nations High Commissioner for Refugees (UNHCR) were invited into the country to provide food and medical care (Smith and Hewison, 1986).

In the wake of this international attention, Papua New Guinea established regulations limiting the mobility of the refugees. The aim of these rules was to contain the refugees along the border until they grew tired of the difficult living conditions and consented to return to home. After a series of military skirmishes in which the Indonesian army pursued members of the OPM across the border into Papua New Guinea territory, a new strategy was developed.

A retired politician, one of the last representatives of Australia's colonial administration, devised a plan in which all of the refugees would be transported away from the border to a largely uninhabited area to the east. According to a UNHCR official, this proposal had a covert agenda:

One of the main reasons for the establishment of the refugee settlement was to promote the economic development of the area. As part of a rubber development scheme, refugees were seen as potentially able to generate the additional production needed in this sparsely-populated region to justify the construction of a rubber processing facility. (Baker, 1992, p. 26)

The refugees would serve as indentured laborers in a large rubber plantation, the profits from which would accrue in part to the author of the plan, who controlled much of the provincial rubber trade (see Hastings, 1986, p. 226). When the refugees learned the details of the plan, however, many rejected it completely: "We came here for independence," one of them told me, "Not to work for white men." Other refugees refused to move because they wanted to stay near the border, which allowed them to maintain close contact with relatives who belonged to the OPM or had remained behind in Irian Jaya. Thus the majority of the Yonggom refugees stayed in the original camps along the border.

In general, Papua New Guinea politicians have shown themselves to be more interested in improving political and economic ties with Indonesia than in helping the refugees. They have made little effort to encourage reform in Irian Jaya, and with few exceptions, have not challenged Indonesia's presence in New Guinea. Relocation of the refugees to permanent settlement camps was prompted by Indonesian border-crossings and economic interests rather than humanitarian issues. Most political scientists writing about the refugees view the situation primarily as a crisis concerning the integrity of international borders (see the essays in May, 1986; Wolfers, 1988). Thus in political discourse, refugees are treated like the proverbial canary in mine shaft, of significance primarily as an indicator of regional stability.

CONCLUSIONS: ETHNOGRAPHY AND THE POLITICS OF REPRESENTATION

Over the last decade, ethnography has been the subject of considerable historical and literary deconstruction, resulting in what has been referred to as a "crisis of representation" (Clifford and Marcus, 1986; Marcus and Fischer, 1986). Recently anthropologists have begun to express concern about the self-paralysis that such criticism threatens to impart. Scheper-Hughes (1992, p. 28) has suggested a "compromise that calls for the practice of 'good enough' ethnography," whereas Watson (in Wolf, 1992, p. 2) has emphasized the importance of "getting the news out."

Another, more compelling reason not to abandon ethnography comes from close examination of alternative modes of representation. In some cases, ethnography may provide a valuable complementary perspective. Anthropologists may also use ethnographic accounts where no alternatives exist: to convey the stories of others across cultural boundaries where they would not otherwise be heard (Behar, 1993), or to show Western readers how they are implicated in the lives of people living elsewhere in the world system (Gewertz and Errington, 1991). Perhaps the most significant use of ethnography, however, is in challenging accounts that ignore or misrepresent the voices and experiences of others to support their own claims.

Advocates of critical and political discourse about the New Guinea border effectively marginalize and dehumanize the refugees in the attempt to gain greater rhetorical power in advancing their respective agendas. In critical discourse, conspiracy theories and millenarian solutions are emphasized rather than dialogue and reform. In political discourse, refugees are of significance because they indicate possible threats to regional security. Neither approach takes refugee viewpoints into account or considers the impact of their discourse on the refugees. In contrast, the goal of person-centered ethnographic accounts of refugee experience is to ensure that refugee perspectives are represented in regional debates.

Anthropologists have become increasingly aware of the political dimensions of their work (Myers, 1986), but the contribution that ethnography can make to political representation is less widely appreciated. As Gewertz and Errington (1991, p. 209) suggest, "it is because ethnography is inherently political that it continues to have potential value." Indeed, it is in contrast to other modes of representation that the political power of ethnographic accounts is fully realized.

EPILOGUE

Recent events in the region and their effect on the refugees from Irian Jaya have reinforced the conclusions of this chapter. On the island of Bougainville, in the North Solomons province of Papua New Guinea, more than two decades of unanswered protests against the Panguna copper mine culminated in an armed insurrection against the mine and the national government. The complaints of Bougainvillean residents centered around a number of related issues, including the devastating environmental impact of the mine, their loss of productive land, the disruption of local patterns of residence and exchange, and their dissatisfaction with the distribution of revenue from the mine. More than five years of military engagement, failed diplomacy, and a prolonged stand-off with the state, which has blockaded the island since 1990, have strengthened the opinion or belief held by many Bougainvilleans that the conflict can only be resolved by secession from Papua New Guinea.

In response, the Papua New Guinea government has actively challenged the legitimacy of calls for Bougainvillean secession:

There is no historical basis for Bougainville as an independent nation. Bougainville, like any other Province, is a colonial creation for convenience of administration. There is no such tribe as Bougainville. (Bernard Narokobi, PNG Minister of Justice, quoted in Spriggs, 1992, p. 269)

Representing Papua New Guinea in a statement to the United Nations Working Group on Indigenous Populations, Charles Lepani has justified Papua New Guinea's use of force against the secessionist movement, arguing that: "Any sovereign state has absolute power to defend its sovereign territory and integrity against internal or external threats" (1992, p. 363). What are the implications of these policies and actions for the refugees from Irian Jaya?

Politically it is difficult to defend the principle of sovereign integrity with regard to one's own state while simultaneously refusing to grant a neighboring state the same rights. Indeed, an observer from Bougainville has described the similarities between Indonesian control of Irian Jaya and Papua New Guinean rule over Bougainville:

The Papua New Guinea government in trying to hang onto the status quo as a necessary prescription for peace is now living in a fantasy, similar to that indulged in by the government of Indonesia. Together they have become modern-day imperialists within the Pacific, claiming territories that clearly do not belong to them geographically, socially or politically. (Havini, 1992, p. 168)

Papua New Guinea also desires the support of Indonesia and other ASEAN member countries in their struggles over Bougainville. The result is that the problems in Irian Jaya have been put on the back burner. Not even renewed clashes along the border with Indonesian troops are likely to change this fact. There is little chance that Papua New Guinea will ever formally endorse the political aspirations of the refugees.

Even the search for a productive middle ground in which Papua New Guinea might work to persuade Indonesia to reform its policies in Irian Jaya, as Wesley-Smith (1987) has suggested, has become increasingly unlikely. Political decisions that directly affect the refugees continue to be formulated with little regard to their needs or concerns. International attention to the problems in Irian Jaya, like media coverage of similar conflicts in East Timor, might be of some benefit. Ultimately, these problems will not be solved until refugee experience is brought to the forefront of political debates that affect them.

NOTES

1. The use of the designation "Irian Jaya" rather than "West Papua" or "West New Guinea" reflects international conventions and is not intended as a political statement.

2. Research support from the National Science Foundation, Fulbright-Hays, Sigma Xi (The Scientific Research Society), The Explorer's Club, and the English-Speaking Union of Philadelphia is gratefully acknowledged. I am further indebted to the Yonggom refugees who trusted me with their stories. I assume full responsibility for any errors of fact or interpretation in this chapter.

3. In Irian Jaya, the Yonggom are known as the "Muyu" or "Muju" (see Schoorl, 1993).

REFERENCES

Arndt, H. (1986). Transmigration in Irian Jaya. In R. J. May (Ed.), *Between Two Nations: The Indonesia-Papua New Guinea Border and West Papuan Nationalism* (pp. 161–174). Bathurst: Robert Brown.

Baker, J. M. (1992). *Ol Refuji Lukautim Ol I Yet:* Community Participation in Refugee Contexts, with Reference to a Case Study of Refugees from Irian Jaya in Papua New Guinea. Unpublished MSc. essay submitted to the London School of Economics and Political Science.

Battaglia, Debbora. (1992). The Body in the Gift: Memory and Forgetting in Sabarl Mortuary Exchange. *American Ethnologist, 19*:1, 3–18.

Behar, Ruth. (1993). *Translated Woman: Crossing the Border with Esperanza's Story.* Boston: Beacon Press.

Cernea, Michael (Ed.). (1985). *Putting People First: Sociological Variables in Rural Development.* New York: Oxford University Press for the World Bank.

Clifford, James and George E. Marcus (Eds.). (1986). *Writing Culture: The Poetics and Politics of Ethnography.* Berkeley: University of California Press.

Cuny, Frederick C. (1983). *Disasters and Development.* New York: Oxford University Press.

DeVoe, Pamela (Ed.). (1992). *Selected Papers on Refugee Issues.* Washington, D.C.: American Anthropological Association.

Desowitz, Robert S. (1987). *New Guinea Tapeworms and Jewish Grandmothers.* New York: Norton. First Publication, 1976.

Dorney, Sean (1990). *Papua New Guinea: People, Politics and History Since 1975.* Sydney: Random House Australia.

Fritzsche, Markus. (1988). Serological Survey on Human Cysticercosis in Irianese Refugee Camps, Papua New Guinea. Inaugural-Dissertation zur Erlangung der Doktorwurde der Medizinischen Fakultat der Universitat Zurich. Institut fur Parasitologie der Universitat Zurich.

Geertz, Clifford. (1984). "From the Native's Point of View": on the Nature of Anthropological Understanding. In R. Shweder and R. Levine (Eds.), *Culture Theory: Essays on Mind, Self, and Emotion* (pp. 123–136). New York: Cambridge University Press.

Gewertz, Deborah B. and Frederick K. Errington. (1991). *Twisted Histories, Altered Contexts: Representing the Chambri in a World System.* New York: Cambridge University Press.

Hastings, Peter. (1986). Prospects: "A State of Mind." In R. J. May (Ed.), *Between Two Nations: The Indonesia-Papua New Guinea Border and West Papuan Nationalism* (pp. 218–231). Bathurst: Robert Brown.

Havini, Moses. (1992). A Bougainvillean Perspective on the Crisis. In R. J. May and Matthew Spriggs (Eds.), *The Bougainville Crisis: 1991 Update* (pp. 161–169). Bathurst: Crawford House Press.

Hopkins, MaryCarol and Nancy D. Donnelly (Eds.). (1993). *Selected Papers on Refugee Issues: II.* Washington, D.C.: American Anthropological Association.

Hyndman, David C. (1987). How the West (Papua) Was Won. *Cultural Survival Quarterly* 11:4, 8–13.

Kirsch, Stuart. (n.d.) Myth as History in the Making along the New Guinea Border. Unpublished Ms.

———. (1991). "The Yonggom of New Guinea: An Ethnography of Sorcery, Ritual and Magic." Unpublished Doctoral Dissertation, University of Pennsylvania.

———. (1989). Field Report from the Ok Tedi: The Yonggom, The Refugee Camps, and the Impact of the Mine. *Research in Melanesia,* 13, 30–61.

Langness, L. L. and Gelya Frank. (1981). *Lives: An Anthropological Approach to Biography.* Novato, California: Chandler & Sharp.

Lepani, Charles Watson. (1992). Statement to the United Nations Working Group on Indigenous Populations, *The Contemporary Pacific,* 4, 360–367.

Marcus, George E. and Michael M. J. Fischer. (1986). *Anthropology as Cultural Critique: An Experimental Moment in the Human Sciences.* Chicago: University of Chicago Press.

Matthews, James. (1992). Hot Spot. *Rolling Stones* (Australia), 473, 71–73, 95.

May, R. J. (Ed.). (1986). *Between Two Nations: The Indonesia-Papua New Guinea*

Border and West Papuan Nationalism (pp. 161–174). Bathurst: Robert Brown.

Myers, Fred R. (1986). The Politics of Representation: Anthropological Discourse and Australian Aborigines. *American Ethnologist,* 13:1, 138–153.

Nietschmann, Bernard and Thomas J. Eley. (1987). Indonesia's Silent Genocide Against Papuan Independence. *Cultural Survival Quarterly,* 11:1, 75–78.

Osbourne, Robin. (1985). *Indonesia's Secret War: The Guerilla Struggle in Irian Jaya.* Boston: Allen & Unwin.

Rosaldo, Michelle. (1984). Toward an Anthropology of Self and Feeling. In R. Shweder and R. Levine (Eds.), *Culture Theory: Essays on Mind, Self, and Emotion* 137–157. New York: Cambridge University Press.

Scheper-Hughes, Nancy. (1992). *Death Without Weeping: The Violence of Everyday Life in Brazil.* Berkeley: University of California Press.

Schoorl, J. W. (1993). *Culture and Culture Change among the Muyu.* Leiden: KITLV Press, Translation Series 23. Originally published as *Kultuur en Kultuurveranderingen in het Moejoe-Gebied,* 1957.

Smith, Alan and Kevin Hewison. (1986). 1984: Refugees, 'Holiday Camps' and Deaths. In R. J. May (Ed.), *Between Two Nations: The Indonesia-Papua New Guinea Border and West Papua Nationalism* (pp. 200–217). Bathurst: Robert Brown.

Spriggs, Matthew. (1992). Alternative Prehistories for Bougainville: Regional, National, or Micronational. *The Contemporary Pacific,* 4:12, 269–298.

Suter, Keith. (1982). East Timor and West Irian. London: Minority Rights Group Report No. 42 (Revised Edition).

Wesley-Smith, Terence. (1987). Lost Melanesian Brothers: The Irian Jaya Problem and its Implications for Papua New Guinea. *Pacific Studies,* 10:3: 27–52.

Whitlam, E. G. (1980). Indonesia and Australia: Political Aspects. In J. J. Fox, R. G. Garnaut, P. T. McCawley, and J. A. C. Mackie (Eds.), *Indonesia: Australian Perspectives,* Volume III. Canberra: Research School of Pacific Studies, The Australian National University.

Whittaker, Alan (Ed.). (1990). *West Papua: Plunder in Paradise.* Indigenous Peoples and Development Series: 6. London: Anti-Slavery Society.

Wolf, Margery. 1992. *A Thrice-Told Tale: Feminism, Postmodernism & Ethnographic Responsibility.* Stanford: Stanford University Press.

Wolfers, Edward P. (Ed.). (1988). *Beyond the Border: Indonesia and Papua New Guinea, South-East Asia and the South Pacific.* Waigani, Papua New Guinea: The Institute of Pacific Studies, the University of the South Pacific.

Index

About the Editors and Contributors

STEPHEN ADAIR is a visiting assistant professor at the University of New Hampshire. He received his Ph.D. from Northeastern University in 1993. His dissertation on the antinuclear movement was entitled "The Culture of Political Economy: A Social History of Seabrook Station."

KEVIN M. CARRAGEE is an assistant professor in the Department of Communication at Worcester State College. He has published articles examining mass communication research and theory in *Critical Studies in Mass Communication, Journalism Monographs,* and the *Western Journal of Communication.*

GINA DADDARIO is associate professor and chair of the Department of Communication Studies at SUNY College at Cortland, in Cortland, New York. She has published articles on women, media, and sport in *Sociology of Sport Journal* and *Women's Studies in Communication.*

MICHAEL R. FRASER is a doctoral candidate at the University of Massachusetts at Amherst. His research interests include the social response to HIV disease, medical sociology, and the study of social movements and social change with an emphasis on gay and lesbian activism in the United States. He is currently undertaking a study of informal caregiving and social support for HIV positive individuals as part of his dissertation research. Recent publications include studies of the AIDS Memorial Quilt, correspondence to Dr. Martin Luther King, Jr., and environmental racism in the United States.

SANDRA JAMIESON is the author of *The Bedford Guide to Teaching Writing in the Disciplines: An Instructor's Desk Reference* (1994), and articles on composition theory and African American literature. She is currently at work on a writing across the curriculum textbook that she hopes will interpellate confident and competent academic writers of all races and social classes (to be published in 1998), and a book-length analysis of the writing subjects created by composition instruction. She is the director of composition at Drew University, where she teaches composition, literature, rhetorical and critical theory, and writing, in addition to training composition instructors. She has also taught at Colgate University and SUNY Binghamton, where she earned her Ph.D.

STUART KIRSCH teaches cultural anthropology at the University of Michigan in Ann Arbor. He is currently at work on a book that examines ritual and myth in contemporary Papua New Guinea. His next fieldwork project is focused on changes in Melanesian perspectives on nature and the environment.

SUSAN LEGGETT is a doctoral candidate in the Department of Communication at the University of Massachusetts—Amherst.

MICHAEL MORGAN is a professor in the Department of Communication at the University of Massachusetts—Amherst. He is co-editor of *Cultivation Analysis: New Directions in the Media Effects Research* (1990) and co-author of *Democracy Tango: Television, Adolescents, and Authoritarian Tensions in Argentina* (1995).

POONAM PILLAI is an assistant professor in the Department of Communication at the Ohio State University and an associate faculty member in the Division of Comparative Studies and the Program in Women's Studies. Her essay, "Environmental Feminism Without Gender: Indigenous Theory in Vandana Shiva's Staying Alive," is forthcoming in *Genders*.

SUSAN ROSS received her Ph.D. in speech communication from Penn State University in 1992 and currently teaches in the Department of Rhetoric and Communication at Hamilton College in New York. Her interest in women's prison writings stems from her ongoing work in the areas of language, culture, and gender. She has published essays on such topics as culture shock, President Reagan's speaking style in China, and the rhetoric of Elizabeth Cady Stanton. Recent publications include "Solitude of Self as Transcendence" in *The Speech Communication Annual,* IX. She has served in the Pennsylvania Prison Society as a volunteer writing tutor and advocate.

ANDY RUDDOCK is a lecturer in media studies at Massey University in Palmerston, New Zealand.

REBECCA SCHNEIDER is a visiting assistant professor of drama at Dartmouth College. She is a contributing editor to *The Dartmouth Review* and has published in various journals as well as in the anthology *Acting Out: Feminist Performances* (L. Hart and P. Phelan, eds., 1993). She is working on a book, *The Explicit Body* (forthcoming in 1996).

JAMES SHANAHAN is an assistant professor in the Department of Communication at Cornell University. His research interests include the effects of television on attitudes about democracy, health, and the environment. His current research deals with the ways in which television conveys messages about environmentalism. His most recent book, co-authored with Michael Morgan, is *Democracy Tango* (1995).

LINDA STEET is an assistant professor of cultural foundations of education in the College of Education at the University of Oklahoma. Her book, *Imaginative Geography: Teaching Orientalism in U.S. Popular Education through* National Geographic, *1888–1988,* is forthcoming. Her current research focuses on the history of public reform schools for girls from 1855 to 1955.

THOMAS STREETER is an associate professor in the Sociology Department of the University of Vermont. His book *Selling the Air: A Critique of the Policy of Commercial Broadcasting in the United States* is forthcoming. Other forthcoming publications include "Audience Theory and Feminism: Property, Gender, and the Television Audience" (with Wendy Wahl), *Camera Obscura;* "Blue Skies and Strange Bedfellows: The Discourse of Cable Television," in *Sixties Television*; and "Some Thoughts on Free Speech, Language, and the Rule of Law," in *Freeing the First Amendment: Critical Perspectives on Freedom of Expression.*

ISBN 0-313-29796-7

HARDCOVER BAR CODE